Islamic Macroeconomics

T0331314

Islamic Macroeconomics proposes an Islamic model that offers significant prospects for economic growth and durable macroeconomic stability, and which is immune to the defects of the economic models prevailing both in developed and developing countries. An Islamic model advocates a limited government confined to its natural duties of defense, justice, education, health, infrastructure, regulation, and welfare of the vulnerable population. It prohibits interest-based debt and money, and requires full liberalization of all markets including labor, financial, commodity, trade, and foreign exchange markets. The government should be Sharia-compliant in its taxation power and regulatory intervention; it ought to reduce unproductive spending in favor of productive spending.

This book is essential reading for students and academics of Islamic economics and finance, economists, practitioners, and researchers.

Dr. Raja M. Almarzoqi was an Advisor at the International Monetary Fund, a faculty member at the Institute of Diplomatic Studies, an Adjunct Professor at Thunderbird Global Business School and King Saud University, Saudi Arabia, a consultant to a number of financial institutions and governments, and a board member of several funds. He has been a conference speaker and writer on a wide range of topics in economics, including Islamic economics.

Dr. Walid Mansour is an Advisor at the Saudi Arabian Monetary Authority. He was Associate Professor of Islamic finance at King Abdulaziz University, Saudi Arabia. He was a research and teaching affiliate at the College of Liberal Arts & Sciences (Kansas University), USA. He has published several articles in internationally refereed journals in various areas, including Islamic finance, corporate finance, and Islamic financial product development.

Dr. Noureddine Krichene was an Economist with the International Monetary Fund, Advisor at the Islamic Development Bank in Saudi Arabia, and Professor of Islamic Finance at INCEIF, Malaysia. He received his PhD in Economics from the University of California, Los Angeles. He is the author of *Islamic Capital Markets: Theory and Practice*.

Islamic Business and Finance Series
Series Editor: Ishaq Bhatti

There is an increasing need for western politicians, financiers, bankers, and indeed the western business community in general to have access to high quality and authoritative texts on Islamic financial and business practices. Drawing on expertise from across the Islamic world, this new series will provide carefully chosen and focused monographs and collections, each authored/edited by experts in their respective field all over the world.

The series will be pitched at a level to appeal to middle and senior management in both the western and the Islamic business communities. For the manager with a western background the series will provide detailed and up-to-date briefings on important topics; for the academics, postgraduates, business communities, managers with western and an Islamic background, the series will provide a guide to best practice in business in Islamic communities around the world, including Muslim minorities in the west and majorities in the rest of the world.

For a complete list of titles in this series, please visit www.routledge.com/finance/series/ISLAMICFINANCE

Islamic Financial Economy and Islamic Banking
Masudul Alam Choudhury

God-Conscious and the Islamic Social Economy
Masudul Alam Choudhury

Labor in an Islamic Setting
Edited by Necmettin Kizilkaya and Toseef Azid

Islamic Macroeconomics
A Model for Efficient Government, Stability and Full Employment
Raja Almarzoqi, Walid Mansour, and Noureddine Krichene

Islamic Macroeconomics

A Model for Efficient Government, Stability and Full Employment

Raja M. Almarzoqi, Walid Mansour, and Noureddine Krichene

LONDON AND NEW YORK

First published 2018 by Routledge

2 Park Square, Milton Park, Abingdon, Oxfordshire OX14 4RN

52 Vanderbilt Avenue, New York, NY 10017

Routledge is an imprint of the Taylor & Francis Group, an informa business

First issued in paperback 2020

British Library Cataloguing-in-Publication Data
A catalogue record for this book is available from the British Library

Library of Congress Cataloging-in-Publication Data
Names: Almarzoqi, Raja, author. | Mansour, Walid, author. | Krichene, Noureddine, author.
Title: Islamic macroeconomics : a model for efficient government, stability and full employment / Raja Almarzoqi, Walid Mansour and Noureddine Krichene.
Description: First Edition. | New York : Routledge, 2018. | Series: Islamic business and finance series | Includes bibliographical references and index.
Identifiers: LCCN 2017020761| ISBN 9781138106482 (hardback) | ISBN 9781315101583 (ebook)
Subjects: LCSH: Economics—Religious aspects—Islam. | Banks and banking—Religious aspects—Islam. | Macroeconomics.
Classification: LCC BP173.75 .A4825 2018 | DDC 339.0917/67—dc23
LC record available at https://lccn.loc.gov/2017020761

ISBN: 978-1-138-10648-2 (hbk)
ISBN: 978-0-367-59180-9 (pbk)

Typeset in Bembo
by Apex CoVantage, LLC

Contents

Figures

Tables

Preface

The classics – David Hume, Adam Smith, David Ricardo, Jean-Baptist Say, and many of their adepts – established the natural mechanisms of an efficient market model including the price-specie flow mechanism and the monetary approach to the balance of payments, the efficiency of free markets achieved by the "Invisible Hand," the Say's law of markets, Ricardo's free trade model, etc. Their illuminating work aimed at rejecting contemporaneous fallacies of large intervention of the state in the economy and showing the loss entailed by this intervention. Yet, until today, their superb free market model remained unpopular among supporters of large government interference, called the statists.

In contrast to the classics, the economic model adopted by many advanced countries is characterized by an extensive intervention of the government in the economy, and by un-natural institutions and laws that prevent free competition in the capital and labor markets. As an example of large-scale intervention, leading industrial countries have been locked, since 2008, into an expansionary fiscal policy, cheap and repressive money policy in form of near-zero interest rates and massive money creation, record public and private debts, explosive asset prices, unstable exchange rates, and heightened uncertainties. The distortions and wealth redistribution caused by these policies are immense. In spite of these unorthodox policies, many industrial countries continued to experience low growth and high unemployment. Had industrial countries adopted a free market model, their economies would have long ago regained sustained prosperity. In sum, the macroeconomic framework of many industrial countries is highly unsustainable and uncertain.

Likewise, a large number of developing countries have been unable to reach autonomous development despite their vast territories and natural resources and large labor surplus, or to promote a safe environment that would attract foreign investment. Ever since they became independent in 1950s, they remained dependent on foreign aid without which they would fall in an economic chaos. Immense resources from official donors and continuous adjustment programs did not help beneficiary countries to industrialize or restore durable growth and financial balances. In many developing countries, real per capita incomes have been stagnant, if not falling. Unemployment and poverty have been aggravating and social life has reached inhumane conditions in terms of crimes, diseases, and shortage of basic necessities and infrastructure. Foreign debt remains a burden. Without full-fledged liberalization and government downsizing, the prospects for many developing countries to reach auto-development remain meager.

In fact, many industrial and developing countries have deeply established an economic model characterized by an oversized government and institutions and laws that stifle the private sector. In light of the economic and social situation in both industrial and developing countries, it appears that the abundance of human and natural resources alone may not secure economic stability and growth. The type of economic model and government adopted by a country are of paramount importance and will determine whether a country will be able to advance or remain in stagnation and suffer economic and social instabilities.

This book proposes an Islamic model that offers significant prospects for economic progress and durable macroeconomic stability and which is immune to the defects of the economic models prevailing both in industrial and developing countries. In a Sharia model, the government has to promote the private sector through fulfilling its natural functions and not through ill-interventions in this sector. A Sharia model opposes absolute, despotic, big government, and un-natural laws. The government has to obey natural laws and deeply establish political and economic freedom. A Sharia model advocates a limited government confined to its natural duties of defense, justice, education, health, infrastructure, regulation, and welfare of the vulnerable population. It fully embraces the classical free market model; with the noteworthy difference, namely the interdiction of interest contracts; such interdiction eliminates interest-based debt and transforms the nature of the banking sector. In line with the classics, an Islamic model requires full liberalization of all markets including labor, capital, and trade and foreign exchange markets. The government has to be Sharia-compliant in its taxation power; it ought to reduce unproductive spending in favor of productive spending. The financial sector, based on interest prohibition, is one of the attractive aspects of a Sharia model. The banking system has two components: (i) a 100 percent reserve depository component; and (ii) a risk-sharing investment banking. Because interest-based money is prohibited, debt money emitted by banks is absent, and debt and money are separated. A vibrant stock market is a natural necessity to mobilize savings, promote risk-sharing investment, and provide liquidity for investors.

The book is not a theoretical book; it is a policy book based on the most recent economic developments in advanced and developing countries; it deals with the most pressing contemporaneous issues and priority reforms in many countries trapped into a rigid statist model; it recommends far-reaching reforms that would curtail the role of the government to its very natural attributions, remove anti-market laws and promote a free-enterprise model, fully liberalize the capital and labor markets, promote a sound money, implement a pro-growth fiscal policy, develop a non-interest banking sector, and enable a full participation of the private sector in infrastructure development. Economic policy deals with first best; yet, first best policies may not be feasible; a country saddled with anti-market institutions, unorthodox policies, and un-natural laws should not obstruct any reform toward economic and financial liberalization and should gradually initiate a process of downsizing the government to its natural attributions, softening anti-market legislation, and repealing all types of oppressive and un-natural laws. Certainly, reforms of deeply rooted popular institutions and laws in labor markets, family matters, money and banking, foreign trade, etc. would rarely be embraced – groups would fight toward preserving their interests – however, inertia would only erode further the growth base, and make the economic situation more unmanageable in many countries in spite of a formidable economic potential.

Acknowledgments

The authors express their great indebtedness and esteem to Professor Ishaq Bhatti of La Trobe University, Australia, whose support enabled the publication of this book.

The authors acknowledge the valuable contribution and very high professionalism of Kristina Abbotts of Routledge whose hard work and generous support were instrumental in the book publication. They extend their deep gratitude to Matthew Ranscombe for his close cooperation in the editing and production of the book. The authors are especially thankful for the continuing support of Routledge in promoting the development of Sharia economics and finance.

1 Nature and dangers of statism

1. Introduction

Economic science established some basic truths:

- Richness can be achieved and poverty can be alleviated only through capital accumulation;
- The only force for growth and technical advance is the private sector;
- The role of the state is to secure for the private enterprise an environment free of crimes and propitious to free markets and competition where individuals can exert to the fullest their natural intelligence and creative capacity.

Economic history fully attested to these truths. Eminent classics, such as Adam Smith, J.B. Say, David Ricardo, and F. Bastiat (2011), noted the government's false interference in the economy and advocated the theory of free markets. In contrast, an extreme ideology developed by the socialists and communists of the nineteenth century called for the elimination of the capitalist bourgeois class and the establishment of a fully state owned and planned economy. Besides millions of lives lost in communist revolutions, the application of this ideology was against the economic and social nature of individuals and had stifled entirely the individual's creative capacity, made the individual depend on the state, and resulted in chronic food shortages and repeated disastrous famines.

Many advanced states had experienced a severe economic and financial crisis during 2007–2009. Years after, economic growth remained slow and unemployment high. These countries became entangled into unorthodox monetary policies and high fiscal deficits. Before this episode, industrial nations suffered the Great Depression of 1929–1939. Today, many developing countries, in spite of their immense natural potential, have not been able to reach auto-development and remained dependent on foreign aid. The Arabic Spring Revolts in 2011 attested to a dramatic failure of an economic model. Disappointed by the total failure of the development model of many countries, including in Latin America, McKinnon (1973) and Shaw (1973) became convinced that abundance of natural resources, vastness of cultivable lands, and abundant labor may not secure economic growth. Comparing post-war Germany, Japan, South Korea, and Taiwan to Latin American countries, McKinnon and Shaw emphasized that a main obstacle to economic development was government un-natural interference in the economy.

The model of extensive government interventions in the economy was often named the statist model. Statism designates a government that neglects its natural duties and intervenes in economic and social areas that do not fall into its natural jurisdiction. A statist government may be called a "big government," or an "inefficient government." It is a government that has stepped beyond its natural duties; it has enacted un-natural legislation and established un-natural institutions that curtail considerably the private sector; it is an over-expanded government that is over-taxing the private sector and a lot of its spending is wasteful. In its extreme version, statism was socialism and communism, whose toll in human lives and economic failure is well known and needs no review.

This chapter reviews some of the literature on the nature of statism and its harmful effects. It covers the following topics:

- Statism: un-natural and unjust intervention of the state in the economy
- The classics' adherence to free market and opposition to state intervention
- Herbert Spencer: the man versus the state
- Lysander Spooner: the natural law and the un-natural statism
- Nock: our enemy, the state
- Mises's human action: the fallacies and dangers of statism

2. Statism: un-natural intervention of the state in the economy

Statism is a form of government that has become omnipotent, extending its intervention to most or all of the economic and social affairs of the country. The more the government expands, the more rigidities are built into the economy, the more the private sector shrinks, the more economic freedom is stifled, the more wealth redistribution is exerted, and the more resources are consumed by the state at the expense of investment and capital, and the more poverty and crime worsen. Freeing itself from the commodity currency, the state has turned money into a costless paper money emitted out of thin air by its central bank and has used extravagant paper currency to expand its size, to finance its ever-rising expenditure, and to freely expand loans to borrowers (Freeman 2016). Inflation has become secular, and is an inherent ailment of statism; inflation tax is often used to finance government expenditure. Interest rates, wages, and exchange rates are often fixed or directly manipulated by the government with attending economic distortions. The government forces a redistribution of income and wealth in favor of its protected groups, through taxation, tariffs, inflation, or price controls, at the expense of taxed groups (Adam Smith 1776). Hence, near-zero interest rates are un-natural and are forced by a government; they amount to a redistribution of incomes and wealth in favor of borrowers at the expense of creditors.

Statism enacts un-natural laws, not to defend the harmonious natural rights of citizens, but to defend the conflicting interests of power groups who may be bureaucrats, military, bankers, industrialists, labor, etc. These laws are unjust and distortive, disable the free market mechanism, and force an excessive taxation on the private sector. A typical example of such un-natural laws was the Corn-Laws (1815–1846)[1] in Great Britain imposed by a power group; they contributed to damage manufacturing and caused a famine in Ireland (1845–1852), which famine forced the repeal of these laws. Other examples of un-natural laws are the mandatory minimum wage laws which created unemployment; the fixation of interest rates at a near-zero level which caused massive debt build-up, bubbles in asset and commodity prices, enormous free wealth to debtors and speculators, and excessive uncertainty; and trade barriers which hurt growth and employment. Un-natural laws severely restricted private enterprise and damaged the economy.

Statism forces the government in areas that do not fall under its natural competence. It acts against the natural laws of the economy and therefore yields injustice, desolation, and poverty. Despite repeated failure, statism still believes that the state is omnipotent and can achieve any of its ideals. To make its intervention effective, the state enacts un-natural and unjust laws such as minimum wage laws, progressive income tax, inheritance tax, price fixation and control, etc. To enforce these laws the state has to increase bureaucracy, the police force, the number of lawyers, judges, clerks, courts, and jails.

Statism has caused severe economic crises and long stagnation as shown by the Great Depression (1929–1939) and the 2008 financial crisis. Statism has established rigid laws and institutions that prevented the free market mechanism and perpetuated unemployment of the labor force. Often, statism has created competing credit expansion and money depreciation among countries,[2] and trade barriers. The impossibility of socialism, as illustrated by the collapse of communism in the 1990s, has shown that statism has been self-defeating and often failed to achieve its design; it has impeded the private sector and economic growth.

Statism has been an evolutive process; it is central to the people's aspirations. The more government people get, the more they ask for. Nock (1935) maintained that a revolution will not change this thinking, and in the aftermath of a revolution, people will even ask for more government than prior to the revolution. Nowadays, statism has become deeply rooted in political, academic, and popular thinking. Today's electorate is far more statist than previous generations, and only statist leaders, who promise more government doles and interventions, are capable of winning popular votes.

Under the influence of political, social, and vested interest forces, countries have evolved from a free market mechanism to statism with rigid and costly economic structures. Each force was moved by a social ideal, such as egalitarism, or a specific class interest, such as labor, farmers, miners, industrialists, or bankers. Each group used power or bribery to prevail. Labor unions proceeded via strikes in key sectors to force their demands; while farmers proceeded by blocking roads to submit the government to their exigencies. Other groups proceeded via electing representatives who would serve their interest. Each class of profiteers succeeded to establish institutions empowered by the state and laws that achieve its design or protect its interest at the expense of non-privileged groups. Each interest group forces a legislation to promote its respective interest regardless of the detrimental consequences on the economy. Often, laws to protect a group penalized another group (Adam Smith 1776). For instance, high tariffs protect inefficient industries and make consumers pay high prices for shoddy products. Moreover, exports are curtailed, since countries exchange commodities for commodities. If a country is precluded to export to a country, then it may not be able to buy from the restricting country. Minimum wages penalize a country twice; there is a loss of output due to institutional unemployment and there is also unemployment compensation to unemployed workers. Similarly, the Corn-Laws in Great Britain had penalized heavily consumers, they had curtailed corn output, caused famine in Ireland, and seriously disrupted manufacturing development.

Statism, be it communism, socialism, or Keynesianism, was un-natural, unjust, and self-defeating in a sense that it never achieved the ends sought by the statists; instead, it made the economy worse off. Statism discourages private investment. Advanced countries are suffering the consequences of statism. However, their industrial basis as well as their reserve currencies allow them to sustain the losses inflicted by statism. In contrast, developing countries that have adopted a statist model are unable to develop and became poorer and too dependent on foreign aid. As few opportunities of livelihood exist, a large number of their labor migrates to more prosperous countries. The reforms are obvious: limit the government to its essential and natural functions, and remove anti-market and un-natural laws and institutions. Yet, statists remained over decades oblivious to any reform that would streamline the role of the state.

3. The classics' adherence to free market and opposition to state intervention

Statism, in the scale and depth as known today, was not known in the nineteenth century and earlier. Nonetheless, some harmful state interventions existed and drew criticism of many writers who attempted to establish the delusion of these interventions and their negative effects on the economy. Some of the state intervention originated in mercantilism doctrine which sought to erect trade barriers and provide bounties to exporters. The Corn-Laws were a typical example for prohibiting imports of cereals in order to enable domestic farmers to sell at high domestic prices.

Locke (1691) severely criticized the British government policy for lowering the interest rate by decree; which policy is presently forcefully applied by advanced countries in the form of near-zero interest rates, massive credit expansion, and sharp currency depreciation. In respect to interest rates, Locke pointed to the fact that the lower interest rates in Holland, which were at about 4 percent, were not dictated by decree; they were equilibrium rates that showed higher real capital abundance in Holland than in England. Fixing the interest rate at 4 percent in England, below its equilibrium rate, would not make capital abundant; instead, it would make it scarcer; it would confer undeserved gain to borrowers and an unjust loss for creditors. A number of borrowers would be excluded. In respect to reducing the silver content of the pound, Locke demonstrated that this measure was a sheer violation of property rights and arbitrary alteration of the standard of value which ought to be kept unchanged. It will increase prices, since traders are interested in the true metal content of the pound, and not its name. If the silver content is reduced by 20 percent, then prices will tend to rise in the same proportion, all contracts made before the currency devaluation are altered, and creditors and rentiers lose in real terms. He strongly rejected a role of the state that deranges contracts and inflicts injustice on a party in favor of another party.

Adam Smith (1776) showed the futility of mercantilism: bounties (subsidies) were distortive and totally unnecessary, and unhampered markets (i.e., the Invisible Hand) never ought to be deranged by state intervention. He maintained that when a country restricts, either by high duties or prohibitions, foreign trade, it necessarily harms its own interest in three different ways. First, by raising the price of all foreign goods and all industrial products, it lowers the price of agricultural products. Second, by affording a monopoly of the home market to its own industrialists, it raises the rate of profit in the industrial sector in proportion to that of agricultural profit, and, consequently, either diverts from agriculture a part of the capital which had before been employed in it, or hinders investment in it. Agriculture may be rendered less advantageous, and industry more advantageous, than they otherwise would be. Third, curtailing imports necessarily reduces exports. If Britain did not import cotton from the United States, the latter cannot buy manufacturing from Britain, since commodities are exchanged against commodities.

Adam Smith advocated free markets and free trade across countries. David Ricardo (1817) fully developed the theory of free trade and comparative advantages, another contribution aimed at demolishing mercantilism. Following the famine in Ireland, caused essentially by the Corn-Laws and government's misguided intervention in the agriculture sector, the Anti-Corn Laws movement finally triumphed with the repeal in 1846 of those foolish laws.

4. Herbert Spencer: the man versus the state

Spencer (1851, 1884) presented the notion of a limited state based on a doctrine of natural rights. His "first principle" enunciated that every citizen is entitled to fullest freedom to exercise his faculties in harmony with every other man's rights to the same freedom. Spencer wanted a reduction of state power over citizens to an absolute minimum, and an enhancement of the private sector, in contradiction with the statist model which expanded too much the state at the expense of the private sector. Spencer stressed that a vital and natural responsibility of the state is to establish the most secure environment by punishing crimes against persons or property; this attribution of the state was deemed as the common sense of mankind. A safe environment is a prerequisite for economic and social advance. Spencer believed that the state should enforce the obligations of contracts; it should make justice costless and easily accessible. Countries where the government is unable to safeguard full security and eradicate lawlessness suffer poverty and social disorder. Beyond enforcing law and order, the state should put no further coercive restraint upon the citizens. All that the state can do for the best interests of citizens is by way of restricting its interventions to its natural attributions. If the state promotes social well-being by positive coercive interventions upon the citizens, any apparent and temporary social good that may be achieved will be at the great cost of real and permanent social good.

Spencer noted the costly errors made by the government through its wrong interventions in the economy. He acclaimed the power of the private sector in creating wealth and inventing new technologies. He stressed that the private enterprise developed the agriculture, the industry, the mining, constructed immense infrastructure in canals, ports, and railroads; invented machinery; and promoted banking, insurance, and capital markets, etc. This truth about private enterprise remains unshakable. The innovative capacity of the private enterprise is inexhaustible. Industrialization has been expanding as the private sector kept inventing airplanes, iphones, computers, cars, satellites, medications, etc. In contrast, Spencer observed that the State, in conducting its judicial attributions, ruins many, misleads others, and discourages away those who need help.

Spencer showed that often government intervention was self-defeating. He exposed the futility of minimum wage legislation which forced business to relocate to a freer environment. He noted that the Spitalfields weavers afforded a case in point. The fixing of minimum wages for the weavers led to a relocation of the textile industry from Spitalfields to cities where labor markets were competitive. He supported the abolition of institutions that harmed the public good. The repeal of the Corn-Laws showed that no good could come from un-natural laws that violated the free market mechanism and protected the interest of some groups at the expense of other groups.

5. Lysander Spooner: the natural law and the un-natural statism

Wary of its harmful and unjust consequences, Spooner (1886) considered statism as dangerous to human rights and freedom, simply because it was un-natural. Spooner realized that the government became an institution to serve the interests of power groups instead of being a neutral institution that would simply establish justice and security, or what he named as the Natural Law. Once the government becomes an instrument for implementing ideologies and serving interest groups it creates conflicts between rival factions and necessarily becomes unjust. Hence, Statists may face opposition from anti-statists groups, unionists may face opposition from entrepreneurs, trade protectionists may face opposition from exporters, inflationists may face opposition from creditors and pensioners, etc. The favors the government showers on one interest group are paid for by taxes or confiscation imposed on a losing group (Adam Smith 1776). Accordingly, the government violates natural human rights pertaining to freedom, property, and trade. It monopolizes money and constantly depreciates its value to reduce debtors' burden.[3]

Spooner (1886) considered that the role of government is to establish justice and should not be used by any party as a policy tool such as achieving full employment of labor or inflating the way out of debt for debtors. He stated:

> If a government is to do equal and exact justice to all men, it must do simply that, and nothing more. If it does more than that to any, – that is, if it gives monopolies, privileges, exemptions, bounties, or favors to any, – it can do so only by doing injustice to more or less others. *It can give to one only what it takes from others; for it has nothing of its own to give to anyone* (Spencer 1886). The best that it can do for all, and the only honest thing it can do for any, is simply to secure to each and every one his own rights, – the rights that nature gave him, – his rights of person, and his rights of property; leaving him, then, to pursue his own interests, and secure his own welfare, by the free and full exercise of his own powers of body and mind; so long as he violates the equal rights of no other person.
>
> (P. 15)

Spooner asserted that men's rights are always harmonious. That is to say, each man's rights are always consistent and harmonious with each and every other man's rights. But their interests constantly conflict; namely, when these interests require government's award of monopolies, privileges, loans, and subsidies. It is the opposing interests that lead to a conflict. The latter is won by the political group that holds more power. For instance, the overly expansionary money policy since 2009 in the United States was imposed by the Administration in power. By fixing the interest rates at near-zero level, this policy penalized the fixed income groups and the creditors, including financial institutions, and showered immense wealth on borrowers and speculators. It created highest uncertainty; its destabilizing effects will unravel over time.

Spooner stated that the true definition of law is that it is a fixed, immutable, and natural principle. He likened the law of justice to the laws of matter such as the law of gravitation, the laws of light, etc. The law of justice should be as unalterable as the natural laws are. For Spooner, many government intervention laws, such as minimum wage laws, trade restriction, inheritance taxes, paper money, price fixation, etc., are not natural laws, and therefore are not harmonious with the interests of all citizens. Spooner contended that the government would have no occasion to take a tremendous responsibility upon itself for managing the economy if it does not intervene in areas that do not fall within its natural duties.[4]

Spooner (1886) deplored that the government's debasing of money was one of the most glaring violations of men's natural right to make their own contracts. He noted that:

> Under the power to coin money, and to regulate its value, the Congress may issue coins of the same denomination, that is, bearing the same name, as those already current by law, but of less intrinsic value than those, by reason of containing a less weight of the precious metals, and thereby enable debtors to discharge their debts by the payment of coins of the less real value.[5]
>
> (P. 67)

Spooner contended that the government has the power to alter the real value of money contracts and defraud creditors; to support his argument, he provided the following statement:

> The contract obligation was not a duty to pay gold or silver, or the kind of money recognized by law at the time when the contract was made, nor was it a duty to pay money of equal intrinsic value in the market. But the obligation of a contract to pay money is to pay that which the law shall recognize as money when the payment is to be made. – Legal Tender Cases, 12 Wallace 548.[6]
>
> (P. 66)

In almost every country, or a group of countries, money is a paper monopoly of the government. Issuing costless money paper has enabled the government to expand to an oversized dimension, maintain an oversized bureaucracy, and tax money holders permanently through an inflation tax. Statist economists, instead of equating inflation to costless paper and government's violation of property rights, they explain it by theories such as demand pull and cost push inflation.

Governments have erected barriers to trade in many countries. The Corn-Laws in Great Britain illustrated how misguided trade restrictions were. Many governments considered their economies as insulated entities from the rest of world and sought autarchy, instead of looking at their economies as naturally integrated parts of the rest of the world regardless of the geographic borders. Spooner maintained that the so-called taxes or duties, which the government levies upon imports, are a practical violation both of men's natural right of property, and of their natural right to make their own contracts. Traders have the right to import and export from other countries without facing trade impediments aimed at protecting local industries.

6. Nock: our enemy, the state

Nock (1935) witnessed the Great Depression; he witnessed also the vast intervention of the state, how it precluded recovery, and prolonged agony. As economic prosperity and social quietness were turned into dislocation and despair, he considered statism as a serious obstacle to the private sector development. Statism allowed the state to take on a vast mass of new duties. But, it still remains the common enemy of all well-disposed, industrious, and decent men. In line with Oppenheimer's theory of wealth appropriation which distinguishes political and economic means for appropriating wealth (Oppenheimer 1908), Nock considered that there are two fundamentally opposed means whereby man may acquire the necessary means for his sustenance. These are work and unrequited transfer: one's own labor and the forcible or voluntary appropriation of the labor of others. He called one's own labor and the equivalent exchange of one's own labor for the labor of others, the "economic means" for the satisfaction of needs. He called the "political means" as the unrequited appropriation of the labor of others. Nock contended that as long as the easy, attractive, superficial ideology of statism deeply influences the citizen's mind, no beneficent social change can be effected, whether by revolution or by any other means.

7. Mises's human action: the fallacies and dangers of statism

Mises (1949) was an advocate of an unhampered market economy which requires the abolition of all laws and institutions that restrict free competition and trade. Economic liberty means: (i) each individual chooses how he wants to cooperate in the social division of labor; (ii) consumers determine what the entrepreneurs should produce; and (iii) no state interference with the operation of the market because such interference must necessarily restrict output and make people poorer.

Mises noted that Western governments had erected trade barriers, conducted a credit expansion and an easy money policy, and introduced price controls, minimum wage rates, and subsidies. They rendered taxation too heavy and they considered high spending as the best way to enhance wealth and welfare. Mises addressed the deliberate lowering of the interest rate and debasement of currency by governments. As post-2008 conditions show, statists forcefully fix the interest rates at near-zero level with no prospect for changing this policy. He noted that a modern central bank offered a government full freedom in terms of money without being constrained by convertibility into gold.

In line with the classics, Mises distinguished the natural rate of interest, which he called the originary rate of interest, and the loan market rate. The former is determined by the time preference of consumers and the productivity of capital; it cannot be altered by a government decree. The loan market rate may be altered by the statists as they will, setting it at near-zero or even significantly negative. The more the statists create a distortion between the natural and the market interest rates, the more injustice and misallocation of resources they inflict. Mises asserted that a credit expansion necessarily creates a stock market as well as an investment boom.

Mises flatly rejected the Keynes theory of effective demand failure which denied that the economy has full automatism for clearing all markets, including the labor markets, and urged an expansionary fiscal and monetary policy to increase the aggregate demand for goods and services and lift the economy from an under-employment equilibrium. This theory contradicts Say's law of clearing markets and flexible prices which maintains that the economy has full automatism to achieve full employment of labor on its own without government's intervention. Keynes's theory of general over-production contradicts the notion of scarcity and immense needs of people around the world that remain unfulfilled. The notion of demand failure is absurd and cannot be taken at face value. If a country has large inventories of unsold goods, such as food, cars, clothing, etc., it may certainly export them, however, at a competitive price.[7] The observation of past crises showed that a crisis happened essentially when savings became too low and shortage of working capital became too acute, triggering a significant rise in interest rates. Keynesians maintain that there are plants and farms whose capacity to produce is either not used at all or not to their full extent, there are large inventories of unsold commodities, and there is mass unemployment. All that is lacking is credit. Additional credit would enable the entrepreneurs to resume or to expand production. In contrast, Mises noted that the mal-investment of the boom has fixed capital in some industries at the expense of other industries in which they were more urgently needed. There is disproportion in the allocation of capital goods to the various branches of industry. This disproportion can be remedied only by the accumulation of new capital and its employment in those branches in which it is most urgently required.

Mises observed that low interest rates and unlimited credit expansion contributed to demolish the gold money and to replace it with paper money emitted by a government central bank. With paper money, and its inherent inflation tax, the government faces no limit on its size and spending. The gold standard makes the increase in the supply of gold depend upon the profitability of producing gold; accordingly, it limits the government's power to resort to inflation. Inflationists showed defects in the gold standard. In contrast, Mises replied that these defects constituted the usefulness of gold money. It prevented large-scale inflationary financing on the part of governments. The gold standard did not fail. The governments destroyed it, because they believed in the fallacies that credit expansion was an appropriate means of lowering the rate of interest and improving the balance of trade.

Mises regretted that, by fully intervening in labor markets, statism has inflicted a loss in the economy by freezing millions of workers who could have contributed to wealth creation. The popular support of pro-labor legislation was based on the fallacy that the wage rates do not depend on labor's productivity. Union leaders appropriate large sums of workers' dues, but can never alter the relation of real wage to productivity. High wages in certain industries could never be due to union leaders; they emanate from high capital intensity and high skills. Likewise, high wages in industrial countries in relation to poor countries could be explained only by productivity and capital intensity and not by unionism.

The market wage rate tends toward a level at which all those eager to earn wages get jobs and all those eager to employ workers can hire as many as they want. It tends toward the establishment of full employment, with no involuntary unemployment. Where there is neither government nor union interference with the labor market, there is only voluntary unemployment. But as soon as the government or the unions fix wage rates above equilibrium rates, institutional unemployment emerges. While there prevails on the free labor market a tendency for involuntary unemployment to disappear, institutional unemployment cannot disappear as long as the government or the unions enforce wages above market-clearing rates. Firmly committed to the principles of interventionism, governments try to remedy institutional unemployment by resorting to measures called full employment policies, which include Keynesian expansionary fiscal and monetary policies, as illustrated by the policies adopted in leading industrial countries after 2008. These policies are such that the cure is worse than the disease.

8. Conclusions

This chapter reviewed some of the criticisms of statism. Such criticism had no impact on policymaking. Instead, with the rise of communism, socialism, Keynesianism, and many power groups and ideologies, statism became the dominant aspect of modern economics. Statism has shaped the economic theory. For instance, monetary economics is based on paper money, and economic policy on interventionism. In spite of its adverse effects on the economy and social well-being, statism is fully embraced and widely taught around the world. For instance, the response to the 2008 crisis was based on a popular Keynesian theory that called for a full-scale government intervention to stimulate the economy and reflate prices.

Statism imposes un-natural laws that confer to interest groups benefits and inflict damage on other groups. Central planning was not able to replace the "Invisible Hand" in any economy; such was the impossibility theorem of socialism, as illustrated by the collapse of socialism in 1990s. Yet, statists will not allow free markets to operate. Statism begets statism. Since the government has imposed laws that preclude free capital and labor markets, Keynesians call on the government to increase its spending to boost aggregate demand for goods and restore full employment. For them, big government is a blessing and an insurance against effective demand failure. Big government will prevent a repeat of the Great Depression say the Keynesians. They call on the state to drastically inflate prices so as to cheat labor by reducing real wages. This is a flagrant contradiction within statism.

Statism, with its institutions, laws, and popular support has become too deeply rooted and will continue to stifle many economies. Today, most politicians, academics, and media firmly believe that the central bank is fully able to restore full employment and economic prosperity and should be mandated to do so; even though the track record of the central bank shows ominous financial crises, unemployment, high inflation, and high uncertainty. Reforms to liberalize the economy are ignored wherever statism has become too vested. For instance, governments rarely rein in large fiscal deficits by reducing spending and limiting their duties to their natural attributions. Economies suffer high inflation, unemployment, impoverishment, and financial disorder, all the natural consequences of statism. Countries that have reserve currencies and face no balance of payments constraint may indulge largely in statism without suffering much of its implications. In contrast, developing countries may suffer considerably the pains inflicted by statism. The latter has two costs: a huge, quantified cost in terms of bureaucracy, inflation, taxation, subsidies, etc.; and a second non-quantified (i.e., unseen) cost in terms of economic losses of the economy.

Notes

1 The Corn-Laws were measures enforced in the United Kingdom between 1815 and 1846, which imposed restrictions and tariffs on imported grain. They were designed to keep grain prices high to favor domestic producers.
2 The US Federal Reserve, by forcing interest rates to near-zero and indulging into quantitative easing at a tune of $4 trillion since 2008, forced the European Central Bank and the Bank of Japan into equally aggressive policies to fend off exporting US unemployment to their respective countries. Such retaliatory action forced a significant depreciation of the euro and yen in relation to the dollar.
3 If the government issues a 30-year bond of $100, equivalent to 100 kilograms of bread. At an inflation rate of 5 percent/year, the government pays only $23 in real terms, or 23 kilograms of bread.
4 This implies that the US Federal Reserve has no need to mount its monumental quantitative money easing to stimulate the economy. The private economy is fully able to restore itself to instant equilibrium without any state intervention.
5 In case of paper money, the state keeps inflating money so debt is paid with depreciated money.
6 The gold clause in a money contract was abolished in 1934 by the Roosevelt Administration in a scheme to eliminate any money role for gold.
7 For instance, there may be a large inventory of unsold houses and commercial property. This does not mean that housing needs are fully satiated. It may mean that the clearing price may be below the initially expected prices and therefore profits will be lower. In fact, near-zero interest rates allow entrepreneurs to maintain large inventories of goods as well as high sales prices for a long period.

References

Bastiat, F., 2011, *The Bastiat Collection*, Auburn, AL: Ludwig von Mises Institute.
Freeman, J., 2016, "The 5,000 Year Government Debt Bubble," *The Wall Street Journal*, September 1, 2016. Available at www.wsj.com/articles/the-5-000-year-government-debt-bubble-1472685194.
Keynes, J. M., 1936, *The General Theory of Employment, Interest, and Money*, London, Palgrave Macmillan, St. Martin's Press, 1970.

Locke, J., 1691, *Some Considerations of the Consequences of the Lowering of Interest and the Raising the Value of Money*, London: Printed for Awnsham and John Churchill, at the Black Swan in Pater-Noster-Row.

McKinnon, R., 1973, *Money and Capital in Economic Development*, Washington, DC: Brookings Institution.

Nock, J., 1935, *Our Enemy, the State*, Caldwell, ID: The Caxton Printers, Ltd., 1950.

Oppenheimer, F., 1908, *The State*, New York: Vanguard Press.

Ricardo, D., 1817, *On the Principle of Political Economy and Taxation*, London: John Murray.

Say, J. B., 1803, *A Treatise on Political Economy*, Philadelphia: Claxton, Kemsen, & Haffelfingee.

Shaw, E., 1973, *Financial Deepening in Economic Development*, Oxford: Oxford University Press.

Smith, A., 1776, *An Inquiry Into the Nature and Causes of the Wealth of Nations*, London: Methuen and Co., Ltd. ed. Edwin Cannan, 1904, Fifth Edition.

Spencer, H., 1851, *The Social Statics*, London: John Chapman.

Spencer, H., 1884, *The Man Versus the State*, Caldwell, ID: The Caxton Printers, Ltd., 1960.

Spooner, L., 1886, *A Letter to Grover Cleveland*, Boston: Benj. R. Tucker Publisher.

Mises, L., 1949, *Human Action*, Auburn, AL: Ludwig von Mises Institute.

2 The government from a Sharia perspective

1. Introduction

In any community, be it a county, a city, or a country, a government is an absolute necessity; it has natural functions and it appears spontaneously and naturally within the community to pool human and material resources and serve the common interests of the inhabitants. Citizens endow the government with powers that will enable it to discharge its functions. Inhabitants pay for the cost of the government and draw considerable benefits from it, such as protection, justice, education, and caring for the vulnerable groups when it is confined to its natural duties.

Notwithstanding, the nature and size of government have been debated by many writers in the past.[1] Today, this topic is of an overriding importance in view of the disastrous effects of big governments, the financial crises, and the failure of governments in many countries to enhance economic development and social equity. The debate on the nature of government has been too controversial. On one side, there is the modern statism which confers an absolute power to the government in managing the economy and family matters. Statism makes government the Supreme Authority, discarding any restraint for its power. On another side, there are the conservatives who fear big government and see it as the source of economic and social problems; by necessity, the more the government expands beyond its natural duties, the less freedom there is; its laws become often unjust and make victims. The conservatives want a minimal government confined to natural domains such as justice, social welfare, education, health, infrastructure, and defense. From past civilizations as well as recent history, a judicious government may contribute tremendously to prosperity and peace; on the other hand, a government could become a powerfully destructive force when it is dominated by statism, socialism, or communism, or when possessed by unruly gangs or military juntas. It could flatten totally a country and displace whole populations, and cause mass killing and famines. Depending on its nature, size, and laws, a government could unleash private sector energies and promote prosperity; or freeze energies and even spread the destruction of life and property. The chapter covers:

- The Sharia duties of a government
- Freedom in Sharia

- Sharia prohibitions
- The size of the government

2. The Sharia duties of a government

A government is an absolutely needed natural entity that emerges spontaneously in any community. Quran and Sunnah have detailed the natural role of the state. There is, in fact, a consensus in every country or community about the basic duties of a government which include justice, defense, security, social welfare, education, health, infrastructure, and regulation. However, in each of these duties, Sharia has prescribed divine laws which are immutable and cannot change over time or across countries. These laws are not man-made, they are intended for the whole of humanity, and are known to be perfect and complete, meaning they dealt with every single aspect of the economic and social life and are most fit for economic prosperity and social justice.[2] They are natural laws, meaning that they preserve the natural rights of life and property. They organize the best economic and social system conducive to peace, security, and wealth creation. Sharia wants to establish the best ethics and highest moral values. The basic idea of Sharia laws is that humans are created by God, and no ruler is allowed to rule over them except according to divine laws.[3] A community which applies Sharia laws is secured total peace and an abundance of wealth. Sharia laws are meant to establish peace, security, and harmony within a community so people can live and work in the safest conditions possible, with no fear of aggression, or loss of life and property. They aim at preserving family life. Both individuals and rulers have to abide by Sharia laws.

A Sharia-compliant government adheres to divine rules: it is not an arbitrary or totalitarian power, it is not the make-up of the electorate or the elected rulers, it is not a dimensionless bureaucracy, rulers are not self-appointed, nor do they govern without concertation (Shura) with the rest of people. The government does not seek to stifle the private sector; instead, it wants to make it a main actor in the economy. It has to obey a set of divine rules, called Sharia, which it can never alter, even if it is an elected or a reformist government. The task of the government is to establish a social environment conducive to wealth creation and economic prosperity. A government should restrain itself to its natural duties and should not expand to areas that do not fail its attributions at the cost of impairing social welfare.

2.1 Justice

The laws of justice, sanctity of life, freedom, human rights, and property rights are fully established in Quran and Sunna, and should never be violated. The preservation of justice, safety, and property rights are the attributions of the government. The latter has to eliminate violence in the society and establish order and law according to Sharia laws. The purpose of Sharia jurisprudence is to achieve maximum safety and social peace at the least cost, which is so essential for economic growth and social stability. Sharia does not want a society to be doubly taxed by crimes: the cost inflicted on victims of crimes, and the cost on taxpayers to run an inefficient justice. The principle of enhancing security and protecting life and property is fully admitted in every country. Violations of private property rights are severely reprimanded by Sharia laws. Moreover, dangerous products such as alcoholic beverages and toxic drugs are forbidden.

Crimes produce victims and harm not only the immediate victims but the whole society. They lead to loss of life and property. Efficiently combating theft, banditry, and larceny is a fundamental element of a Sharia economic model, without which a country would be doomed to social disorder and economic stagnation. More specifically, work values deteriorate, trust disappears, and insecurity grows to alarming levels. In many countries, labor markets have suffered considerably from the prevalence of crime and deteriorating work values, which pushed farmers and employers in many industries to fear employing workers, shut down farms and plants, or push for capital-intensive modes of production, substituting machinery for labor.

Economic and social life involve a multitude of contracts. There are sale contracts such as the sale of houses, stocks, cars, computers, and airplanes; there are rent contracts such as rent of houses, office space, and cars; there are loans and debt contracts; there are bills, and many other contracts that arise in the daily transactions. A basic attribution of the government is the enforcement of duly agreed contracts and to hold responsible a party who fails to fulfill its contractual obligations. This is a basic attribution of the government. Duly agreed contracts have to be reinforced by the government. Commercial transactions have to be recorded in contracts written by a legal notary in the presence of witnesses. In the absence of a legal notary, collateral can be taken, which should be remitted when the obligation is fulfilled. If contracts are not reinforced, economic activity will suffer, and disorder spreads as contracting parties negate on their obligations. For instance, if a tenant refuses to pay rent or vacate the house, the landlord will suffer loss of income. With government force, the contract is either respected or the property is immediately vacated.

Being in charge of justice, the state has to abide by Sharia laws which are meant to establish a very safe environment, protect life and property, enhance business, eliminate crimes, and minimize enormously the cost of justice. Modern states maintain huge jail facilities and an increasing number of inmates which, in itself, shows a defective and too costly justice. Crimes can flourish and abound only with defective and un-natural laws and judicial systems.

2.2 Defense and security

A priority of the government is security and defense.[4] Defense has been a main reason for a government. Each city or country was susceptible of invasion and spoilage. The community has to collectively maintain an army, well trained and equipped to fend off external attacks. Besides defense, internal security is the duty of the state. Security force, fire stations, and emergency rescue are the duties of the state. Security forces are necessary for ensuring the safety of traffic, apprehending criminals, and responding to emergencies, including natural disasters. Sharia laws aim at ensuring perfect security conducive to social peace and sustained economic development. The lack of security in many developing countries has considerably penalized investment and growth.

2.3 Social welfare

Sharia addresses explicitly social welfare and mutual responsibility among the inhabitants of a region or cross-regions. A priority of the government is to attend to the well-being of the vulnerable persons in terms of sustenance, health, and shelter; these include the handicapped persons, the aged persons, the orphans, the widows, the sick, etc. Sharia has made it mandatory upon people to pay *Zakat* (see Chapter 4) as a way to provide for the needs of disinherited groups. Allah (SWT) made *Zakat* the third pillar of Islam. Contrary to all other economic systems, Sharia has built in a perfect safety net against poverty and social inequities. *Zakat* is a prerequisite for economic growth. By fully establishing *Zakat*, a Sharia economic model could easily eradicate poverty, build social and economic infrastructure, and achieve higher economic growth and employment. A Sharia economic model cannot be established without the full discharge of *Zakat*. The Prophet (PUH) said *Zakat* does not decrease wealth; rather, it increases it. He (PUH) warned against withholding *Zakat*. Refusal to pay *Zakat* will cause economic losses, as is explicated in many parts of the Quran. *Zakat* is not a favor of the rich to the poor; it is a right of the poor in the wealth of the rich.[5]

 Zakat is distributed to eligible recipients. Historical experience has established that if *Zakat* is fully paid, absolute poverty will completely disappear in the country where it is applied for two major reasons. First, Allah (SWT) will multiply wealth when *Zakat* is paid. Second, *Zakat* is fairly sufficient to satisfy the needs of the poor and the needy. Besides obligatory *Zakat*, *infaq*, defined as voluntary contributions, has been highly praised by Allah (SWT) and His Messenger (PUH). Generally, *infaq* is destined only for good causes such as building Mosques, hospitals, and infrastructure, or for defense or natural disasters. It is never meant to finance government waste.

2.4 Education

Science and knowledge are a priority of Islam. The latter is a religion of science and enlightenment. Allah SWT stressed the value of knowledge and science. It is only with science and knowledge that well-being is enhanced and natural resources are valorized. The Prophet (PUH) established teaching to the community as well as learning and memorization of the Quran. The first action of the Prophet (PUH) was to build the Quba Mosque upon his arrival in Medina and, a few days later, His Mosque (al-Masjid al-Nabawi), both were centers of teaching and learning. A priority of the state is to establish education and science; without science, there can be no human progress and improvement in well-being. Education cannot be spread without schools. Hence, the multiplication of Mosques and schools should be a priority of the government. Although this priority was undertaken essentially by individuals as well as groups of individuals, it could be a priority of the state to spread education and knowledge without charge.

2.5 Health

Health is a priority attribution of the state to which large amounts of resources have to be devoted for the construction and operation of hospitals and primary care centers. Free health services have to be available for vulnerable populations. Likewise, basic medicine, such as vaccination, has to be free for all the population. The financing of health should be part of the government budget. The government has to reduce unproductive public expenditure and increase health expenditure. The cost of health should also be covered through developing wide social insurance systems financed by beneficiaries' contributions, *Zakat* funds, charity donations, employers' contributions, and social security and pension funds' contributions.

2.6 Social and economic infrastructure

The production of public goods, such as Mosques, schools and hospitals, bridges, roads, etc., serves a common interest; these goods involve indivisibilities and economies of scale. Their production may require the authority of the state. For instance, building a highway or railroad requires expropriation of land over hundreds of miles, which can be done only through state authority and compensation. Sanitation infrastructure is essential to prevent dangerous diseases such as cholera or malaria. Infrastructure, in the form of schools, hospitals, roads, etc., contributes to economic growth and enhances the community welfare. These public goods could be provided by the state as well as the private sector. Hence, in many instances, such as roads, schools, hospitals, water, sanitation, etc., an active role of the state is necessary to enhance the social welfare. The state is explicitly allowed to use *Zakat* money for the purpose of building infrastructure, such as schools, hospitals, roads, etc., all belonging to a category eligible for *Zakat* money. Infrastructure could also be built through charitable organizations. For instance, a hospital, school, Mosque, etc. may be built and operated through private charitable organizations and may cover their expenses from income of endowments. Infrastructure may also be built by the private sector on a market basis.

2.7 Moral values and code of conduct

Sharia law authorizes the government to protect moral values, encourage high ethical values, politeness, and responsible behavior. In Quran 3: 104, Allah says: "Let there arise among you a group of people inviting to all that is good and forbidding the evil." The state has to protect the youth as well as the whole population against evil and promote good manners and civism.

2.8 Municipal services and protection of the environment

Sharia law entrusts the state with the obligations to preserve the hygienic standards, clean the streets, treat waste, and protect the environment. Fulfilling this obligation prevents against epidemics, plagues, and protects life. Littering streets is forbidden. The state is responsible for the collection and treatment of the waste at a cost to be paid by the inhabitants who directly benefit from this service.

2.9 Regulation (Hisbah)

Regulation is an inherent aspect of the justice function of the government. For safety as well as the protection of property rights, the state has to perform a regulatory role. This role is never meant to interfere with price mechanism and economic freedom. For instance, the state has the responsibility to verify that the weights used for weighting merchandise are exact, i.e., one kilogram mass is exactly one kilo, and is not diminished by the trader. However, the government cannot prevent the trader to set freely his price. Similarly, the state cannot allow just anyone to become a heart surgeon. This will be disastrous; it has to strictly regulate the profession and allow only those who are certified by medical schools to practice the profession. In traffic, environment pollution, etc. it is a mandatory responsibility of the government to attend to the safety of air, sea, and road traffic and the environment. The government has also a regulatory role in planning cities and infrastructure. It may force compliance with zoning standards. For instance, a gas station may not be allowed within a residential area, or near a school or hospital, because of the emission of toxic gasses and risk of fire. The government regulates the money, and ensures that the coin conforms to the standard with no counterfeiting. It regulates the construction of buildings, and fire and safety standards.

There are industries that pollute. The government may relocate them and impose anti-pollution regulations. Industrial zones and inflammable products storage have to be regulated. Similarly, cars emit pollution. The government may force users to install anti-pollution devices and to have an emission inspection every year. Regulation of traffic such as traffic lights, speed limits, vehicle inspection, and car insurance all fall under the regulatory authority of the government. Medicine and many other professions require licensing. The finance industry also requires regulations. The purpose of regulations is to protect the community against fraud and to prevent harmful externalities that endanger the environment (Say 1803). Urban anarchy is harmful and has to be combated. Similarly, protection of farmland, rivers, forests, and other natural resources is part of the state's regulatory role.

The state has to prevent the sales of alcohol, illicit products, gambling, and many other immoral trades that are strictly forbidden by Sharia. The state has to reinforce competition rules and eliminate any restriction to entry in a market place or industry. Regulatory duties, called Hisbah, were conducted during the lifetime of the Prophet PUH and His Successors. These duties were never meant to interfere with free markets; they were aimed at punishing fraud or establishing a safe and social business environment.

3. Freedom in Sharia

While the restrictive confines of Sharia are very well known to all people and are simply understood, Sharia grants political freedom and opposes any form of dictatorship and oppression. It condemns torture. It grants freedom of choice, possession, and trade, and condemns any restraint which was not authorized by Sharia. Hence, prohibition of trade in gold and silver is anti-Sharia and a form of despotism. Similarly, restrictions on foreign trade and foreign exchange are anti-Sharia. Price and wage controls are distortive and may not be permissible. In many countries, government imposes high commodity taxes which naturally create arbitrage opportunities. It calls traders who seize these opportunities as smugglers; it jails them and inflicts on them high penalties (Adam Smith 1776).

4. Sharia prohibitions

Sharia prohibits interest-based debt. This is not a novelty since this prohibition existed in previous divine laws. It prohibits trade in alcohol beverage and gambling. These activities are dangerous and are strictly forbidden. They are a source of injustice, misconduct, and crimes. There is a great economic loss that arises from these activities and social disorder. While interest, alcohol, and gambling were explicitly named and considered as among the most serious violations of Sharia, the latter prohibits also trade in products that are known to be harmful, such as pork meat, drugs, and tobacco. Sharia prohibits bribery.[6] The latter corrupts the judicial system and leads to injustice or the protection of interest groups at the expense of other people. Bribery has existed at all times; rulers are bribed to make laws or institutions that protect the interest a group of persons; without this bribery, the bribing group would not reap benefits.

5. The size of the government

A major problem in many countries is a too-bloated government, most of it wasteful, and a source of economic and social chaos. In many developing countries, the bureaucracy has become the dominant class. Civil servants and army salaries may absorb up to 70 percent of tax revenues in some countries. Very little government saving is left for infrastructure. Being poorly paid, bureaucrats turn to bribery to supplement their salaries. The government has become an outlet for unqualified employees and a disguised, handsomely paid unemployment. The size of government has expanded through the multiplication of administrative jobs as well as inefficient and corrupt judicial laws. More government begets more government. Many democratic countries started with a very small government; however, their lawmakers kept creating laws, which necessitated more bureaucracy and enforcement agencies. In parallel, as the government became too big, it had to establish a bigger taxation administration and phenomenal tax laws, which even the most sophisticated experts can never understand or grasp. Hence, it has to tax heavily to maintain huge bureaucracy, army, and enforce un-natural laws. All would have been unnecessary if the government remained within its initial constitutional powers and renounced making useless, un-natural laws.

The creation of government jobs and the expansion of spending programs are very easy; however, the general population has to pay for it through taxes, debt, or money printing. Consequently, poverty and unemployment have been increasing as resources are consumed by unproductive bureaucracy instead of being invested in the economy. In some countries, the size of the police and security forces are too bloated; yet, the number of jails and inmates keeps increasing to reach two and half million in a single country, or tens of thousands in many other countries. All the spending on security forces, the justice system, and jails could be drastically reduced if governments prevented the sources of crimes; refrained from intervening in domains that do not fall under its competence, and applied Sharia laws. Anti-market labor and trade laws and un-natural family laws made governments intervene in areas which are not its natural attributions and created a huge legislative body for their enforcement.[7]

Sharia laws aim at a Sharia-based and efficient government, which will prevent crowding out of the private sector as well as distortions to the market as a result of unconstrained government. The government cannot expand expenditure in a heedless manner far beyond its resources. The government has no authority to impose taxation beyond the laws of Sharia. A government that has unlimited authority of taxation will keep inventing new taxes, increasing existing taxes, and will keep enlarging its size, as has actually occurred in most countries, until it reaches an incredible size and possesses vast powers. Eventually, it will print money ex-nihilo as a taxation instrument. A Sharia-compliant government has no authority to expand spending beyond what is affordable from *Zakat*, royalties, user fees, donations, Sharia-compliant taxes, etc. It has to prioritize spending towards education, health, and infrastructure construction. It cannot print money ex-nihilo to finance its expenditure. It cannot borrow with interest. It has necessarily to curtail its expenditure to conform strictly to Sharia-compliant revenues. The government has therefore to cut down its size to comply with its budget restraint. It has no right to shower doles and maintain unproductive political spending.

Justice is a crucial area of the government; yet, its cost was meant to be considerably low if the government applies Sharia law. A main goal of Sharia is to minimize drastically the cost of justice by maximizing its efficiency and deterrence. The government should never interfere in areas that do not fall under its jurisdiction. Arresting a trader who sells gold or who carries foreign currency is no crime from Sharia perspective. The state incurs a cost to the judge and then to keep the trader in jail; in turn, the trader loses his property and his family suffers poverty and dislocation. If the government strictly applies the Sharia law to cope with widespread thefts, it would reduce drastically theft and theft-related killings; likewise, applying the death penalty will tremendously reduce murders. If the government refrains from intervening in labor markets through awkward legislation it will have no occasion for justice spending. Similarly, if the government prevents the selling of alcohol and dangerous products, the number of road fatalities will be reduced, and so will be the number of crimes. The cost of justice is extremely high in many countries simply because the state applies un-natural and unjust laws of its own making and discards the divine laws.

In the area of infrastructure, the government should encourage full participation of the private sector in areas where such participation is highly feasible such as in education, health, water, electricity, sanitation, dams, railroads, etc. This participation would contribute to reduce significantly the size and cost of the government. It will increase significantly the supply of infrastructure as well as the efficiency with which this infrastructure is managed and maintained.

In some countries, the government wants to create full employment. It reduces interest rates to zero, and hikes its spending and bureaucracy to a huge number. The unlimited size of the government has become a hurdle to economic growth. A big government spreads economic and social chaos. It has a huge debt; it keeps inflating money to pay for wasteful expenses. Social life in many countries is disorderly; and crimes are rising. From a Sharia perspective, the government has no right to interfere with markets, it has no right to print money out of thin air, and it has no right to jerk up its spending beyond its Sharia-compliant revenues. The government is never meant to enslave or to direct or plan the life of individuals. An individual should be responsible for his own life, family, and livelihood. If a chieftain promises free food, housing, and clothing to all village members, everyone in the village will cheer the decision as the most formidable and just decision of an outstanding chieftain; however, soon, everyone in the village will perish of famine and economic disorder, simply because the chieftain decided to disable the law of nature. Such is indeed the policy of many governments.

6. Conclusions

A state emerges naturally within a community to serve common, and not private, interests of its members. Many common interests bind community members. Among the most pressing needs are freedom, security, protection of life and property, and mutual solidarity. The joint commitment of the inhabitants enables them to establish a security and defense apparatus against crimes and outside invasion; it enables people to establish social programs that attend for the needs of the vulnerable groups. The government is obligated to apply the Sharia law, which is a divine law, prescribed by the Creator of the Universe. The regulatory authority also serves a common interest in enhancing safety and averting fraud and crime. In sum, the state has to organize the safest and most enticing environment for the private sector. Many countries were not able to promote a secure environment as a fundamental prerequisite for their development; consequently, they continue to suffer stagnation and poverty.

We observe that the Prophet (PUH) and His Successors established political and economic freedom, precluding any form of violation of free enterprise, and private property rights. Without political freedom, there will be no security and enthusiasm for private sector development. Dictatorship has never been favorable to economic development as experienced by countries which were ruled by dictators. We observe that neither the Prophet (PUH) nor His Successors spent money on building entertainment places (theaters, cultural activities, celebrations, parties, etc.). Most importantly, neither the Prophet (PUH) nor His Successors practiced arbitrary taxation and confiscation as in modern governments to meet, what is known, as pressing inflexible government spending. We observe that the Prophet (PUH) severely condemned idleness, praised the virtues of work, trust, honesty, and high quality of work. If the state provides the right environment, education, justice, and free markets, wealth will become abundant, as clearly stated by Allah (SWT) in many verses of the Quran (e.g., Al-Araf, 7: 96).[8] If the state wants to emphasize economic development, full employment, wealth and material values while neglecting Sharia laws of justice and free markets, only poverty and misery will spread, as has happened in many countries in recent times.

The state, as established by the Prophet (PUH), is bound by rules prescribed by the Sharia as to its natural duties, spending, and sources of revenues. It cannot exceed its limits and functions without imperiling political and economic stability, freedom, and natural human rights. It cannot use state money for rulers and public officials' privileges beyond their just remuneration; nor can the state confiscate property or impose arbitrary tax obligations beyond Sharia rules. All the work of a modern state is to strive to secure the high pay of its bureaucracy and army often at the expense of poor people. Despite large deficit and increasing debt, the state keeps taxing, borrowing, and printing money to pay regularly for its unproductive spending at the expense of productive spending.

Democracy is no guarantee against statism, big, disorderly, and bankrupt governments. Well-conceived constitutions cannot restrain government powers. Democratic states are the least to observe any fiscal or monetary discipline or recognize any limit to statism; they suffer large financial disequilibria, and out-of-control government size and spending. A Sharia-based government has to be confined to its natural fields; in taxation, it cannot exceed the financial revenues allowed by Sharia. This implies an active role of the private sector in the economy and sustained prosperity. A Sharia-based government has a double limit on its size: (i) its legislative domain is virtually determined by Sharia laws: it cannot violate or add to these laws; and (ii) its resources are limited by *Zakat*, *infaq*, royalties, and other Sharia-compliant revenues. These two checks do not exist for a conventional government that has been made into a big government with extensive arbitrary powers and amazing spending.

Sharia laws are natural laws aimed at preserving peace, harmony, and prosperity. They purport to establish a safe and crime-free environment that enables economic prosperity, enforces contracts, and forbids all forms of injustice and aggression. It is natural to forbid murder, theft, or alcohol. In many countries, driving under the influence is forbidden simply because of a huge number of road fatalities caused by alcohol. Sharia laws aim at attaining the most peaceful community at the least cost. It is totally unjust to make the poor pay for criminals, such as in the form of jailhouses and oversized judicial system. Jails are totally inhumane and ineffective against crime; they represent a huge futile cost for the community. Judicial systems absorb more resources than devoted to education or health. Some countries have a small number of poorly equipped hospitals; yet they have jails that incarcerate thousands of criminals.

Bastiat (1877) discussed the cost of wrong laws; there are seen costs which are the high number of murders; the loss of property stolen by thieves, and the cost of the judicial system. There is an unseen cost which is the lost investment and prosperity due to fear from crime and insecurity.

A Sharia model postulates two basic principles for the government:

- The government has to remain within its natural duties, discharge efficiently these duties, and contain its size.
- It has to secure an environment that is free of crime by strictly Sharia laws in reprimanding crimes.

However, often governments have neglected their natural duties; they have stepped beyond Sharia confines and often made legislation that was not natural, such as forbidding trade in gold or silver, or punishing traders in parallel markets for highly taxed commodities. Adam Smith noted that offenses of this kind are not true offenses and penalizing traders who take risks to profit from arbitrage opportunities is not fair. In addition, in many countries, the environment is so infested with crimes that private activities are seriously impeded.

Sharia laws are perfect, they are divine, and the Creator knows best what fits His Creation.[9] Man-made laws are failing and causing increasing and alarming crimes in most of countries. They are too costly, inhumane, unethical, and inefficient. Many countries are entangled into vicious circles of higher justice cost and higher crime rates and insecurity.

Notes

1 The US Declaration of Independence 1776, and the US Constitution 1789. See also James Mill (1825), "Government", Encyclopaedia Britannica.

2 Quran 6: 38: We have neglected nothing in the Book. Quran 16: 89: And we have sent down to you the Book as an exposition of everything.

3 Quran: 5: 44: And whosoever does not judge by what Allah has revealed, such as the disbelievers. Quran: 4:45: And whosoever does not judge by that which Allah has revealed, such are the wrong-doers. Quran 4:46: And whosoever does not judge by what Allah has revealed such are the rebellious.

4 Security is a fundamental prerequisite to economic prosperity. In the Quran (2: 126 and 14: 35), the Prophet Ibrahim implored Allah (SWT) to make the Holy Land secure, i.e., free of crime and transgression.

5 *Zakat* is essentially destined to eight categories of eligible recipients, as specified in the Quran (9: 60): Alms are for the poor and the needy, and those employed to administer the funds, for those whose hearts have been recently reconciled to truth, for those in bondage and in debt, in the cause of Allah, and for the wayfarer; thus is it ordained by Allah, and Allah is full of knowledge and wisdom.

6 Quran 2: 188: And do not consume one another's wealth unjustly nor give bribes to rulers that you may knowingly consume part of the property of others sinfully.

7 Imagine Mr. A hired a worker for one hour and paid him $8 instead of the minimum wage of $9.25. The state would arrest Mr. A, state lawyers and Mr. A's lawyers are employed, judges and clerks are used, and hundreds of pages of legal work are created. Mr. A pays $50,000 for legal fees, he pays a compensation of $1,000,000 to the worker, and he is sentenced to 10 years in jail. More jail personnel is hired, and a jail cost is paid for 10 years. Mr. A's family of a wife and five children are without a breadwinner, children drop out of school, the family cannot rent a home, and finally becomes homeless. Such is the law in many countries. So many people are jailed, deported, or fined huge penalties because they paid less than the minimum wage or kept their workers some extra time beyond the government time.

8 And if the people of the towns had believed and had the *Taqwa* (piety), certainly, We should have opened for them blessings from the heaven and the earth, but they belied (the Messengers). So We took them (with punishment) for what they used to earn (polytheism and crimes, etc.).

9 Quran 5: 50: Do they seek the judgement of the days of ignorance? And who is better in judgement than Allah for a people who have firm faith.

References

Bastiat, F., 1877, *The Bastiat Collection*, Auburn, AL: Ludwig von Mises Institute.
Mill, J., 1825, "Government", *Encyclopaedia Britannica*.
Smith, A., 1776, *An Inquiry Into the Nature and Causes of the Wealth of Nations*, London: Methuen and Co., Ltd., ed. Edwin Cannan, 1904, Fifth Edition.

3 Sharia free market model

1. Introduction

Natural mechanisms of any system or body cannot be altered without causing losses. Laissez-faire doctrine advocates free markets, including free processes of exchange, production, pricing, and wealth accumulation. The government should cause no distortions in the form of monopolies, interest rate control, minimum wages, tariffs, subsidies, and quotas. These distortions have caused inefficiencies (Smith 1776; Say 1803; Mill 1808; Ricardo 1817; Mises 1949).

Adam Smith elaborated the theory of the "invisible hand," according to which free markets lead to most efficient allocations of resources within and across countries. Mises established the impossibility of socialism; manifestly illustrated by the collapse of the communist model in the 1990s. Laissez-faire advocates adhere to free enterprise and free prices in the creation of wealth and its distribution among individuals and nations. Free markets are efficient. Free wealth accumulation by entrepreneurs can never hurt workers; it can only improve their lots.

Sharia model opposes alterations of the free natural mechanism of exchange, production, and wealth accumulation. All product and factor markets have to be free. Sharia strictly opposes wage and price controls.[1] Product and factor prices have to be determined by the market with free choice of traders. Any honest wealth accumulation in a free market is praised and is perfectly legitimate. Sharia model repudiates the principle that consumption, and not production, is a way to richness. Any intervention of the government which impairs free markets is detrimental; it can only transfer free gain to one group at the expense of another group.

This chapter addresses the micro-equilibrium of commodities and labor as well as the macroeconomic equilibrium of the economy; it covers:

- The neoclassical pricing theory: the free market equilibrium
- Welfare effects of taxes and subsidies
- Say's law: main principle of free markets
- The Keynesian, classical, and Sharia models of macroeconomic equilibrium

2. The neoclassical pricing theory: the free market equilibrium

Value theory stipulates that a marketable product (e.g., wheat) has a market where demand and supply meet. The demand for a marketable product is downward sloping in terms of the price of the product and the supply of the product is upward sloping in terms of price where price is a money price per unit of the product (e.g., $/bushel). (Figure 3.1A). A free market has a clearing price P_0 that equates the demand of the product with its supply. At a higher price P_1 there is an excess supply of wheat. At a lower price P_2 there is an excess demand of wheat. Observe that both excess supply and excess demand are relative notions; neither implies an absolute abundance nor an absolute shortage of wheat. Either glut or shortage disappears as price veers to equilibrium price P_0. Either would persist if government disables the market mechanism through minimum or maximum price legislation.

Trade benefits each trader. There are gains that arise from trade. This principle is illustrated by Edgeworth box (Figure 3.1B). Consider two traders A and B and two products cloth and wheat. Let A possess only wheat and no cloth; and B possess cloth and no wheat. Trader A does not want to be without cloth, and B does not wish to starve; both gain from trade. The initial endowments of A and B are shown by E_0. With free trade, an equilibrium is reached at E_e where A consumes AW of wheat and AC of cloth; and B consumes BW of wheat and BC of cloth. Trader A moves to a higher indifference curve I^e_A and B moves also to a higher indifference curve I^e_A. The trading process between A and B is described by Figure 1C and 1D. At price P_1 there is excess supply of wheat.

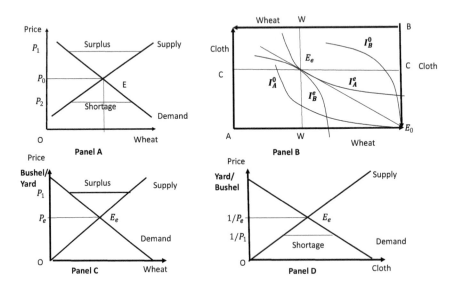

Figure 3.1 Free markets

Say's law postulates that there is necessarily excess demand for cloth at price $1/P_1$, which means that B is ready to offer only a small quantity of cloth for such a low price of cloth in terms of wheat. Both A and B gain by renegotiating the terms of trade until they reach the equilibrium price *Pe* and the equilibrium allocation E_e (Figure 3.1B, 3.1C, 3.1D).

The competitive equilibrium is called the first fundamental theorem of welfare economics. Arrow and Debreu (1954) have established the mathematical existence of a general equilibrium and its uniqueness. Market prices are efficient, provide information, such as the constantly changing social preferences, the production technologies, and availability of resources. The social value of any enterprise is measured by the value of profits under unhampered prices. If an enterprise is making less than the normal profit or is making losses, then obviously that enterprise is socially inefficient, and its capital is being consumed. It is worthwhile for the community that resources be employed in most profitable enterprises. Free competition among enterprises is the mother of creation, including creative destruction. Free competition among enterprises and nations lead to technological progress, new products appearing, older products disappearing, gains in productivity, and higher wealth. Private sector adapts to the cost of resources; it economizes on resources that become dearer, such as crude oil, with energy saving technologies and products. The private sector uses resources according to their true price. Government control of prices can make a loss-making firm profitable, such as through near-zero interest rates, inflation, and subsidies. Government-controlled prices misdirect resources and penalize social welfare.

Demand and supply analysis applies for labor as for any commodity and enable to determine equilibrium wages. The demand for labor is a derived demand from profit maximization. Given all other factors of production such as fixed capital, raw materials, and factor and product prices, a firm employs labor until the value of the marginal product of a unit of labor is equal to nominal wage rate. The labor demand curve is downward sloping; if nominal wage drops, a firm will recruit more labor to maximize its profits. Inversely, if nominal wage rises, a firm lays off labor to maximize its profit.

The supply of labor is derived from utility maximization that includes labor and leisure. If labor time rises, leisure time decreases, des-utility of labor increases, and a higher wage rate is required for encouraging labor to renounce leisure. If the wage rate drops, labor will cut down labor time in favor of leisure. The equilibrium of the labor market is obtained with free interplay of demand and supply of labor. In a free market, this equilibrium is defined as a full employment equilibrium. It will determine the level of national output for given capital and land.

The same analysis applies at the margin for capital. An additional unit of capital is saved. Its saving is upward sloping with the rate of return. An additional unit of capital is invested; investment is downward sloping with the rate of return. An equilibrium rate of return is obtained with the interplay of free capital markets for savings and investment. At the equilibrium rate of return, savings and investment are equal.

The neoclassical theory of income distribution postulates that income from production is distributed into two parts: wages that remunerate labor and profits that remunerate capital; the latter include rent, interest, and normal profits. We assume income Y is produced by two primary factors labor L and capital k according to $Y = F(K,L)$. The wage rate is $p\dfrac{\partial F}{\partial L} = w$ and the profit rate is $p\dfrac{\partial F}{\partial K} = r$. Income is equal to the sum of wages and profits:

$$Y = wL + rK$$

The distribution of income is a free market distribution which depends on the wage rate determined in the labor market and the profit rate determined in the capital market. If the production function is a Cobb-Douglas function of the form $Y = A.K^{\alpha}L^{1-\alpha}$, then the relative share of capital is α and that of labor is $(1-\alpha)$. Labor unions cannot change these shares. If unions increase wages, the entrepreneurs substitute capital for labor and lay off labor which will increase the marginal product of labor to equate the higher unions' wage. If the government intervenes both to prevent layoffs and force higher wages, then the enterprises will see its profits eaten up by labor. It will no longer be able to invest in replacing capital and save for new investment. If the government allows layoffs, however, then it taxes enterprises with a higher corporate tax to pay for unemployment benefits, and the result will be identically the same: the profits in the economy are reduced by labor to the detriment of capital and new investment. Subsidizing unemployment is a dangerous policy of the government. It penalizes an economy twice: it consumes capital, and it deprives it from the output that could have been produced if labor markets were free from unions and government intervention.

3. Welfare effects of taxes and subsidies

Governments rely heavily on commodity taxes to generate revenues for their expenditures (Ibn Khaldoun 1377). Besides the revenue purposes, a government uses taxes and subsidies for policy purposes such as providing incentives for new investment, or subsidizing consumers, or protecting farmers, or encouraging exports and discouraging imports. Every tax or subsidy is distortive; it changes the competitive equilibrium and yields a suboptimal equilibrium.

Figure 3.2A illustrates the equilibrium of the bread market; the free market equilibrium is quantity Q_e and price P_e. We assume that this equilibrium is part of a general equilibrium in the economy, where consumers, after taking into account their incomes, tastes, and all other expenditures on housing, clothing, cars, etc., have decided to consume Q_e of bread at a price P_e per bread. We observe that this equilibrium is optimal. The consumer surplus is the triangle AP_eE_e; the producer surplus is the triangle BP_eE_e. The government introduces a unit subsidy per bread to help the poor. This action in fact serves no social purpose and cannot help the poor; it is only distortive. It requires a high administration cost; moreover, it creates changes in spending patterns and occasions a taxation that was not needed. The government fixes a subsidized price P_c per bread; the demand for bread increases to Q_s. To supply this quantity, the producer has to sell bread at P_s per bread, of which the consumer pays P_c and the government pays a subsidy equal to P_s-P_c. The welfare effects of the subsidy are shown in Table 3.1. Consumer surplus increases by the area $P_sP_cE_eE_c$; the producer surplus increases by the area $P_sP_eE_eE_s$; the government spends the area $-P_sP_cE_eE_s$; the national welfare decreases by the area $-EeEcEs$.

The area $PsP_cE_eE_s$ represents the amount of subsidy on bread that has to be paid out of taxation. Observe that this important sum did not exist in a competitive equilibrium. Now it introduces a totally unnecessary spending in the budget. Except in a country where government revenues are plentiful, such as royalties from natural resources, this expenditure has to be financed from new taxes, which reduce consumption and investment of those who have to pay, or it crowds out spending on health, education, or infrastructure (Smith 1776); or it has to be financed through debt, or through arrears or default on debt. Assuming it has to be financed by workers through a tax on their wages, which is the most plausible case, then the poor worker ends up subsidizing the bread consumption of the rich consumers. It is possible that the poor worker be a net

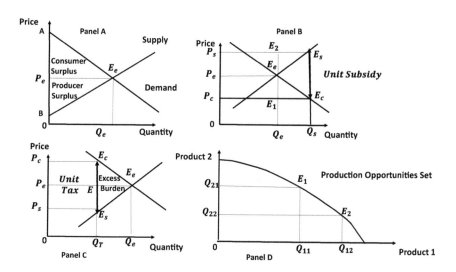

Figure 3.2 Subsidy and tax distortions

Table 3.1 Welfare effects of a subsidy

Consumer surplus = area = $P_cP_eE_eE_c$	Producer surplus = area = $P_sP_eE_eE_s$	Government Revenue = area = $-P_sP_cE_eE_s$	National Welfare= area = $-EeEcEs$.

Table 3.2 Welfare effects of a tax

Consumer surplus = area = $-P_c P_e E_e E_c$	Producer surplus = area = $-P_s P_e E_e E_s$	Government Revenue = area = $P_s P_c E_c E_s$	National Welfare = area = $-E_e E_c E_s$

loser if the amount of taxes far exceeds his additional consumption of bread. This is not the only distortion. Since the supply of bread has to increase, it has to be imported, or supplied at the expense of relocation of resources from the production say of clothing to the production of wheat, Maize, barley, etc. The relative price of these items has increased in terms of clothing, and therefore it is less profitable to produce clothing and more profitable to produce food items. The distortions could be numerous. Assuming some consumers make net gains from the subsidies, they will utilize their economies to spend more on other commodities that are less essential than bread, such as movies, etc., and these may have to be imported and their price may be raised.

Let the government impose a unit tax, either to discourage the consumption of a commodity or to gain tax revenues for its budget. Figure 3.2C illustrates the effect of a unit tax. The demand is reduced from Q_e to Q_T; *the price paid by the consumer is P_c, the price received by the producer is P_s, the difference P_c-P_s is the unit tax.* The welfare effects of a unit tax are depicted in Table 3.2.

Consumers lose a surplus equal to the area $P_c P_e E_e E_c$; likewise, producers lose a surplus equal to the area $P_s P_e E_e E_s$. The area $P_s P_c E_c E_s$ is the amount of tax received by the government. The triangle $E_e E_c E_s$ is called the excess burden of the tax, which is the net loss of national welfare from the unit tax.

Figure 3.2 illustrates the tradeoff effect of a subsidy or a tax. A subsidy would encourage a reallocation of production resources toward the subsidized industry. The opportunity cost of a subsidy would be the lost output of the non-subsidized industry. If the production of the subsidized product is inelastic, there will less exports and more imports of the subsidized product. The opportunity cost would be the lost foreign exchange which could have been used for investment. Likewise, a tax discourages production of the taxed industry and therefore reallocated resources toward the non-taxed industry. The consumers may gain in terms of additional consumption or producers from additional exports of non-taxed industry products.

4. Say's law: main principle of free markets

Say's law of markets is a main principle of free markets within and across countries. Under free market assumptions, commodities are exchanged for commodities; the production of commodities creates a market for the produced commodities. Money is essentially a medium of exchange: there can be no demand failure (Say 1803), only partial gluts corresponding to partial deficits that may appear in an economy. If a commodity is produced in abundance, another commodity or set of commodities may happen to be in shortage and do not offer a market for the abundant commodity. Say's law is formulated as the sum of excess demands and excess supplies in an economy add to zero, therefore ruling out general over-production and aggregate demand failure, i.e., an excess of savings over investment. The flexibility of prices regulates commodities markets, wages, and interest rates of the capital markets. If there is an excess saving over investment, free interest rates will decline and increase investment to close the gap. Inversely, drying up of capital will cause interest rates to rise.

The authors of Say's law, including J. B. Say (1803), Ricardo (1817), James Mill (1808), and J. S. Mill (1848) explicitly maintained the impossibility of over-production of all commodities; they feared the theory of under-consumption, which disgraced saving and asserted that an economy can grow rich with consumption and not with production. This theory has been known as Keynesian economics since 1936, which B. Anderson (1945) qualified as more dangerous than Marxism. Proponents of Say's law explicitly opposed any intervention of the government to increase consumption via money printing and disabling the free market mechanism. Say (1803) maintained that:

> The same principle [i.e., Say's law] leads to the conclusion, that the encouragement of mere consumption is no benefit to commerce; for the difficulty lies in supplying the means, not in stimulating the desire of consumption; and we have seen that production alone, furnishes those means. Thus, it is the aim of good government to stimulate production, of bad government to encourage consumption.
>
> (P. 139)

Albeit Say's law is indubitably true in a barter economy, laissez-faire economists, including Say, Ricardo, J.S. Mill, Mises, etc., maintained that Say's law is true in a monetary economy, i.e., a general glut is impossible in either a barter or money economy. In Figure 3.1C and 3.1D, if wheat and cloth are the only commodities in the economy, then we cannot have excess supply in both wheat and cloth with or without money. Ultimately, commodities are exchanged for commodities both in domestic and international trade. The role of money is explicated by Say (1803):

> Should a tradesman say, I do not want other products for my woolens, I want money, there could be little difficulty in convincing him that his customers could not pay him in money, without having first procured it by the sale of some other commodities of their own.
>
> (P. 133)

J.S. Mill feared the doctrine of consumption which called for a large government expenditure for the purpose of encouraging industry; he stressed that production created wealth and that consumption needed no stimulus. He maintained that all which is produced is consumed, either for the purpose of investment or consumption.[2] A person who saves provides capital for investment. The policy of government to encourage consumption reduces saving; it promotes unproductive consumption at the expense of investment and erodes the capital base. Mill stressed that so long as there are unsatisfied needs in basic necessities or even in luxuries, there is always a need for investment. He maintained that nothing can be more absurd than the notion that investment should aggravate poverty. He reiterated the principle that commodities constitute the market for commodities, and that a general over-production of commodities is not conceivable: only some commodities may be produced in surplus; however, at the expense of shortages in some other commodities.

Statists attacked Say's law which postulated both self-regulating markets and the impossibility of general over-production of commodities. Marx (1862) and Keynes (1936) considered Say's law erroneous – markets cannot self-regulate and the economy suffers under-consumption and the general glut of commodities – both called on the state to intervene in the economy and prevent mass–unemployment due to general glut and demand failure. In Marxism, the state should abolish property and markets altogether. In Keynesian economics, the state should inflate money and credit, prevent any deflation of prices and wages, spend as much as possible since saving is harmful to employment, and depreciate currency so that full employment and prosperity can be maintained in a durable way. Keynes considered that consumption, not production, was the essence of prosperity and full employment.

5. The Keynesian, classical, and Sharia models of macroeconomic equilibrium

Business cycles show that full employment output could fall quickly to under-employment output and the unemployment rate could rise from 2–3 percent to as high as 20–25 percent as witnessed in the US during the Great Depression (1929–1939) (US Bureau of Labor Statistics). An economy that operates at full employment revels in prosperity; in contrast, mass–unemployment entails loss of output and end of prosperity. A stylized fact of cycle theory showed that a depression was preceded by an inflationary boom fueled by a cheap money policy and the creation of fictitious credit that has no real saving backing (Gouge 1833; Carroll 1850). Credit expansion causes asset price bubbles, credit contraction causes a crash of these prices and perhaps bank failures, in turn, it causes an economic recession.[3]

Juglar (1862) observed that financial crises were frequent; he statistically analyzed their causes, which were invariably unchecked credit followed by a contraction of deposits. They were peculiar only to countries with developed fractional reserve banking and absent elsewhere. Each crisis was brief, there was no government intervention, and the classical model of free markets was fully operational. There was a liquidation process of unsafe banks, no bailouts of banks and enterprises; unprofitable projects were discarded; interest rates rose significantly; prices fell and so did wages; and economic recovery was prompt. Juglar showed that prosperity was far higher after the crisis than before. The full relevance of the classical model of free markets can be illustrated by the fast economic recovery following the 1907 and 1921 crises in the United States, with the economy recovering promptly to full employment and fast growth without government intervention. The government did not have to print or borrow one single penny for the economy to reach quickly full employment thanks to the self-adjustment of free markets.

In contrast, statism has become too rooted since the crisis of 1929. The policies of cheap money and super fiscal expansion, lowering of interest rates, and increasing minimum wages were severely criticized by Hayek (1931), Robbins (1934), Mises (1949), and Etienne Mantoux (1937) who believed that free markets would restore full employment with no need for fiscal and money policies.

The contrast between pre- and post-1929 is striking. In the pre-1929 era, the economy recovered promptly in every financial crisis, without any money or fiscal actions. The government did not have to print or borrow any money, did not have to interfere with wage, price, and interest rates mechanisms, and real incomes were rising. After 1929 (e.g., 2008 crisis), the recovery became too slow, the government had to borrow heavily and print money out of thin air, unemployment subsidies were monumental, there was too much unjust redistribution of wealth, and real incomes were falling. Uncertainties were too exacerbated.

5.1 Keynesian approach to full employment: fiscal spending and money inflation

Keynesian economics apply to an economy like the US economy where the government has disabled the gold standard and replaced it with a government inconvertible paper, controls labor and capital markets, imposes downward rigidity of wages, and uses inflation to promote employment and growth. They do not apply to a free market economy. Keynes mounted an attack on the classics in an effort to discredit them and refuted Say's law according to which a general over-production was impossible and money hoarding did not harm the economy since both prices and wages were perfectly flexible.[4] In fact, Keynes's diagnosis of a financial crisis was opposite to the nature of the crisis as well as statistical data. Fisher (1933, 1936) and Soddy (1934) did not attribute the crisis to a demand failure, but to an evaporation of debt money by 28 percent. Labordere (1908) showed that a crisis could appear only when saving became too low; this truth is confirmed consistently by the collapse of banks during the nineteenth century when there were heavy imports and withdrawals of specie from the banks to make foreign payments.

Keynes showed flaws in a government-controlled economy that would prevent self-recovery to full employment, except with full-scale government intervention. These flaws were the following:

- Investment was interest-inelastic; low interest rates would not increase investment.
- Absolute liquidity preference; at low interest rates, demand for money became infinitely elastic; money was hoarded for speculation.
- Prices and nominal wages were downward rigid and money illusion prevailed. This rigidity arose from monopoly and union powers and led to involuntary unemployment.

According to Keynes, these flaws force the economy into an under-employment equilibrium and preclude market automatism for self-recovery. Keynes described under-employment equilibrium as a state of equilibrium in the goods and assets markets and involuntary unemployment in the labor market. Keynes considered deflation as harmful and strongly opposed it: it hurts debtors, ignites deflationary expectations, and cause a drop in output and employment.

Because of the downward stickiness of nominal wage and money illusion assumed by Keynes, the labor market could not clear. Labor unions and the government refused to cut the nominal wages that existed at the peak of the boom regardless of the prevailing mass-unemployment. Keynesians claim that a nominal wage cut would reduce labor's revenues and spending, and in turn would reduce aggregate demand for commodities. In addition, a nominal wage cut would reduce the price level; consequently, depressed prices would elevate real money supply, and higher money supply entails a drop in interest rates. However, in view of an interest-inelastic investment together with a high preference for liquidity, any decline in interest rates would induce no rise in borrowing and spending.

Keynesians maintain workers' money illusion; they concur that a decline in real wages would cause higher labor demand. They recommend a rise in prices as a means to cut real wages and hike labor demand. An increase in prices elevates profits and encourages hiring workers. In addition to a decline in real wages, Keynesians recommend higher government spending which would hike output via a multiplier effect and therefore cause higher employment. The joint effect of lower real wage and higher government spending would re-establish full employment.

5.2 The classical approach to full employment: perfect price and wage flexibility

The classical model was a natural model that worked over centuries before 1929 and cannot be demolished by statists without painful consequences. It relies on free market forces, perfect competition, and perfect price-wage flexibility for equilibrating the labor, goods, and assets' markets. The interest rate, wages, and the price level are determined in such a manner that the aggregate demand for goods and services is equal to full employment output and the desired ratio of money to securities is equal to actual ratio of money stock to outstanding securities in the economy.

The classical model considers a Walras's (1874) tatonnement process. Based on full information, in addition to the wage and price flexibility, all markets, including the labor market, can attain full employment equilibrium;[5] under-employment equilibrium is not conceivable in the classical model. The equilibrium price-wage vector is efficient; it exploits relevant information only markets possess. To justify deflation, the classics introduced the real-balance effect (Pigou-effect) in the income-expenditure model.[6] Hence, in addition to income, the consumption function depends on real wealth including real monetary wealth (Metzler 1951). Price-wage deflation augments real cash balances, which, in turn, augments consumption. Via the real wealth effect, deflation no longer diminishes aggregate demand as claimed by Keynesians. An increase in real wealth would augment consumption and reduce saving. In contrast to Keynes' theory, price-wage deflation would augment aggregate demand and would restore full employment.

In classical economics, the cheap credit and money expansion caused a forced saving and excessive investment in capital goods accompanied by shortfalls in consumer goods (Mises 1953). In a post-boom, the entrepreneurs attempt to correct the mal-investment that occurred during the boom; they re-allocate resources to consumer goods and remedy the losses in consumption that were incurred by forced saving.

5.3 Sharia approach to full employment: inherent financial stability and free markets

A Sharia model has many fundamental properties that make it immune to financial instability as well as to the price and wage rigidities of the Keynesian model. A Sharia model forbids interest-based contracts. This interdiction has a major implication on the structure of banking. Theoretically, a Sharia banking system is a two-tier banking: (i) a 100 percent reserve banking for safe depository and domestic and international payments; and (ii) a risk-sharing, equity-based banking for financing trade and investment. This two-tier banking had been strongly proposed by many eminent writers such as Hume (1752), Gouge (1833), Carroll (1850s), Walker (1873), the Chicago Plan (1933),[7] Irving Fisher (1936), Simons (1948), and many others. In Sharia banking, money is separated from debt. Banks cannot create or destroy money; they only intermediate between savers and investors. A fictitious expansion of credit is prevented. Therefore, high fluctuations in asset and commodities prices are also prevented. Prices and wages tend to be stable, and the risk for major inflation or deflation is negligible.

In addition to inherent financial stability, a Sharia model imbeds full flexibility of wages and prices. Laws and institutions that interfere with the competitive market mechanism are not Sharia compatible. Hence, all markets, including the labor market, face no hurdle for clearing. Full employment is established like in the classical model via the Walras's tatonnement mechanism.

Say's law of markets applies in a Sharia model; therefore, expansionary fiscal and monetary policies are not needed. The central bank is not allowed to expand credit and depreciate money to increase employment and pervert the price and wage mechanism. Moreover, the central bank cannot set the interest rate, since the latter is replaced by the profit rate in the economy, which is determined by market forces. Inflation has a redistribution effect, to which a Sharia model is opposed.

In view of the vital role of the labor market, Sharia requires that the government should remove any practice that undermines free competition such as minimum wages or unemployment benefits. In many countries, structural rigidities in labor markets have contributed to high unemployment and have become too damaging to the economy.

6. Conclusions

Sharia model is a purely free market, with non–interest-based debt or money. It repudiates any control of any market by the government or an interest group which hinders free competition. It opposes the doctrine of under-consumption that calls on the government to spend and eliminate deficient demand. Consuming without producing is dangerous for society and amounts to an injustice against those who strive to earn an income; workers, creditors, and pensioners may lose real income through money expansion. Many governments control the price of production factors: labor and capital; they set wages at higher than equilibrium wage which penalizes employment and growth. They set the interest rates at near-zero or even negative rate, which redistributes income from creditors to borrowers and reduces capital in the economy. The government has no right to create or destroy money. Such action violates Sharia law. Sharia model does not endorse either out-of-thin-air money creation, or wage and rate of return fixation.

Competitive equilibrium prices, wages, rates of returns, and exchange rates are efficient; they provide a true measure of social value and cost of resources, and the best opportunities for allocating resources. The impossibility of socialism means that no government agency, no matter how omnipotent it may be, can replicate the market, or possess the market's information, or alter the laws of nature. Disabling free markets can only cause losses and inefficiencies. Unless financed from manna from heavens, subsidies serve no social purpose and may violate the equity principle of a Sharia model. The poor who are targeted by subsidies may end up as the big losers by paying a large share of the subsidies. Unhampered private markets are able to produce priority goods such as food and energy at low real cost with no need for subsidies.[8] Some producers whose products have become less competitive or obsolete may fight for subsidies to make them profitable. Likewise, corporations harmed by high labor wages may fight for subsidies and bailouts. In these cases, subsidies harm the economy. A Sharia model allows no unrestrained commodity taxes. However, taxes to cover the cost arising from the consumption of a product are quite legitimate, such as taxes on vehicles, fuel, tires, etc., to cover the cost of roads and their maintenance. Similarly, taxes on tobacco to cover the medical expenses of tobacco-related cancers are quite legitimate.

Many countries have become too entangled in institutions and legislation that disable competitive markets and have built too many structural rigidities that have slowed growth and spread economic disorders. Full liberalization of the economy would be adamantly resisted. Many authors such as Smith, Simons, Mises, Rothbard, and Hayek advocated a laissez-faire system; yet their message became buried under the glory of statism. Mises stated that Keynes did not teach us how to perform the miracle of turning stones into bread, but how to eat the seed corn. Such will be the inevitable consequences of the present Keynesian policies in many industrial countries.

Notes

1 The Prophet PUH strictly condemned price fixation when He (PUH) was asked to fix food prices during a severe food shortage. In fact, such action would be dangerous; it could precipitate a famine. Food inventories may be exhausted rapidly, or withheld. Further, the additional supply of food from farms or imports may be discouraged.
2 Implicitly, this statement refers to the national product identity: $Y = C + I$, where Y is the national product, C is consumption, and I is investment.
3 The debate whether monetary or real factors caused the Great Depression was unsettled. Irving Fisher (1933) contended that cheap money led to over-indebtedness, then to debt deflation and asset price crash. Robbins (1934) explained that the Great Depression was caused by a cheap money policy in the form of low interest rates and abundant credit that fueled stock market speculation in the United States.
4 A fall in prices due to money hoarding increases the purchasing power of money and benefits consumers. If wages are flexible, a fall in prices will be accompanied by a fall in wages and profits are not affected. However, if wages are inflexible, then a fall in prices causes unemployment.
5 The Walrasian mechanism is based on wage and price adjustments to equilibrate. In opposite, because prices and wages are rigid, the Marshallian mechanism is based on quantities' adjustment to clear markets.
6 The classics believe that deflation arising from productivity gains and higher output is beneficial; however, price deflation arising from money deflation is pernicious and hurts debtors.
7 The Chicago plan (1933) proposed 100 percent reserve banking and investment banking to separate money from debt. It was advanced by University of Chicago economists during the Great Depression. The plan was endorsed by eminent economists such as Irving Fisher, Frank H. Knight, Lloyd W. Mints, Henry Schultz, Henry C. Simons, Garfield V. Cox, Aaron Director, Paul H. Douglas, and Albert G. Hart.
8 In fact, agricultural products were produced at an increasingly lower cost in the United States, which permitted a release of labor to industry and services. Such release would not be possible if agricultural products remained costly in labor time.

References

Arrow, K., and Debreu, G., 1954, "Existence of an Equilibrium for a Competitive Economy," *Econometrica*, 22: 265–290.

Carroll, C. H., 1965, *Organization of Debt Into Currency and Other Papers*, Edited With an Introduction by Edward C. Simmons, D. Van Nostrand Company, Inc. Princeton, NJ.

Cobb, C. W., Douglas, P. H. (1928). "A Theory of Production" (PDF). *American Economic Review*, 18 (Supplement): 139–165.

Fisher, F., 1933, "The Debt-Deflation Theory of Great Depressions," *Econometrica*, 1(4): 337–357.

Fisher, I., 1936, *100% Money*, New York: Adelphi Company.

Gouge, W., 1833, *A Short History of Paper Money & Banking*, New York: Augustus M. Kelley Publishers.

Hayek, F. A., 1931, *Prices and Production*, New York: Augustus M. Kelly, Publishers.

Hume, D., 1752, *Political Discourses*, Edinburgh: Printed by R. Fleming, for A. Kincaid and A. Donaldson.

Ibn Khaldoun, 1377/1985, *Al Muqaddimah*, Beirut: Dār al-Qalam.

Juglar, C., 1862, *Des Crises Commerciales et leur Retour Periodique en France, en Angleterre, et aux Etats Unis*, Paris: Guillaumin.

Keynes, J. M., 1936, *The General Theory of Employment, Interest and Money*, London: Macmillan.

Labordere, M., 1908, "Autour de la Crise Americaine de 1907," in *La Revue de Paris*, Paris: Paul Brodard.

Mantoux, E., 1937, "La Théorie générale de M. Keynes," *Revue d'économie politique*, 51(6): 1559–1590, Paris: Librairie Sirey.

Marx K., 1863, *Theories of Surplus Value*, Moscow: Progress Publishers.

Metzler, L., 1951, "Wealth, Saving, and the Rate of Interest," *Journal of Political Economy*, 59(2): 93–116.

Mill, J., 1808, *Commerce Defended*, London: C. and R. Baldwin, New Bridge Street.

Mill, J. S., 1848, *Principles of Political Economy*, New York: D. Appleton and Company.

Ricardo, D., 1817, *On the Principles of Political Economy and Taxation*, London: John Murray.

Robbins, L., 1934, *The Great Depression*, New York: Books for Libraries Press, Freeport.

Say, J. B., 1803, *A Treatise on Political Economy*, Philadelphia: Claxton, Kemsen, & Haffelfingee.

Simons, H., 1948, *Economic Policy for a Free Society*, Chicago: University of Chicago Press.

Smith, A., 1776, *An Inquiry Into the Nature and Causes of the Wealth of Nations*, London: Methuen and Co., Ltd., ed. Edwin Cannan, 1904, Fifth Edition.

Soddy, F., 1934, *The Role of Money*, London: George Routledge and Sons Ltd.

Von Mises, L., 1949, *Human Action*, Auburn, AL: Ludwig von Mises Institute.

Von Mises, L., 1953, *The Theory of Money and Credit*, New Haven: Yale University Press.

Walker, A., 1873, *The Science of Wealth*, Philadelphia: J. B. Lippincott.

Walras, L., 1874, *Elements d'Economie Politique Pure*, Paris et Lausanne, 1926: translated by W. Jaffe, 1954, *Elements of Pure Economics*, Homewood: Richard D. Irwin, Inc., 1954

4 *Zakat*

A mandatory redistributive principle of a Sharia model

1. Introduction

Sharia established an advanced social safety net, called *Zakat*, which addresses effectively and equitably the welfare of the vulnerable groups in the community. Islam made *Zakat* a third pillar of the religion; it is an obligation upon individuals to pay *Zakat*. Such obligation has been stressed over and over in both the Quran and Sunna. The collection and distribution of *Zakat* is entrusted to the government; however, it may be performed directly by concerned individuals. Sharia is forceful about property rights, full freedom, free competition, and free enterprise. Yet, at the same it attends with extreme care to the well-being and comfort of vulnerable people. The human aspect of growth and the bondage among society is a fundamental pillar of Sharia. Besides *Zakat*, which is mandatory, Sharia encourages "*infaq*," defined as voluntary charity to both reduce poverty and contribute to education and health.

Sharia puts a great emphasis on caring for the orphan, widow, sick, and handicapped. It elevates the moral and human standards of the community. Many countries have a social safety net. Well known were the "Poor Laws" in England, a codified legislative system from the medieval epoch that obligated the government to address the well-being of the vulnerable people. An organized social system, such as *Zakat*, would protect against desolation, suffering, mendacity, and homelessness. It reaches those who are in dire need, such as orphans, blind people, etc., and secures their rights for livelihood. While government consumer subsidies profit the rich and poor alike, *Zakat* is directly destined to the eligible recipients.

Zakat is an obligation of the eligible payer and a full right, and not a privilege, of the poor. *Zakat* has too many moral and economic virtues. From the moral perspective, it establishes a feeling of mutual protection and solidarity where no person, no matter how poor or sick, feels abandoned. From an economic view point, *Zakat* is very fair, it is never meant to impoverish the rich nor to institutionalize poverty by making a large section of population welfare recipients, leaving very few to labor to produce food and other necessities. In contrast to modern tax system, it does not make the poor pay for the rich or for government bureaucracy. *Zakat* levies selectively from eligible payers and distributes directly to eligible recipients. *Zakat* cannot become due if a minimum of the *Zakat* base (called *Nissab*) is not attained, or if the minimum time of one year required for the possession of an item subject to *Zakat* is not attained. *Zakat* is very clear in terms of its conditions and ratios.

Zakat is so conceived that it effectively reduces poverty, it is defined such that it can be paid promptly upon harvest, and its rates are not prohibitive and would not incite evasion. *Zakat* covers basic food items that constitute the basic diet of the poor people and the necessity for their survival. These food items include cereals and meat. Wheat, barley, maize, corn, rice, etc. are subject to *Zakat*, which is levied and distributed to the poor in physical quantities.

The institutionalization of *Zakat* accelerated over the last 15 years in various regions of the world, such as the Gulf region, Western Africa, and Southeast Asia. This increase stems from the willingness of the governmental authorities to benefit from the preponderant role of *Zakat* as an alternative, self-contained tax system that spurs a comprehensive vision of social welfare. The collection of *Zakat* funds by institutionalized collectors has efficient economic and social actions on society.

Zakat institutions play a role in macro- and micro-economic policies that aim at the alleviation of poverty. Governments enforce public policies in order to increase growth, create wealth, and, accordingly, reduce poverty. *Zakat* institutions can enforce measures and re-allocative channels in order to guarantee the success of public policies. For instance, *Zakat* institutions can re-allocate financial resources optimally in a way that improves human capital, educational and health facilities, and peculiar programs for the poor. In addition, such institutions can also boost the micro-economic policies through measures that improve the entitlements that go to households.

This chapter covers:

- *Zakat*: definition and purposes
- Institutionalization of *Zakat*'s collection and allocation
- *Zakat* and micro- and macroeconomic policies

2. *Zakat*: definition and purpose

The literal meaning of *Zakat* is growth and increase. The direct linguistic meaning consists in purification. Maududi (1988) argues that the direct religious meaning is related to the purification of sins and spiritual maladies as result of paying *Zakat*. He considers that an individual's wealth is not pure if he does not pay the right of Allah from the wealth bestowed by Him. This religious definition is not dissociated from the economic implications on individuals and society. Although the payment of *Zakat* stems from a spiritual incentive to obey Allah's rules, it entails a redistribution of income from payers to recipients, which contributes to the alleviation of social inequities.

Al-Qaradawi (1999) argues that *Zakat*

> is not purely a worship, for in addition to being a worship it is a defined right of the poor, an established tax, and an ingredient of the social, and economic system of the society. The reasons for enacting zakat are, in general, known and clear.

Zakat is one of the five pillars of Islam. It is almost the only worship that has crucial implications on individual and society for a sustainable socioeconomic justice. Such justice can be achieved through judicious policies of savings, aggregate investment, wealth creation, and poverty alleviation.

Kazi et al. (2014) claim that the establishment of *Zakat* payment has several objectives including the following:

- Securing the living of vulnerable people, of whom some may be too vulnerable and may perish if left without social protection.
- Eradication of poverty and maintenance of socioeconomic justice.
- Safeguard of wealth from the jealousy of the others, the poor in particular.
- Purification of one's wealth and removal of one's stinginess.
- Keeping thankful to God for His bounty.

There are eight categories of recipients of *Zakat*:

- The poor living without resources of livelihood (*al-fuqaraa*).
- The needy that cannot provide their basic needs (*al-masakin*).
- *Zakat* collectors (*al-amilyn alayha*).
- The category of those sympathetically expected to convert to Islam (*al-muallafatu qulubuhum*), recent converts to Islam, and potential followers that defend Islam.
- The category of slaves' freedom (*fir-riqab*).
- The category of debtors (*al-gharimin*) who are unable to honor their financial commitments.
- The category of Muslims who defend a religious cause in the path of God (*fi sabilillah*).
- The wayfarers and travelers who need a financial assistance (*ibnu al-sabil*).

Avoiding the payment of *Zakat* "unleashes" social disorders similar to the instability that happened in the Arab World and started from Tunisia on December 17, 2010. Allah Says in Surat *Tau'bah* (Chapter 9: 103):

> Take sadaqah (obligatory alms) out of their wealth through which you may cleanse and purify them, and pray for them. Indeed, your prayer is a source of peace for them. And Allah is (All-) Hearing, (All-) Knowing.

The payment of *Zakat* is an obligation: there is a set of Sharia conditions that a Muslim must satisfy such that *Zakat* becomes eligible. This set includes the following: (i) being Muslim; (ii) being major; (iii) rational and lucid; and (iv) owner of a wealth beyond a minimum level called *nisaab*. If the first three conditions are easily met, the fourth condition is most dealt with by Sharia scholars and Islamic economists. *Nisaab* is defined as the minimum amount of a commodity or money subject to *Zakat*. There are several *hadiths* (citations by Prophet Mohammed, peace be upon him) that agree on the fact that *Zakat* is due only after a whole lunar year (354 days) passes and *nissab* is reached. Kazi et al. (2014) provide the following quantitative amounts of wealth:

- Grains, dates, and olives, all have the same *Nissab*, five Awsuqs, equivalent to 675 kilograms.
- Sheep, 40; cows, 30; camels, 5.
- Gold: the *nissab* for gold is 3 ounces or 100 grams.
- Silver: the *nissab* for silver is 21 ounces or 700 grams.
- Cash money: the *nissab* for cash is an equivalent to the value of the *nissab* of silver or gold.

Imam Malik (Al Muatta, Book 17, *Zakat*) provided a description of the rules of *Zakat*. He stated that *Zakat* is on three things: the produce of plowed land, gold and silver, and livestock. *Zakat* has to be paid on 20 dinars of gold coins, in the same way as it has to be paid on 200 dirhams of silver. There is no *Zakat* to pay on gold that is clearly less than 20 dinars (in weight) but if it increases so that by the increase the amount reaches a full 20 dinars in weight then *Zakat* has to be paid. Similarly, there is no *Zakat* to pay on silver that is clearly less than 200 dirhams in weight, but if it increases so that by the increase the amount reaches a full 200 dirhams in weight then *Zakat* has to be paid.

For all crops, there is an identical *nissab* of five awsuq, about 675 kilograms, below which no *Zakat* is taken. Regarding crops from land that is watered by rain or springs or any natural means there is *Zakat* to pay a tenth. On irrigated land, there is *Zakat* of a twentieth to pay. The tenth that is taken from olives is taken after they have been pressed, and the olives must come to a minimum amount of five awsuq. If there are less than five awsuq of olives, no *Zakat* has to be paid. Olive trees are like date palms insofar as there is a tenth on whatever is watered by rain or springs or any natural means, and a twentieth on whatever is irrigated.

Imam Malik said minerals from mining are dealt with like crops, and the same procedure is applied to both. *Zakat* is deducted from what comes out of a mine on the day it comes out, without waiting for a year, just as a tenth is taken from a crop at the time it is harvested, without waiting for a year to elapse over it. Regarding un-earthed treasure, he said that there is a *Zakat* of a fifth on buried treasure if the treasure is extracted without the expense of capital and labor. If expenses are incurred, then there is no *Zakat* on it.

Regarding livestock, on 24 camels or less *Zakat* is paid with sheep, *Zakat* is one sheep for every five camels. On grazing sheep and goats, if they come to

40 or more, up to 120 heads, *Zakat* is one sheep. For 30 cows, *Zakat* is one cow in its second year.

The mandatory redistribution of *Zakat* ensures an equitable and stable reallocation of wealth among members of society. There is no coercion for paying *Zakat*; it is left to the judgment of the payer. However, the divine retribution for not giving *Zakat* could be serious. There are several injunctions that can be derived from *Qu'ran*[1] and *hadiths* from *Sunnah* showing the retribution for not giving *Zakat*. Allah Says in Surat *Tau'bah* (Chapter 9: 34–35):

> As for those who accumulate gold and silver and do not spend it in the way of Allah, give them the "good" news of a painful punishment on the day it (the wealth) will be heated up in the fire of hell, then their foreheads and their sides and their backs shall be branded with it: "this is what you had accumulated for yourselves. So, taste what you have been accumulating."

Wealthy individuals in Muslim societies must not avoid the payment of *Zakat* not only because of the retribution they may face but also because of the disequilibria and social gaps that stem as an ineluctable result on all levels. Their moral and human values become degraded. *Zakat* is the most efficient method of channeling fairly financial resources in a society in a way that minimizes any potential economic and social turbulence. Metwally (1997) considers that the technique of "co-operative forces" and not the technique of "opposites" should be used to achieve equilibrium in different levels.

3. Institutionalization of *Zakat*'s collection and allocation

As viewed from a modern practical perspective, *Zakat* can be seen as a reliable substitute to the conventional tax system. Indeed, it can play an appropriate fiscal device in a sophisticated public finance platform. According to Yusoff and Densumite (2012), *Zakat* is able to be a trustworthy system in a welfare economy that deals with issues related to social security entitlements, social assistance grants for childcare, food subsidy, education, health care, housing, and public transportation.

The Prophet PBUH founded the Bay-Al Mal, a treasury which received the *Zakat* and distributed it to eligible recipients. Hence, the *Zakat* institutions find their roots in the instructions given by the Prophet Mohammad PBUH to collect and distribute *Zakat*. The four rightly guided rulers (Abu Baker, Omar, Uthman, and Ali) who ruled the first 40 years after the death of the Prophet PBUH buttressed the institutionalization of *Zakat* collection through an organized mechanism under the control and regulation of the state. It is noticeable that modern *Zakat*'s experts and Sharia scholars, such as Al-Qaradawi, reject the idea to merge the secular budget with the budgets of *Zakat* institutions.

The existing *Zakat* institutions classify the needy and poor as the principal beneficiary category of recipients. Orphans and families without support are mainly added to this category. These groups are considered "below poverty" and represent situations where typical, family-based social support systems have broken down, requiring the support of other social mechanisms (Minor 2014b).

The institutionalization of *Zakat* became an attractive research route for academicians and an interesting policy-making tool for policymakers in Muslim economies. Whilst most studies in the past concentrated on the role of *Zakat* from the philosophical aspect, an increasing number of current empirical studies are focusing on the performance of *Zakat* institutions in alleviating poverty (Hairunnizam 2014). *Zakat* has become officially institutionalized since the early 1970s. The first official institutions appeared in Egypt and Saudi Arabia in 1971. Minor (2014a) considers that the observed smooth increase in the number of official *Zakat* institutions is due to the orientation of governmental authorities across the Muslim world to manage the collection and use of *Zakat* funds. Although with the outstanding success of *Zakat* institutionalization at the level of officials and governmental authorities, there is a twofold challenge over the upcoming years. On the one hand, there still is some disconnection between *Zakat* institutionalization and development finance. On the other hand, the proportion of practicing Muslims who hand over their due *Zakat* to institutions is very small. The first challenge is related to the role *Zakat* institutions can play in conjunction with supranational development institutions to build coordinative programs aiming at enhancing economic and financial development in the least-developed Muslim economies. The second challenge is related to the involvement of the general public in the endorsement of *Zakat* institutions.

Guermat et al. (2003) conducted a survey in the Gulf region to provide evidence on the incongruence between the official *Zakat* practices and the corresponding theoretical aspects. The objective of the study is the explanation of the beliefs and orientations of Muslim individuals regarding the collection of *Zakat*. The results show that there is a consensual trend among *Zakat* payers to not deliver their due *Zakat* to official institutions. This behavior can be explained by two reasons. The first reason is related to the individual responsibility towards God. The second reason is related to the preferences of *Zakat* payers to deliver it in channels they consider as the best to them.

Al-Qaradawi (1999) maintains that governments should be in charge of the collection and redistribution of *Zakat* funds. Besides the organizational aspect, the redistribution of *Zakat* by a governmental institution preserves the dignity of recipients. Although the most developed *Zakat* institutions are in the region of Gulf, there are few studies that deal with the size of collected funds, the channels of distribution and the efficiency of their managerial activities. However, an extensive number of journal articles focused on Malaysia where *Zakat* management is under the control and jurisdiction of each state's government. Sanep et al. (2006) confirm that some Malaysian states privatized their corresponding *Zakat* institutions in order to improve the distributive performance to recipients.

The Malaysian's State Islamic Religious Councils are the governmental authorities that are accountable of *Zakat* collection and allocation in their respective states according to peculiar needs and specificities. The government of Malaysia is expected to play an important role in promoting good governance within such institutions (Wahab and Abdul Rahman 2011). More than a decade ago, Rahman (2003) proposed that the Malaysian government should pioneer and enforce financial management practices, including audit and accounting norms[2] on *Zakat*, and performance indicators of the managerial system.

Since *Zakat* institutions manage the collected funds of the general public for purposes of charity, they must satisfy various norms of managerial efficiency, accountancy and financial disclosures, and optimal allocation. Most of existing empirical studies and policy reports tackle the procedures used by *Zakat* institutions to collect and allocate funds. However, there is a scarcity in the studies dealing with the governance and economic efficiency of official *Zakat* institutions (Wahab and Abdul Rahman 2011). The governance of *Zakat* is related to the ability to implement efficiently managerial norms and techniques to collect and allocate funds properly. The economic efficiency indicates whether the institution is allocating optimally the collected funds in a way to maximize the satisfaction and quality of life of recipients.

Wahid et al. (2004) explored the effect of *Zakat* allocation on the quality of life of recipients. The authors consider that an effective *Zakat* distribution should result in a better quality of life in terms of food, education, health, involvement in social life, transportation facilities, and shelter. Wahid et al. (2004) used a logit model and examined the answers of respondents from three Malaysian states. The general results do not confirm a perfect satisfaction with the allocative policy adopted by *Zakat* institutions, except for educational services and involvement in social activities. The results of the authors show that the educational services and received income are the most affected factors by the distribution policy relative to the other factors. This can show that the quality life of poor who are beneficiaries of *Zakat* is significantly affected by the policy choices in terms of education and income. *Zakat* institutions have to determine which aspects of life need to be prioritized.

Wahab and Abdul Rahman (2011) studied three types of efficiency of *Zakat* institutions in Malaysia over 2003–2007. The authors used the non-parametric data envelopment analysis (DEA) to assess the technical, pure technical, and scale efficiencies. For this purpose, 10 independent variables were used, namely number of branches available, number of staff, total *Zakat* payment system offered, dummy of operational website, dummy of computerized *Zakat* system, board size, meeting per year, audit committee, decentralization, and corporatization. The authors find that the variables "*Zakat* payment system" and "decentralization" are consistently affecting the three types of efficiency during the period of study under consideration. Jamaliah et al. (2012) developed a composite performance measurement which comprised of a financial index, an employee index, a *Zakat* recipient index, and a *Zakat* payer index to measure the quality performance of *Zakat* institutions and the intended impact on recipients' satisfaction.

Yusuf and Derus (2013) conceptualized a model of the determinants driving the individual decision to deliver *Zakat* to institutions. The authors define the adoption of corporate *Zakat* collection as the individual's own estimated probability that she uses or will use corporate *Zakat* services. The model includes a set of variables that reflect the adoption of *Zakat* collection by official institutions, namely compatibility, image, visibility, result demonstrability, voluntariness, complexity, relative advantage, and trust. The proposed model identifies the factors that influence the adoption of corporate zakat. For instance, the authors consider that the variables trust are positively and negatively related to the adoption decision. This means that a high level of trust and a low level of complexity are favor to the adoption.

Ahmad et al. (2015) explore how the recipients of *Zakat* transmit information among themselves and how this can affect their satisfaction of the managerial efforts of *Zakat* institutions. The authors use three independent variables, namely services quality, environment offices, and waiting time to explain the dependent variable, namely the level of satisfaction of *Zakat* recipients. The results of the authors show that the respondents are satisfied by the quality of services and unhappy because of the long procedure time.

Salleh (2015) studies how *Zakat* institutions in Brunei can integrate financial inclusion into the services they provide. Financial inclusion is defined as the delivery of financial products and services at reasonable costs to low-income categories of society. The objective of Salleh is to examine whether *Zakat* institutions in Brunei are efficient enough to be able to embed financial inclusion into the services they offer to recipients. The contribution of the author consists in exploring the untapped role of *Zakat* institutions in developing Sharia-compliant personal finance solutions "through facilitating financial inclusion and the saving modes of *zakat* recipients" (P. 150).

4. *Zakat* and micro- and macroeconomic policies

A variety of supranational financial and economic institutions spurred different macro-programs that aim at the reduction of poverty in the globe. For example, the United Nations' (2000, P. 4) Millennium Development Declaration claims that no efforts will be spared

> to free our fellow men, women and children from the abject and dehumanizing conditions of extreme poverty, to which more than a billion of them are currently subjected. We are committed to making the right to development a reality for everyone and to freeing the entire human race from want.

Poverty eradication and fight of famines and malnutrition in the globe are the central objectives that were enounced during the 2000 United Nations meeting.

In his Preface of the United Nations' (2015) Millennium Development Goals report, Ban Ki-moon, Secretary-General of the United Nations, documents that several significant achievements have reached several targets. However, large gaps need to be filled to solve the sub-development issues. The United Nations argues that

> yet major gaps remain in reducing vulnerabilities for many developing countries, including least developed countries (LDCs), small-islands developing States and other low-income countries. Access to essential medicines at affordable prices remains highly problematic, with many households squeezed out of the market due to high prices and limited availability. And while the rapid expansion of information and communication technologies (ICTs) has allowed several billion people in developing countries to join the information society, a major digital divide is still in place, with more people offline than online and particularly poor access in Sub-Saharan Africa.
>
> (P. 5)

The Millennium Development Goals have not been reached in 2015. The particular poverty issue requires a specific attention. As reported by *The London Economist*,[3] what happened globally has been dominated by the dynamics of poverty in two countries, namely China and India. In 1990, 62 percent of the world's poor population lived in these two countries, the geographical distribution of poverty in the globe changed significantly. The poverty in China decreased from 62 percent in 1990 to 16 percent in 2015. Although this favorable decrease confirms the success of the United Nations' development goals, the poverty in least developed countries did not decrease over the same period. Unequal distribution of income and the unfair creation of value in the world led to a deterioration of poverty indicators in Sub-Saharan Africa.

Based on the previous discussion, it turns out that the actions taken by the United Nations did not reach all goals. Specifically, the issues of poverty, unequal distribution of income, and social injustice require the efforts of other quasi-governmental institutions to reach such goals. *Zakat* is an efficient additional device. Several recent theoretical and empirical contributions in macroeconomics showed that the alleviation of poverty is effective when *Zakat* is used in addition to macroeconomic policies. For example, Ahmed (2008) shows that the simulation of various *Zakat* schemes shows that poverty cannot be eliminated without a proper use of *Zakat* in an effective way. The point is not to claim that *Zakat* can – independently of macroeconomic policies – alleviate poverty. In contrast, the Ahmed argues that there is a complementarity because this enhances growth and redistributes optimally the aggregate income.

The macroeconomic policy spurring economic growth is made up of an assortment of measures, institutional reforms, and supplementary supportive facilities that aim at alleviating poverty. The measures encompass incentives policies, regulatory policies, and appropriate fiscal and monetary policies. The equal redistribution of wealth through public policies is supposed to provide the poor categories of society to be endowed with equal opportunities. The salient public policies consistent in the government spending on education and human capital. The micro-economic policies can be divided into two categories. The first category is related to enhancing the income-generation process for this category. The second category is related to the unproductive households that lack the required resources to survive perpetually above the level of poverty. For the latter category, the transfer of wealth through charitable endowments and/or social security measures by the government would be necessary for alleviating their poverty.

The role of *Zakat* institutions can be complementary to the aforementioned macro- and micro-economic policies. Their role can be summarized in the optimal reallocation of financial resources to guarantee the success of the macro- and micro-economic policies. For instance, *Zakat* institutions can re-allocate financial resources optimally in a way that improves human capital, educational settings, health facilities, and peculiar programs for the poor. In addition, such institutions can also boost the micro-economic policies through measures that improve the entitlements that go perpetually to the productive and unproductive households. The reallocation of financial resources to productive households with the most sophisticated financial inclusion mechanisms is an illustrative example in this regard.

5. Conclusions

Zakat is a pillar of a Sharia model; it is obligatory of eligible individuals. Those who do not pay *Zakat* are considered sinners that have degraded moral and human values. *Zakat* cements the social bondage within a community. Its purpose is to promote social and economic progress within a country. It ensures a broader sharing of vulnerable groups in the society's produce and wealth; it therefore enhances their dignity and sustenance. *Zakat* is meant for eligible recipients: those who are vulnerable, such as the orphans, the aged, the handicapped, etc. A lot of vulnerable people do not have the health for work and should not be denied a living. *Zakat* secures for them such living and averts suffering. *Zakat* is not supposed to be given to the healthy, unemployed people. *Zakat* is also meant to provide resources for the government to provide social services such as education, health, and infrastructure. We note that besides mandatory *Zakat*, there is voluntary contribution (*infaq*) for those who would like to finance community projects such as schools, hospitals, infrastructure, and research. The establishment of *Zakat* foundations would organize effective channels for collecting and distributing *Zakat*. These foundations will act to increase the number of *Zakat* payers and recipients; they will also design projects in education and health that would enhance the poor's welfare.

Notes

1 There are at least 27 passages in *Qur'an* where the obligation to pay *Zakat* and the order to pray occur jointly. See Metwally (1997).

2 The Accounting and Auditing Organization for Islamic Financial Institutions (AAOIFI) enacted Financial Accounting Standard 9 (FAS 9) to standardize the recognition, measurement, and disclosure of *Zakat* in financial reporting. The recognition is related to the timing of revenues and expenses. The measurement deals with the principles determining the amount at which the values of assets and liabilities are reported in financial statements. The disclosure requirement is related to the type of information to be made available.

3 See www.economist.com/blogs/dailychart/2010/09/millennium_development_goals

References

Ahmed, H., 2008, "Zakah, Macroeconomic Policies and Poverty Alleviation: Lessons From Simulation on Bangladesh," *Journal of Islamic Economics, Banking and Finance*, 4(2): 81–105.

Ahmad, Raja Adzrin Raja, Othman, Ahmad Marzuki Amiruddin, and Salleh, Muhammad Sufiyudin, 2015, "Assessing the Satisfaction Level of Zakat Recipients Towards Zakat Management," *Procedia Economics and Finance* 31: 140–151.

Al-Qaradawi, Y., 1999, Monzer Kahf (transl.) *Fiqh az-Zakat*. King Abdulaziz University, Saudi Arabia. Available online at: http://monzer.kahf.com/books/english/fiqhalzakah_vol1.pdf.

Guermat, C., Al-Utaibi, T., and Tucker, J. P., 2003, "The Practice of Zakat: An Empirical Examination of Four Gulf Countries." Discussion Paper. Exeter University, Department of Economics.

Hairunnizam, W., 2014, "Localization of Malaysian Zakat Distribution: Perceptions of Amils and Zakat Recipients." PhD thesis. University of Malaya, Malaysia.

Jamaliah, S., Ghani, E. K., Zawawi, S. N., and Yusof, S.N.S., 2012, "Composite Performance for Zakat Organizations," *British Journal of Economics, Finance and Management Sciences*, 4(1): 50–59.

Kazi, T. M., Hassan, K., Alam, M. F., Kazi, S., and Rafiq, F., 2014, "Opinion of the Zakat Recipients on Their Food Security: A Case Study on Bangladesh," *International Journal of Islamic and Middle Eastern Finance and Management*, 7(3): 333–345.

Maududi, A. A., 1988, *Maashiaati Islam*, Lahore: Islamic Publication.

Metwally, M. M., 1997, "Economic Consequences of Applying Islamic Principles in Muslim Societies," *International Journal of Social Economics*, 24(7/8/9): 941–957.

Minor, A., 2014a, "Zakat and Development Finance: Filling the Gaps". Available at: http://aiddata.org/.

Minor, A., 2014b, "Faith in Finance: The Role of Zakat in International Development." MA Thesis, The University of Texas at Austin.

Rahman, A.R.A., 2003, "Zakat on Business Wealth in Malaysia: Corporate Tax Rebate, Accountability, and Governance," *Journal IKIM*, 11(1): 37–50.

Salleh, A. M., 2015, "Integrating Financial Inclusion and Saving Motives Into Institutional Zakat Practices," *International Journal of Islamic and Middle Eastern Finance and Management*, 8(2): 150–170.

Sanep, A., Hairunnizam, W., and Adnan, M., 2006, "Penswastaan institusi zakat dan kesannya terhadap pembayaran secara formal di Malaysia," *International Journal of Management Studies*, 13(2): 175–196.

Wahab, N. A., and Abdul Rahman, A. R., 2011, "Efficiency of Zakat Institutions and Its Determinants." 8th International Conference on Islamic Economics and Finance, Doha, Qatar.

Wahid, H., Ahmad, S., and Nor, M.A.M., 2004, "Kesan Bantuan Zakat Terhadap Kualiti Hidup: Kajian Kes Asnaf Fakir dan Miskin ("The effect of zakat aid on the quality of life:

The case of the poor and needy recipients")," *The Journal of Muamalat & Islamic Finance Research*, 1(1): 151–166.

Yusoff, M., and Densumite, S., 2012, "Zakat Distribution and Growth in the Federal Territory of Malaysia," *Journal of Economics and Behavioral Studies*, 4(8): 449–456.

Yusuf, M. O., and Derus, A. M., 2013, "Measurement Model of Corporate Zakat Collection in Malaysia," *Humanomics*, 29(1): 61–74.

5 Fiscal policy from a Sharia perspective

1. Introduction

Public finance mismanagement disrupted many economies; it caused poverty, mass-unemployment, inflation, and debt crises. Fiscal deficits caused external deficits and large foreign debt. Many countries remained in poverty and social disorder simply because public finance remained a stumbling block to economic growth. Pressing, public, unproductive spending[1] and large fiscal deficits lead to high taxation and a monetization of these deficits, i.e., inflation tax, or high debt.

Ricardo (1817) recognized the necessity which the government has for money to pay for its operations, and therefore to tax its subjects. Without taxes, the government cannot exist, the community remains in a primitive state, such as herdsmen and tribes; the economy cannot develop. However, taxes should not reach a point where they become an obstacle to economic growth. He stated that the most perfect knowledge of the economic science is to direct governments to right measures in taxation. Ricardo was for a limited government; his growth theory predicted that ominous public debt will keep the economy in stagnation. Ibn Khaldoun (1377) laid down the principles of modern fiscal theory in a macroeconomic framework. He meticulously described how public finance mismanagement necessarily resolved in economic decline, and a relocation of men and capital to countries suffering less fiscal taxation.

Sharia recommends sound fiscal management. A government indulges in fiscal mismanagement when it is free to tax anything, at any rate, and spends tax revenues in a wasteful manner. Sharia prescribes clear rules that limit the taxation power of the state, and the nature of its spending; the latter has to remain within its natural duties. The notion of a rigid and ever-expanding government is incompatible with Sharia. Sharia prohibits interest-based financing of the government budget. By prohibiting fiscal mismanagement, Sharia directs capital resources to best productive uses, reduces the cost of capital, and promotes employment and growth. This chapter covers:

- Diversity of budget structures
- Theories of taxation: excessive taxation a way to economic decline

- Taxation from a Sharia perspective: restraint and equity
- Expenditure policy: reduce unproductive spending
- Fiscal balance: a requisite for sound public finance
- Government debt: an index of waste

2. Diversity of budget structures

Table 5.1 shows a diversity of budget structures. The budget structure of a country is a deep-rooted legacy inherited from past generations and legislation (Ibn Khaldoun 1377). It is the result of power of past and present rulers. Governments vary widely in their power to appropriate part of the GDP. The share of government revenues may be as low as 12.9 percent and as high as 53.5 percent. The share of taxes could be as low as 8 percent of GDP. High taxation could repress the private sector (Ibn Khaldoun 1377; Ricardo 1817). The marginal cost of additional revenue could become very high (J.B. Say 1803). Historically, high taxation might become too unpopular and lead to a revolt.[2]

Table 5.1 Comparative fiscal structures in 2014 (in percent of GDP, unless otherwise indicated)

Country	Rev.	Exp.	Sal.	Trans.	Cap.	Def.	Debt	Growth	Un.	Inf.
France	53.5	57.5	...	...	...	-4.0	95.6	0.2	10.3	00.6
United Kingdom	41.3	47.1	10.1	15.9	...	-4.8	92.1	3.2	60.5	10.9
Japan	33.0	40.3	60.1	21.0	30.6	-7.3	246.2	-0.1	30.6	20.7
Italy	48.1	51.1	10.1	23.3	...	-3.0	132.1	-0.4	12.7	00.2
Germany	44.6	44.0	70.7	24.7	...	0.6	74.7	1.6	50.0	00.8
Spain	37.8	43.6	10.8	18.8	00.1	-5.7	98.0	1.4	24.5	-0.2
US	31.1	36.0	...	...	...	-4.9	106.4	2.4	60.2	00.6
Sweden	50.3	52.2	14.4	18.5	...	-1.9	41.8	2.6	80.1	00.1
Argentina	28.9	25.2	7.7	9.0	20.5	-4.4	133.9	9.0	12.1	40.4
Malaysia	20.7	24.2	6.0	5.3	30.7	-3.9	56.4	5.9	30.0	30.1
Mexico	21.9	26.1	6.0	3.0	40.7	-4.2	47.8	2.4	40.8	30.9
Brazil	24.1	24.5	4.3	4.1	10.5	-0.4	64.2	0.0	50.4	60.4
India	19.6	27.3	...	...	30.9	-7.7	67.3	4.6	...	10.5
Tunisia	24.5	28.1	12.7	7.0	...	-4.1	56.2	2.4	...	50.6
Morocco	28.3	33.2	12.8	3.6	...	-4.9	66.2	2.9	9.2	10.6
Chad	25.5	31.5	70.1	5.3	14.1	-6.0	30.2	3.6	...	00.4
Burundi	28.3	29.9	60.7	4.3	11.0	-1.6	29.8	4.7	...	70.5
Mauritania	24.3	36.3	80.4	5.7	13.8	-4.7	78.4	6.4	...	30.5
Uganda	13.0	16.7	30.5	...	70.0	-3.8	28.9	4.5	...	60.7
Bangladesh	12.9	16.9	20.1	3.9	40.8	-4.0	38.8	6.0	...	60.8

Rev = government (g) revenues, which may include, besides taxes, revenues from natural resources, social contributions, and grants; Exp = g total expenditure, which include both current and capital expenditure; Sal = g salaries; Trans = g transfers and subsidies; Cap = g capital expenditure; Def = g deficit; Debt = g debt; Growth = real gross domestic product growth (%/year); Un = unemployment rate, % of active labor force; Inf = rate of consumer price index change (%/year).

Source: International Monetary Fund; International Financial Statistics

Generally, governments may resort to an inflation tax as a more subtle mean of taxation, when forcing more taxes becomes too costly to levy and too unpopular. The government may push inflation taxation until the value of paper money becomes worthless (Cagan 1956).

Table 5.1 shows that total government expenditure vary among countries. A government may spend as much as 57.5 percent of the GDP; or as low as 16.7 percent of the GDP. Table 5.1 shows that high government spending may not imply high real economic growth or high employment and low government spending may not imply low economic growth. In fact, as shown in Table 5.1, the unproductive feature of government spending may become too apparent when government wages reach 12 percent or 14 percent of the GDP, or when subsidies and transfers range between 7 percent and 24.7 percent of the GDP. Table 5.1 shows that real economic growth may be low or even negative in high spending cases, and high in low spending cases. Likewise, unemployment may reach as high as 24.5 percent and may hover around 10 percent in high-spending countries. Noticeably, price inflation could be high in high-spending cases. Both low growth and high inflation imply that high government spending may be too wasteful and is consuming capital that could have been invested in the private sector and generated higher supplies of commodities.

Table 5.1 shows that fiscal deficits were pervasive and could be as high as 8 percent of the GDP. This implies that a government may have little or no control over its spending. It seems in this case that spending is pulling both taxes and public debt. A government may be facing expenditure pressure, and will resort simultaneously to more taxes and more debt to satisfy its expenditure programs. Table 5.1 shows that governments with high spending have both high fiscal deficits and high public debt. The latter may be as high as 246.2 percent of the GDP and may hover around or exceed 100 percent of GDP.[3] In contrast, governments with low spending tend to have lower fiscal deficits and lower public debt, which could be as low as 28.9 percent of GDP. High government spending may not be growth-oriented. In fact, capital spending could be low in high spending cases, and relatively high in low spending cases. Often, fiscal deficits exceeded capital spending, implying that governments were not able to tame their unproductive expenditures. In these conditions, investment in the economy is necessarily diminished in amount equal to government dissaving and growth is impeded consequently (Ricardo 1817).

Table 5.1 shows that many countries are trapped in a structural budget deficit that will continue to cripple their economies for decades to come (Ibn Khaldoun 1377). The budget may be so unmanageable that a return to a fiscal balance may expose the country to serious upheavals, since such a return would necessitate eliminating most of the unproductive spending. Strong fiscal reforms may become politically unattainable. As Ibn Khaldoun brilliantly asserted, the country may become entangled in economic decline, which is, similar to senility, incurable. The ruling dynasty remains in agony until extinction.[4]

Sharia does not agree with disorderly budgets that are excessive in taxation and wasteful in spending. It is for a limited government that obeys
divine rules and establishes perfect security and order. The mission of a
government is to implement the divine rulings without alteration; government governs best which governs least. The government has no right to
impose taxes indiscriminately, or to inflate money, or finance unproductive
expenditure that only impoverish people and increase dependence on debt.
Moreover, Sharia does not agree with interest-based debt. A government
violates the law that prohibits interest if it borrows with interest to finance
its expenditure.

3. Theories of taxation: excessive taxation a way to economic decline

The *Encyclopaedia Britannica* defines taxation as "that part of the revenues of a
state which is obtained by the compulsory dues and charges upon its subjects."
Taxation has been one of most important aspects of any country's political life
throughout centuries since it is the cost to maintain the government. Hence,
taxation has been the concern of the rulers who are constantly under pressure
to raise money; and the citizens who have to pay taxes. The government may
also carry out taxation by money printing. In this case, the government perse-
cutes no taxpayer. Although, money printing finances government spending in
the same way as money obtained through taxation, it is politically more attractive, since no taxpayer is directly subject to taxation. The government may also
carry taxation through indebtedness, since debt means future taxation in form
of higher taxes, inflation tax, or even default.

Taxation is distortionary; it causes changes in the distribution of incomes
(Smith 1776; Ricardo 1817; Seligman 1902; Ramsey 1927). If efficiently
used, taxation would contribute to economic growth (Bastiat 1850). If mis-
used in waste, such as financing unproductive expenditure, taxation may
become ruinous to the economy (Ibn Khaldoun 1377). Controversies in
taxation have been too pervasive. The debate of taxation evolves around primarily the notions of macroeconomic stability, equity, ability-to-pay taxes,
ability to shift taxes, incidence of taxation, and notion of optimal taxation.
The latter notion is not unique; Ricardo defined optimal taxation as the one
that raises minimum revenues and does not penalize capital. Ramsey (1927)
defined it as the one, which for a given amount of tax revenue, minimizes
the loss of consumer and producer surplus, i.e., the deadweight loss, from
taxation.

Ibn Khaldoun elaborated a penetrating analysis of taxation that is very
pertinent to modern fiscal theory and describes closely the fiscal crises of
many contemporaneous countries. He dealt with fiscal unsustainability,
caused solely by unrestrained unproductive spending, in relation to economic
growth, employment, and social peace. He considered fiscal unsustainability

as the only cause for the ruin of a civilization. It ruins the productive base and leads to the confiscation of property by the state. While natural disasters such as pestilence, or even wars, were incidental, fiscal unsustainability might be too durable and incurable. Ibn Khaldoun described a pattern of taxation inherent to vanished civilizations which seemingly could not be reversed by any ruler since the pattern evolved over many generations of rulers and citizens.

At the beginning of a government, taxation was just and modest; it financed productive expenditures highly desired by the citizens such as justice, security, education, and infrastructure. Assessments were small and tax yield was relatively adequate and in balance with government expenditure. A phase was reached where the size of the government was too overburdening; the number of people whose livelihood depended on taxes became too large. Unproductive expenditure kept rising. Taxation was constrained by the ability of taxpayers to pay taxes, and became far outpaced by unproductive expenditure. A final phase was reached where the ruler kept increasing existing tax rates, inventing new taxes, and resorting to property confiscation in order to finance still expanding expenditure. In this phase, economic activity was simply vanishing, and consequently, taxes were falling rapidly. Ibn Khaldoun maintained that this final phase was the senility of the dynasty and could not be cured in the same way the senility of the human body was also irremediable. In this phase, the dynasty vanished.

Ibn Khaldoun (1377) stated that:

> It should be known that at the beginning of the dynasty, taxation yields a large revenue from small assessments. At the end of the dynasty, taxation yields a small revenue from large assessments. Heavy taxes become an obligation and tradition, because the increases took place gradually, and no one knows specifically who increased them or levied them. The assessments increase beyond the limits of equity. The result is that the interest of the subjects in cultural enterprises disappears, since when they compare expenditures and taxes with their income and gain and see the little profit they make, they lose all hope. Therefore, many of them refrain from all cultural activities. The result is that the total tax revenue goes down, as the number of the individual assessments goes down. Often, when the decrease is noticed, the amounts of individual imposts are increased. This is considered a mean of compensating for the decrease. Finally, individual imposts and assessments reach their limit. It would be of no avail to increase them further. The costs of all cultural enterprise are now too high, the taxes are too heavy, and the profits anticipated fail to materialize. Thus, the total revenue continues to decrease, while the amounts of individual imposts and assessments continue to increase, because it is believed that such an increase will compensate for the drop in revenue in the end. Finally, civilization is destroyed, because the incentive for cultural activity is gone. It is the

dynasty that suffers from the situation, because it is the dynasty that profits from cultural activity.

(Chapter 36, P. 352)

Ibn Khaldoun stressed that history teaches that unproductive government spending ruined civilization. There was no other cause in Ibn Khaldoun's theory that would ruin a country other than excessive taxation to finance unproductive spending. He maintained that the historical facts proved that a government inevitably suffered losses through injustice and hostile acts in form of excessive taxation or requisitions. Ibn Khaldoun stated that, on the account of these evil consequences, the religious law prohibited all such unfair activities, i.e., unproductive spending and excessive taxation. The religious law legalizes mutual consent in trading, but forbids depriving people of their property illegally. The purpose is to prevent such evil consequences, which would lead to the destruction of civilization through disturbances or the lack of opportunity to make a living. He maintained that the strongest incentive for the private sector is to lower as much as possible the amounts of individual imposts levied upon persons capable of undertaking productive enterprises. In this manner, such persons will be psychologically disposed to undertake them, because they can be confident of making a profit from them. He (Ibn Khaldoun 1377) stated that:

> It should be known that the finances of a ruler can be increased, and his financial resources improved, only through the revenue from taxes. The revenue from taxes can be improved only through the equitable treatment of people with property and regard for them. This makes their hopes rise, and they have the incentive to start making their capital bear fruit and grow. This, in turn, increases the ruler's revenues in taxes.
>
> (P. 359)

Adam Smith (1776) noted that public stock and public lands, the two sources of revenue which may peculiarly belong to the sovereign or commonwealth, were both insufficient funds for financing the necessary cost of any great government; it remains that this cost must, to some large extent, be financed by taxes levied on private incomes in order to provide a public revenue to the sovereign or commonwealth. The incomes of individuals arise, ultimately, from three different sources: rent, profit, and wages. Every tax must finally be paid from these revenues. Smith formulated four maxims with regard to taxes in general: (i) the subjects of every state ought to contribute towards the support of the government, as nearly as possible, in proportion to their respective abilities; (ii) that the tax to be paid by each individual should be certain and not arbitrary; (iii) that it should be payable at the time and in the way most convenient to the payer; (iv) that the cost of collection should be as small as possible.

Smith was wary of the shortcomings of taxation. First, there is the tax administration cost which absorbs a considerable amount of the tax revenues. Second, a tax may have disincentive effects. Third, tax evaders may incur penalties that may ruin their business. Fourth, tax collectors may undertake audits which may be distressing for the taxpayer under examination.

Smith described taxes upon rent, profit, wages of labor, and taxes upon consumable commodities. The impossibility of taxing people in proportion to their revenue led to taxes upon consumable commodities. The state not knowing how to tax, directly and proportionally, the revenue of its subjects, seeks to tax it indirectly by taxing their spending.

J.B. Say (1803) dealt with the criteria for a less injurious taxation, the collection cost of taxation, its effects on capital accumulation and growth, and desirability of indirect taxation in relation to direct taxation. Say maintained that there are but two ways of obtaining resources, namely, creating oneself, or taking from others. The best scheme of finance is to spend as little as possible; and the best tax is always the lightest. The best taxes, or, rather those that are least bad, are (i) the most moderate in their ratios, (ii) least attended with those vexatious circumstances that harass the taxpayer without bringing anything into the public treasury, (iii) apply impartially on all classes, (iv) least injurious to reproduction, and (v) favorable to the national morality; that is to say, to the prevalence of habits, useful and beneficial to society (P. 452).

Say stressed the advantage of moderate taxation. Taxation, pushed to the extreme, may impoverish taxpayers without increasing tax revenues. Thus, the taxpayer is diminished of his revenues and the treasury of its revenues. However, if taxes are used in productive spending such as in infrastructure and education, they will contribute to increase economic growth.

Two methods are applied to tax revenues – direct, and indirect taxation. The former is defined as a tax on revenue; the latter is defined by tax rates on consumption articles and services. Indirect taxation is levied at each act of purchases, and is paid by individuals according to their spending amounts. Indirect taxation has the advantage of avoiding the shortcomings of direct taxation such as the inability to assess the taxpayer incomes or persecution of tax evaders. It enables the government to promote the consumption of basic goods and discourage luxuries.

Ricardo (1817) considered that taxes were distortive, and there were no taxes which had not a tendency to lessen the power to accumulate. All taxes must either fall on capital or revenue. If they affect capital, they may reduce the productive capacity of the country. If they affect revenue, they may reduce savings or compel the taxpayers to save the amount of the tax by reducing their consumption. He noted that if taxes are constantly used to finance government's unproductive expenditure, then the country's productive capacity will be eroded. Ricardo stressed that governments should encourage people to increase both their income and capital, and avoid taxing capital.

Rothbard (1962) considered that the greater the amount of taxes imposed on the producers – the taxpayers – the lower the marginal utility of work will be, for the returns from work are forcibly diminished, and the greater the marginal utility of leisure forgone. In the market economy, net incomes are derived from wages, interest, rent, and profit; and in so far as taxes strike at the earnings from these sources, attempts to earn these incomes will diminish. The laborer, faced with a tax on his wages, has less incentive to work hard; the capitalist, confronting a tax on his interest or profit return, has more incentive to consume rather than to save and invest. The landlord, a tax being imposed on his rents, will have less incentive for property development.

Initiated by Ramsey (1927), optimal taxation became a major topic of fiscal theory. Ramsey stated:

> The problem I propose to tackle is this: a given revenue is to be raised by proportionate taxes on some or all uses of income, the taxes on different uses being possibly at different rates; how these rates should be adjusted in order that the decrement of utility may be a minimum?
>
> (P. 47)

A simplified version of the Ramsey rule is the "inverse-elasticity rule." This rules states that tax rate on goods should be inversely related to their elasticity of demand. That is, the ratio of the tax rates as a percentage of the initial prices are inversely related to the elasticities of demand. So, all else equal, more elastic goods should have lower tax rates. More inelastic goods should have higher tax rates. The tax mix should be adjusted until the excess burden per dollar of revenue raised, at the margin, is equal across commodities. Using an intertemporal Ramsey model, Chamley (1986) showed that capital income tax is a double taxation of saving and that optimality requires a zero capital income tax.

4. Taxation from a Sharia perspective: restraint and equity

The government has no legal right to impose any levy, except those compliant with the Sharia laws, or to print money out of thin air, or to borrow with interest.[5] Sharia is not compatible with fiscal mismanagement. The financial resources of the government arise essentially from the following: (i) income from its own property and stocks, such as royalties from natural resources, public land, public enterprises, and sovereign funds investment; (ii) *Zakat* revenues; (iv) Sharia-compliant taxes; (iii) voluntary contributions and official and private grants; (iv) cost recovery and users' fees; and (v) non-interest based loans.

In respect to property taxes, county and municipal taxes levied on properties are perfectly legitimate to pay for municipal infrastructure and services, schools, and fire protection. Inheritance tax is not Sharia-compliant; it abrogates the inheritance laws of Sharia.[6] Income taxation should be regulated by Sharia laws. Progressive income taxation violates Sharia. For instance, *Zakat* ratios are fixed and are not progressive. Likewise, sales taxes, commodity taxes, and customs duties have to be Sharia-compliant. For instance, social equity may require the taxation of some commodities. Typically, cars and roads are complementary products. Taxes on cars, petroleum, and transport-related engines and parts are a form of users' fees, the proceeds of which are destined to the building and maintenance of roads. Hence, only road users pay this tax, in proportion to their road use as measured by fuel consumption. Similarly, the consumption of water may be subjected to a tax for sanitation and water treatment. Municipal fees for street pavements, garbage collection and treatment, etc. are quite legitimate. Pollutant industries may have to incur additional costs to prevent environment damage from polluting substances. Important revenue may be derived from user fees and cost recovery for marketable services. For instance, all recordings of property and contracts, civil matters, etc. are covered via fees, called stamp fees. Passport issuance is covered by fees.

5. Expenditure policy: reduce unproductive spending

Often, government spending is the driving force for taxation. Spending is a measure of effective taxes. Debt which finances spending has to be paid out of taxes. Government spending is classified into productive and nonproductive. Productive spending enhances infrastructure and human capital (education, health); it maintains security, justice, and defense. This spending, besides adding to fixed capital as well as human capital, contributes necessarily to economic growth. Without security and the prompt reinforcement of contracts, economic activity will be impaired (Davenport 1913).[7] Unproductive spending simply consumes capital and reduces economic growth. Under this category there are subsidies, useless ministries, useless embassies, and useless administration that intervenes in every aspect of social and economic life, etc. Unproductive spending crowds out productive spending and leads necessarily to deficits and even high inflation. As Ibn Khaldoun noted, the economy gets entangled in an incurable trap of decline with unproductive spending expanding, capital eroding, and the tax base shrinking.

A large part of productive spending may be delegated to the private sector and would not require increasing taxes for its financing. In fact, social equity should require a large participation of the private sector in the productive spending. This is the case of many types of infrastructure such as schools, universities, hospitals, water, sanitation, ports, airports, dams, bridges, canals, etc. Productive spending may be financed through voluntary contributions as well as the establishment of endowments (*Awqaf*). By enhancing private sector participation, the supply of economic infrastructure will be enhanced, and the country will suffer less shortage of health, education, and utilities infrastructure. In contrast, unproductive spending is financed essentially through more taxes.

Sharia does not allow the state to undertake any expenditure it wishes; spending should be within its natural functions and should be subject to revenues and non-interest financing; spending programs should not be rigid and nonresponsive to revenue shortfall. Social spending on the poor should target the vulnerable groups such as the handicapped, the orphans, the aged, the sick, etc. Social spending on education and health are highly praised. Subsidies have to be eliminated. Spending should be prioritized. Productive spending should have priority over unproductive spending. While the latter should be downsized considerably in light of revenue constraint, productive spending has to increase in efficiency. For instance, education towards the needs of the economy such as medicine would be preferred to education in fashion, movies, music, and sports. The latter should be provided by private schools.

Many countries became trapped in overwhelming unproductive spending that has inflicted damage to their economies. The government shows no flexibility for downsizing itself. These countries became too indebted and had no success in increasing further their taxes to finance unproductive spending.

6. Fiscal balance: a requisite for sound public finance

Table 5.1 shows that most countries have fiscal deficits; this is an indication of unproductive spending; productive spending can be more than fully financed by taxation. Moreover, productive spending keeps generating growth and therefore more revenues, whereas unproductive spending erodes the tax base and enlarges the deficit. From the perspective of growth and macroeconomic stability, it is desirable that fiscal position be in equilibrium with alternating small deficits and surpluses. Moreover, even though the budget may be brought into equilibrium from intense taxation, it is far preferable that fiscal balance be achieved through downsizing unproductive spending.

Table 5.1 clearly demonstrates an inherent defect in fiscal policy which keeps generating sizeable deficits. Namely, in the budgeting exercise, most governments increase their spending to any politically desired level, with little attention to their revenue. The government manages to cover deficits through more debt, or inflation tax. This policy is deficient and has serious implications on growth and social equity. It creates financial disorder in the economy. Very few governments observe fiscal balance, and very few have a constitutional law requiring such balance.[9] Fiscal equilibrium has many advantages. It helps to reduce unproductive spending and to redeploy labor and capital to the private economy to generate economic growth and employment and reduce poverty. It prevents debt and therefore intergeneration injustice. The cost of capital will be reduced as government borrowing is reduced. Fiscal deficit explains most of the external deficit; hence, fiscal balance will enable the restoration of an external equilibrium and will reduce exchange rate depreciation.

7. Government debt: an index of waste

Table 5.1 shows most countries are indebted, some heavily indebted, and some in debt crises. Government debt may reach 250 percent of the GDP, and often exceeds 100 percent of the GDP. Government debt may be an index of government waste; it shows how rigid a government may be in respect to its finance. The government may be under pressure to finance unproductive spending, and pays little attention to long-term burdens, distortions, and inequity aspects of debt. From a distant past, e.g., Roman Empire, government debt was not easy to service. Recent experiences showed that government debt was either canceled or renegotiated with large discounts. In fact, contrary to an entrepreneur who borrows money to build a factory and generate a stream of income out of which to pay the debt and interest, the government borrows to finance unproductive spending with no trace of capital accumulation out of which to service debt.

Ibn Khaldoun postulated that, once embroiled in fiscal deficits, a government is powerless to eliminate unproductive spending and to prevent the debt build-up. Adam Smith noted that governments resorted to debt to finance fiscal deficits. Public debt may rise rapidly due to war or profligacy. Its repayment may require higher taxes or new taxes. However, he noted that high debts were rarely paid. Often, government fell in default or resorted to money inflation to reduce its real debt.

> The raising of the denomination of the coin has been the most usual expedient by which a real public bankruptcy has been disguised under the appearance of a pretended payment. If a sixpence, for example, should, either by act of parliament or royal proclamation, be raised to the denomination of a shilling, and twenty sixpences to that of a pound sterling; the person who, under the old denomination, had borrowed twenty shillings, or near four ounces of silver, would, under the new, pay with twenty sixpences, or with something less than two ounces.
>
> (Smith 1776, P. 769)

Adam Smith (1776) noted that debasing was injurious to creditors:

> A pretended payment of this kind, therefore, instead of alleviating, aggravates, in most cases, the loss of the creditors of the public; and, without any advantage to the public, extends the calamity to a great number of other innocent people. It occasions a general and most pernicious subversion of the fortunes of private people; enriching, in most cases, the idle and profuse debtor, at the expense of the industrious and frugal creditor; and transporting a great part of the national capital from the hands which were likely to increase and improve it, to those who are likely to dissipate and destroy it.
>
> (P. 770)

Governments, in all times, when in bankruptcy, have often inflated their way out of debt. Adam Smith showed that through money debasement a debt of £128 million might be reduced all at once to £5.3 million. In fact, the German hyperinflation of 1919–1923 showed that government debt could be wiped all together through currency extinction. The fiscal theory of the price level postulates that the government may be compelled to inflate the price level in order to reduce the real burden of its debt. In view of the record levels of public debt in many industrial countries, central banks may keep interest rates very low and attempt to increase prices in order to reduce the debt burden and afflict the creditors.

Churchman (2001) described plainly Ricardo's hostility to public debt and his doctrine for limited taxation and balanced budget. With respect to public debt, Ricardo made two related policy recommendations: (i) under no circumstances should government expenditure be financed by borrowing; and (ii) existing government debt should be redeemed immediately. He feared that heavy taxation would cause capital flight. He believed that repealing the Corn-Laws and paying off debt would be highly favorable to the United Kingdom's prosperity. Ricardo urged that some solutions should be used to liquidate the public debt and eliminate its ill-effects to the extent that it distorted prices and caused many persons to relocate in other countries in order to avoid the taxation which it entailed.

Ricardo rejected the equivalence of debt and taxation. In Ricardo's view, tax financing of government expenditure was preferable to debt financing because the former would tend to the restraint of government waste. Debt deferred the tax burden and thus allowed the government to spend without a pain on taxpayers. Public loans thus tended to encourage high, unproductive spending, which was, by its nature, detrimental to capital formation. Government borrowing thus deluded taxpayers in respect to the true burden of government expenditure. Furthermore, it deluded them as to the extent of their own wealth. Ricardo analyzed the harmful effects of public debt on investment. These effects were these: (i) the unproductive nature of public expenditure and the possibility for profligacy in using loan financing; (ii) the decrease in private investment as saving is diverted to government borrowing; and (iii) capital flight to evade heavy taxation to service the debt. By rejecting the applicability of Ricardian Equivalence, Ricardo argued that government borrowing reduced capital formation. He contended that government borrowing concealed the true size of public expenditure and thus encouraged unproductive expenditure, afflicting the country's economic well-being.

Buchanan (1999) addressed defects of public debt such as the intergenerational injustice, the unproductive aspects of public spending financed by debt, the violation of fiscal prudence, and the deferment of the true costs of public expenditure. In regard to intergeneration injustice, he contended that future generations pay a public debt which arose from spending decisions in which they did not participate. In addition, to the extent that public debt may finance current consumption, it becomes unjust as it draws income from those who are not beneficiaries of the expenditure and who cannot be involved in budgeting decisions that lead to a debt build-up. In view of the intergeneration injustice, a government often repudiated debt of past governments as irresponsible management which creditors should not have consented to.

Among the shortcomings of the public debt is that it allows the government to undertake large expenditure without an immediate tax burden on the taxpayers. For instance, the government may finance large subsidies and transfer programs with debt. Hence, this expenditure does not immediately afflict taxpayers. Its burden is postponed into the future when interest and the principal of the debt have to be paid. Moreover, if public debt finances public consumption instead of public investment, it reduces investment. In this instance, fiscal prudence has been twice violated. First, the government has not applied a cash management principle which requires it to pay for current spending out of its tax revenues. Second, the government has not applied the borrowed funds to productive investment in infrastructure. Buchanan likened the financing of current government expenditure by debt to cutting the apple trees for firewood, thereby diminishing forever the income stream from the plantation. Buchanan disdained public debt build-up for it diminishes private investment, increases interest rates, necessitates additional taxes to service it, and may cause a debt crisis where the government fails to pay its creditors. Many governments had used public debt for current spending, or in unproductive infrastructure and reached debt unsustainability, with high level of indebtedness coupled with deteriorating poverty.

Buchanan recommended a constitutional law that requires fiscal balance. Budgets should obey financial discipline, and should not be out of control under the influence of political forces. The government should observe not only financial constraints but also priority and balance constraints. It should increase the efficiency of its expenditure. To adhere to a constitutional balanced-budget principle, the government should apply full flexibility in its budgeting process and trigger immediate balancing measures such as tax increases or expenditure cuts. Buchanan considered that these cuts should apply to all categories of spending, including civil service wages, with a view to enforcing the budget balance rules. In line with Ricardo, Buchanan thought that Ricardian equivalence does not hold because of fiscal illusion.

Notwithstanding, fiscal discipline requires that public debt should finance only investment projects that are socially profitable, i.e., their social rate of return exceeds the interest rate, and contribute to growth and enlarge the tax base. In these conditions, the debt contributes to build a productive capital which provides an income stream for repaying the debt service. Intergeneration equity is not violated, since future generations will benefit from the infrastructure built by the previous generation.

Sharia does not allow interest-based debt. The government should achieve a current surplus to be used in capital expenditure. To finance its investment projects, the government may apply Islamic financing such as *sukuks*,[10] or risk sharing with the private sector.

8. Conclusions

Table 5.1 shows that scarcely public finance is managed on sound principles of fiscal balance. Most governments indulge in fiscal mismanagement, the consequences of which are impoverishment, inflation, unemployment, and social instability. Ibn Khaldoun postulated that excessive taxation was not reversible, and was the cause for the collapse of previous civilizations. The contribution of excessive taxation to the collapse of the Roman Empire was widely documented in economic literature. Smith described plainly that a government may inflate to reduce real value of debt in case of bankruptcy. This practice is widely applied by governments in the distant past as well in present times and has been called the fiscal theory of the price level. Hayek (1978) called for ending the unholy marriage between fiscal and money policy and recommended fiscal balance.

Sharia provides a framework for sound public finance and sets restrictions on both taxation and spending power of the ruler. Taxation has to be Sharia-compliant. The government may encourage the private sector participation in infrastructure, which would reduce taxation. The spending of the government has to be flexible, and subjected to many criteria of resource availability, priority, productivity, and intergenerational equity. Fiscal deficits should not be financed by interest-based debt. They should be financed through non-interest financing. Many governments are too deep in fiscal mismanagement, and for decades, have become accustomed to fiscal deficits; fiscal unsustainability becomes incurable. Governments do not understand the principles of sound public finance, and even if they do, they cannot implement them without setting a country ablaze, since too many beneficiaries would be denied a rent from fiscal profligacy.

Notes

1 Unproductive spending absorbs resources and contributes little or nothing to national output. It has a negative rate of return. Productive spending, such as a port, hospital, university, etc., contributes to national output and has a positive rate of return. If unproductive spending is reduced in favor of productive spending, economic growth will improve considerably.

2 Take, for example, the US Declaration of Independence and the ensuing American Revolution. Revolts caused by oppressive taxation were thoroughly analyzed by Ibn Khaldoun.

3 The rate of return on such high public debt is forcibly very low and often negative in real terms. This is so because the government sets interest rates at near-zero bound. Second, high government debt is a debt that has been used to finance government consumption; it has contributed to no capital base, and therefore there is no installed capital that would produce a high return for the holders of government debt. Pension funds, insurance companies, and many other institutional investors earn negligible return when government debt is high.

4 Hume stated that: "Historians inform us, that one of the chief causes of the destruction of the Roman state, was the alteration, which Constantine introduced into the finances, by substituting a universal poll-tax, in lieu of almost all the tithes, customs, and excises,

which formerly composed the revenue of the *empire*. The people, in all the provinces, were so grinded and oppressed by the *publicans,* that they were glad to take refuge under the conquering arms of the barbarians; whose dominion, as they had fewer necessities and less art, was found preferable to the refined tyranny of the Romans" (P. 82).

5　Holy Quran 4:29–30: O you who believe! Eat not up your property among yourself unjustly except it be trade amongst you, by mutual consent, and do not kill yourselves. Surely, Allah is most Merciful to you. And whoever commits that through aggression and injustice, We shall cast him into the Fire, and that is easy for Allah.

6　Quran 4:2: And unto orphans their property and do not exchange your bad things for their good ones; and devour not their property by adding it to your property, this is a great sin.

7　Davenport stated that social conditions affect product. The effect of the social situation upon the productive power of the laborer may be great. The bearing of science and invention needs perhaps no further emphasis. Important, likewise, and sometimes in an equal degree, are the safety and security of the individual and of his property, his freedom of choice, his immunity from different forms of injustice and exploitation. No society which, through disorder, crime, war, or over-taxation, unsettles the connection between industry and reward, can fail of enfeebling its productive forces. Security of life, property, and investment are essential to high economic efficiency (The Economics of Enterprise, P. 9).

8　Source: International Monetary Fund, Article IV Consultation, Staff Report, 2015.

9　A balanced-budget amendment is a constitutional rule requiring that a state cannot spend more than its income. It requires a balance between the projected receipts and expenditures of the government. Balanced-budget provisions have been added to the constitutions of most US states, the Basic Law of Germany, the Hong Kong Basic Law, Spain, Italy, and the Swiss Constitution. It is often proposed that a balanced-budget rule be added to the national United States Constitution. Most balanced-budget provisions make an exception for times of war, national emergency, or recession, or allow the legislature to suspend the rule by a supermajority vote.

10　*Sukuk* Islamic bonds are structured in such a way as to generate returns to investors without infringing Islamic law (which prohibits riba or interest). *Sukuk* represents undivided shares in the ownership of tangible assets relating to particular projects or special investment activity.

References

Bastiat, F., 1850, *The Bastiat Collection*, Auburn, AL: Ludwig von Mises Institute.

Buchanan, J., 1999, *The Collected Works of James M. Buchanan*, Indianapolis, IN: Liberty Fund.

Cagan, P., 1956, "The Monetary Dynamic of Hyper-Inflation," in Friedman, M. (ed.). *Studies in the Quantity Theory of Money*, Chicago: University of Chicago Press.

Chamley, C., 1986, "Optimal Taxation of Capital Income in General Equilibrium With Infinite Lives," *Econometrica*, 54: 607–622.

Churchman, N., 2001, *David Ricardo on Public Debt*, New York: Palgrave Macmillan.

Davenport, H., 1913, *The Economics of Enterprise*, New York: M. Kelley Publishers.

Hayek, F. A., 1978, *Denationalization of Money: An Analysis of the Theory and Practice of Concurrent Currencies*, London: Institute of Economic Affairs.

Hume, D., 1752, *Political Discourses*, Edinburgh: Printed by R. Fleming, for A. Kincaid and A. Donaldson.

Ibn Khaldun, 1377/1985, *Al Muqaddimah*, Beirut: Dār al-Qalam.

Ramsey, F. P., 1927, "A Contribution to the Theory of Taxation," *Economic Journal* 37: 47–61.

Ricardo, D., 1817, *On the Principles of Political Economy and Taxation*, 3rd edition, London: John Murray.

Rothbard, M., 1962, *Man, Economy, and State, With Power and Market*, Auburn, AL: Ludwig von Mises Institute.

Say, J. B., 1803, *A Treatise on Political Economy*, Philadelphia: Claxton, Kemsen, & Haffelfingee.

Seligman, E.R.A., 1902, *The Shifting and Incidence of Taxation*, London: Palgrave Macmillan.

Smith, A., 1776, *An Inquiry Into the Nature and Causes of the Wealth of Nations*, London: Methuen and Co. Ltd., ed. Edwin Canan, 1904, Fifth Edition.

6 Nature of money in Sharia

1. Introduction

Money is the pillar of commerce and the specialization and division of labor within and across countries. Oresme (fourteenth century) and Copernicus (1526) maintained that if the government debases money, it will inflict damage to trade and property. Without money, any economy will collapse into starvation and social disorder.[1] Money was a commodity, an equivalent in labor and capital content to another commodity in exchange, which enters the circulation, as any other commodity, via production and exchange.[2] Its price in relation to other commodities obeyed strictly the laws of supply and demand. Although many commodities served as money, gold and silver superseded all commodities, and became universal money throughout the centuries in all countries (Smith 1776; Gouge 1833; Mises 1953; Rothbard 1962). Today, in all countries, money is fiat inconvertible paper emitted by a central bank; it is a monopoly of the government. In addition, credit money is emitted by both the central bank and the banking system. All money supply, defined as currency in circulation and credit money, is regulated by the central bank within its monetary policy framework. Generally, the central bank increases money supply via many channels[3] to attain a target consumer price inflation rate, e.g., 3 percent per year.

There are two notions of money: money as an instrument of trade and money as a unit of account (Einaudi 1936). In any country, money has a unit of account as well as a physical shape in form of a paper or coin. The money of account could be the same or different from money as an instrument of trade. The money of account in the United States is the dollar. All prices and values of merchandise and property and all accounts are expressed in dollars. Money is defined as the cash in circulation; it is perfectly liquid, and unanimously accepted in all transactions.[4] Previously, it included gold and silver coins. Presently, it is government currency. Money substitutes may be less liquid. They depend on the advancement of banking and the technology of payments. They include credit, credit cards, bills of exchange, and commercial effects that are allowed by law to circulate through endorsement. Money substitutes are the most important instruments of payments in advanced financial systems. As money substitutes advance, an economy may reach a cashless payments' system.

The chapter covers the following:

- Controversies in money
- Origins of money: money as a commodity and a unit of account
- Money is gold and silver
- Nature of government inconvertible paper
- The debate Locke versus Lowndes
- Theories of optimum money
- Sharia money

2. Controversies in money

Money is one of most controversial topics in political economy where conflict between schools of thought is too predominant.[5] Controversies evolve around the nature of money, money as a market commodity, money as a costless paper emitted by a bank or the state, money as a credit, the conflict between inflationism and sound money, the confusion between money and capital, and the use of money as a policy tool. A controversy opposed the currency school and the banking school: the former wanted currency to be fully backed by gold; the latter considered that money has to be elastic in accordance with the needs of business for credit and at the same time convertibility into gold has to be preserved. Questions such as what is money, what is the pound, and what is the dollar have been repeatedly formulated; yet, the answers were diverse and reflected divergent views in respect of money. There was an evolution process from money as a commodity with intrinsic value to money as inconvertible paper, a nominal standard with zero intrinsic value.

Sharia establishes a sound money policy. It bans strictly interest transactions. Consequently, it bans interest-based debt money which displaced gold and silver (Gouge 1833; Carroll 1850). Being inherently inflationary, inconvertible paper money may not be Sharia-compliant. Sharia strictly forbids altering the standard of measure be it meter, ton, or liter. Once the standard of measure has been defined, it should become immutable (Locke 1691; Liverpool 1805). Hence a gold dinar defined at 4.25 grams should remain unaltered. Sharia prohibits the creation of money ex-nihilo by the government or the banking system. The latter may regulate money through minting, preventing counterfeiting, and insuring the quality of coin.

Sharia considers money and financial intermediation as two related aspects of the payment mechanism in an economy or across economies. They were inseparable aspects of a money system. Financial intermediaries, which include banks, clearing houses, etc., were needed to increase the efficiency of money and economize on its use. Financial intermediaries do not create money; they create substitutes for money, which have to be convertible, by law, into money.

3. Origins of money: money as a commodity and a unit of account

Today's money is an inconvertible government paper. Prior to reaching this form, money originated as a commodity to reduce transactions costs. Money was not invented by any government and existed independently of any government. It was inherent to trade and emerged as a traded commodity selected by the market to economize on the transaction cost involved with barter trade. Merchants have devised instruments to facilitate trade, such as money, institutions for safekeeping money and financial intermediation such as banks, and instruments to save on the use of money such as bills of exchange, clearing houses, and credit cards. Only 2 percent of local transactions were settled in gold in the United Kingdom during the 1890s. Today, many economies tend to a cashless payment system via electronic credit means.

Smith (1776) noted that trade preceded money, and money was a medium for advancing trade. He maintained that in any economy there are a large number of industries, products, and specialized producers. Each producer wants to sell his surplus product against other products, essential for his survival, which he does not produce. The shoemaker needs to sell his shoes to obtain wheat, and medicines. Trade takes place between local and foreign producers. In barter trade, commodities are exchanged directly against each other, say a pair of shoes is exchanged against 10 pounds of corn. Imagine the shoemaker needs a coat. He offers 10 pairs of shoes to the tailor. The latter happens to need corn flour; moreover, he has no need for such a large number of pairs of shoes. The wants of the shoemaker and tailor do not coincide; moreover, there is a problem of indivisibility of some commodities, which makes it difficult to exchange a coat for shoes, a car for coats, or an airplane for cars.

The barter trade existed widely prior to the use of money, and may still exist in conditions where money becomes scarce due to inflation; however, it was too inefficient. The information and transaction cost for making wants coincide was too high; moreover, there were divisibility issues, where some commodities could not be divided to fit commodities in exchange. Smith (1776) noted that traders, and not the government, had selected spontaneously a commodity, or a few commodities, that intervened in most of the exchange transactions to circumvent the inconvenience of barter trade and allowed the producers to specialize and exchange their products against all the rest of local and foreign products. Smith cited few examples of commodities used as medium of exchange: these were salt, cowry shell, tobacco, vampum, rice, fur, etc. Carl Menger (1892) contended that money was the most saleable commodity, i.e., liquid commodity, whereby each trader would sell it instantly against any other commodity.

The supplier of the selected commodity was the one who created money on a profit criterion. The chosen commodity had an intrinsic value, it needed labor and capital for its production. The basic feature of the chosen commodity was liquidity, i.e., general acceptability in every transaction, provided its intrinsic qualities were not altered. Each trader ceded his produce against a valuable equivalent, with a certainty that money would be accepted by every trader, would preserve value, and would enable him to purchase any good or service he wished to acquire. A stock of money was held among traders and served in all exchange transactions. It had a velocity which defined the work it performed. Exchanges became indirect; for instance, wheat was exchanged for money. The shoemaker faced no longer the problem of double coincidence of wants. With the proceeds of 10 pairs of shoes, he could easily exchange money for a coat.

Accordingly, money originated as a medium of exchange embodied in a marketable commodity that was willingly acceptable by all local and foreign traders to circumvent the direct barter trade and allow commodities to exchange indirectly via the commodity money. This commodity is sufficiently divisible, without losing its intrinsic value, to solve the indivisibility issue arising in barter trade. As a commodity, money may increase or decrease in quantity, but it is stable in value, and in adequate supply to enable an increasing number of exchange transactions.

Locke (1691), Liverpool (1805), Mises (1953), and Rothbard (1962) maintained that money of account is an imaginary name, and money is a real commodity, and that once the relation between money and unit of account is set by law it should never be altered by the government or by traders. Thus, if a sovereign is defined as 7.32 grams, the US dollar as 25.8 grains, and the dinar as 4.25 grams, this relation should become invariant. The United Kingdom law retired all sovereign coins which lost 0.747 grains from their mint weight. Money cannot be a measure of value if this relation becomes variable.

Lord Liverpool (1805) defined money in terms of two properties: a standard of value and an equivalent in exchange meaning that it is as valuable in exchange as the commodity for which it is exchanged. For instance, the buyer of a computer finds the computer as worthy as an ounce of gold he possesses. Lord Liverpool defined these two properties of money as follows:

> The money or coin of a country is the standard of measure, by which the value of all things is regulated and ascertained; – and it is itself, at the same time, the value, or equivalent, for which goods are exchanged, and in which contracts are generally made payable.
>
> (P. 9)

Gold is an equivalent commodity because it embodies labor time and material cost. A gold money, e.g., gold dollar, is a standard of measure because its unit weight and fineness are fixed, and its exchange value is not subject to frequent fluctuations.

Sharia strictly forbids the altering of weights and measures. Quran 11:84:

> And to Midian people, we sent their brother Shuaib. He said: O my people worship Allah, you have no other god, but Him, and give not short measure

or weight. I see you in prosperity and verily I fear for you the torment of a day encompassing. And O my people, give full measure and weight and reduce not the things that are due to people, and do not commit mischief in the land, causing corruption.

This Sharia ruling is repeated often in Quran and Sunnah. Quran 6:152: "and give full measure and full weight with justice." Quran 17:35: "And give full measure when you measure, and weigh with balance that is straight. That is good and better in the end." Quran 55:9: "And observe the weight with equity and do not make the balance deficient." Sharia ruling in regard to integrity of measures and weights is part of the ruling regarding the sanctity of property rights, often emphasized in Quran and Sunnah. Money, if corrupted, can be turned into a grandiose stealing scheme, which would deprive victims from substantial real wealth. For instance, if a creditor made a loan in money equivalent to a farm of 1,000 hectares. If repaid in inflated money that bought him four eggs, as in the German hyperinflation (1923), then he lost unjustly his wealth.[6] Sharia requires that altered coins be destroyed.

Commodity money performs essential functions. It is a medium of exchange that circulates commodities within and across countries. It is a standard of value. To serve as a medium of exchange, money has to be a standard of value; that is, it measures the value of a commodity or a service against which it is exchanged. Hence, each commodity is priced in terms of money. The value of each commodity is defined as the number of units of that commodity that exchange for one unit of money, or the number of units of money that are exchanged for one unit of the commodity. By being a standard of value, money becomes a common denominator for all commodities in the economy.[7] To be a standard of value, money has to preserve value. Gold and silver were stable standards of value; meaning that the value of gold or silver was relatively stable. Hence, a unit of money plays the same role as a meter. The latter has to keep the same length to fulfill measurements. If it shrinks or extends, traders will no longer accept it as a standard of measurement. It causes chaos in transactions and designs and mappings. If money depreciates, traders will reject is as a standard of value.[8]

Money cannot be a medium of exchange without being a store of value and standard of deferred payments.[9] Since exchanges are not instantaneous transactions and varying time intervals occur between sales and purchases operations, i.e., payments are deferred to the future, the medium of exchange has to be a store of value and a standard of deferred payments. The property of a store of value cannot be dissociated from that of medium of exchange. If a commodity loses its value, as measured against all the rest of commodities, during the time interval separating sales and purchases, or loan disbursement and repayment, it would not qualify to be a medium of exchange. For instance, paper money in hyperinflation becomes worthless, simply because it does not hold any value through depreciation. Any holder of money will lose wealth during the time interval he is holding the money. If money loses value at a regular or fast speed, it will end up by being rejected and will be extinguished as has happened at the end of many hyperinflations.

Money substitutes are distinctly different from money. Money may be coin or paper and circulates from hand to hand among traders; the identity of the traders is totally irrelevant. Money substitutes are personal credit, in form of offsetting credit, checks, credit cards, bills of exchanges, financial papers, and are far more efficient than money in large transactions. They are promises to pay money. They are expressed in money terms.

4. Money is gold and silver

Gold and silver are not by nature money, but money consists by its nature of gold and silver. Gold and silver have been used as universal money, common to all countries, throughout history. Monetary organization was similar across nations: it consisted of adopting a monetary law defining the unit of account, the standard of value in weight and fineness, and types of coins in terms of weights and shapes to be allowed to circulate. To circulate as money, gold and silver had to be coined in a standard shape. Coins were standardized and stamped so they became instantly identifiable and circulated with perfect confidence in trade. Coinage saved on transactions cost and enhanced the confidence in money. The trader who ceded his valuable commodity knew with certainty that he was receiving a true money according to the specifications prescribed by the law and understood by all traders. The trader had to incur no cost in verifying the authenticity, weight, and fineness of the coin. We emphasize here that the King, or the government, did not create money. Money was created by the producer of the commodity money on pure profitability basis and with no subsidies such as the silver subsidies under the Bland-Allison Act (1878); he brought it to the market and surrendered it in exchange for other commodities or properties. The gold and silver are produced as long as they are profitable, bullion may be brought to the mints and turned into coins, or to a bullion dealer and exchanged for coins. The government only certified the conformity of the coin to the prescribed law and protected traders against counterfeiting, or money debasing. In any modern economy, if the government withdraws from being a money supplier, and lets the private economy again supply money, as it did in the nineteenth century, then the market will choose no other money except gold and silver. Paper money will circulate only as a pure representative of gold. It will never circulate as a privately produced money.

The market verdict settled spontaneously over centuries for gold and silver money. Only government changed this verdict. For Gouge (1833), money was metallic, saying that:

> The high estimation in which the precious metals have been held, in nearly all ages and all regions, is evidence that they must possess something more than merely ideal value. It is not from the mere vagaries of fancy, that they are equally prized by the Laplander and the Siamese. It was not from

compliance with any preconceived theories of philosophers or statesmen, that they were, for many thousand years in all commercial countries, the exclusive circulating medium. Men chose gold and silver for the material for money, for reasons similar to those which induced them to choose wool, flax, silk, and cotton, for materials for clothing, and stone, brick, and timber, for materials for building. They found the precious metals had those specific qualities, which fitted them to be standards and measures of value, and to serve, when in the shape of coin, the purposes of a circulating medium.

(P. 10)

He added that there was:

No instance is on record of a nation's having arrived at great wealth without the use of gold and silver money. Nor is there, on the other hand, any instance of a nation's endeavoring to supplant this natural money, by the use of paper money, without involving itself in distress and embarrassment. All writers are agreed that six requisites are essential to a good kind of money, viz., portability, uniformity, durability, divisibility, cognizability, and stability of value. Long experience has taught mankind that these qualities are best embodied in the metal gold.

(P. 17)

Aristotle elaborated on the theory of money; he deemed that gold and silver had natural properties that made them the best forms of money. They made commodities commensurable and made prices expressible in gold or silver units. As common denominators, gold and silver money made commodities comparable. Having intrinsic values, traders invented gold and silver money units that supplied a measure on the basis of which just exchange could take place. Aristotle stated that every commodity could be valued in money. He described the properties of a good money. It must be durable, portable, divisible, and malleable. Money should be easily divided or recombined with no loss in its intrinsic value.

Gold and silver were natural commodities and became money from a natural market process. The producer of gold was as any other producer who operated on profitability, with no subsidies; gold and silver were produced at a profit. In case of loss, their production is discarded. The producer brought gold to the market in the same manner as a car manufacturer brings cars to the market. The laws of value applies to both gold and cars. In contrast, the issuer of paper money brings nothing to the market; he exchanges his bits of paper against cars, food, houses, etc. His bits of paper obey no laws of value and no natural control process, other than counterfeiting or coercion (Walker 1873). The market chose gold and silver as money essentially because of their scarcity. Gold's value and purchasing power are stable over time, as its supply grows slowly and it cannot be created ad infinitum, as paper or digital currency can be. The scarcity of gold and silver was never an impediment to trade. Instead, it enabled trade to flourish among nations over the centuries, simply because trade was an exchange of commodities against commodities, and it was the volume of commodities that determined trade, and never the volume of gold or silver. In fact, money was a veil which cached the actual trade of commodities for commodities.

Gold and silver are scare metals. Very few countries produce these metals. Over the centuries, their production has never ceased; sometimes, it rose at a high pace when new mines were discovered. Today, gold and silver continue to be extracted from mines. In contrast to paper, the scarcity of gold and silver is a basic property that makes them suitable as money. Gold and silver cannot be produced in millions of metric tons, as can wood, stones, gravel, and coal. If men wanted an inflationary commodity, they would never have chosen gold or silver. Because of the slow rise of their stocks, gold and silver provided a stable measure of value. An inflationary commodity cannot serve as a measure of value as much as a shrinking rod cannot be used to measure length or distance. With gold or silver, prices were stable and did not change violently. Durability is an essential property of a currency. Without this characteristic, there can be no exchange, saving, and capital formation. Durability means that money remains a store of value until it is used again in trade. A commodity, used as medium of exchange, has to be durable and capable of storing value. In fact, a medium of exchange has to store value. There is always a time period of varying length between transactions. A worker saves part of his income with a view to buying a house in the future. Gold and silver are durable, unalterable, and have a stable and predictable value. They can be stored even in the ground and cannot be altered. In fact, quantities of gold were found in ships that sunk deep in the sea centuries before; the gold thus found had practically no erosion.

Gold and silver bullion are assayed and certified by specialized agencies and banks and cannot be counterfeited. Similarly, gold and silver coins were milled and stamped and could not be counterfeited. Paper can easily be counterfeited on a large scale. Gold and silver possess the main properties of a money, which are these: value in exchange, intrinsic value; stability of value; homogeneity of material; durability; divisibility without diminution of value; large value in small compass; and adaptability to coinage. Gold and silver fulfilled five essential functions of money as they are recognized today: a medium of exchange; a common denominator; a standard of value; a store of value; and a standard of deferred payments. Because of these properties, gold has always been considered an ideal store of value and thus, and ideal medium of exchange. Among all commodities produced from earth, gold and silver were found by the human race, centuries ago, as the best fit for money for both local and international trade. Because of their natural attraction, they were valued as a commodity before being chosen as money. While some commodities served in domestic trade such as cowries shells, wampum, tobacco, salt, iron, and silk, only gold and silver were everlasting and universal monies.

5. Nature of government inconvertible paper

Government inconvertible money arose from bankruptcy. A government with balanced budgets would never need it. Imposed by force, inconvertible paper is a taxation means, highly inflationary, and causes impoverishment. By its nature, inconvertible paper cannot circulate, except by compulsion. Paper money allowed the government to become giant in size, wage wars, interfere in all aspects of the economy, maintain an endless inflation tax, spread poverty, and often become an obstacle to human and economic development. Inconvertible paper cannot circulate along with gold. Therefore the government had to banish this natural money out of circulation, and made it a crime to use it as a currency. In contrast to gold coins, which were defined in terms of weight and fineness, paper money is a "thing-in-itself" and has no intrinsic value. Paper money is emitted by a simple procedure: print and spend, a 100 percent seigniorage. Governments debased metallic money:[10] with paper, they faced practically no limit in debasing money.

Horrifying hyperinflations are where governments printed money until paper became worthless and the economy became without money. Historical hyperinflations, namely the John Law's System (1716–1720), the US continental money (1775–1783), the French Assignats (1790–1796), and the German mark (1919–1923) ended in disorder, starvation, and economic decline. In each case, governments were bankrupt. They used paper as unlimited taxation instrument to confiscate property and wipe out totally their debts. The more they printed money, the less real seigniorage they extracted. Table 6.1 shows the characteristics of hyperinflations (Cagan 1956). Paper money vanished within 10 to 26 months. Prices were rising faster than printing, and within a few months the currency became not worth a continental, i.e., worthless. Real money fell to almost zero, a phenomenon called the death of money.

The unrestrained paper issuance may be illustrated by the quantitative easing of the US Federal Reserve (Fed), who went on a spree of money creation during 2009–2014, expanding its credit from \$0.7 trillion to about \$4.4 trillion, to

Table 6.1 Characteristics of hyperinflations

	Austria	Germany	Greece	Hungary	Poland	Russia
Number months of hyperinflation	11	16	13	10	11	26
Monthly price inflation dP/P (%)	47	322	365	46	81.4	57
Monthly money inflation dM/M (%)	30.9	314	220	32.7	72.2	49.3
Real money, end inflation (M/P) (base = 1)	0.252	0.00741	0.00277	0.185	0.0357	0.00775

Source: Cagan 1956

re-inflate the economy (Figure 6.1); this credit hyperinflation was out of thin air and undertaken at near-zero interest rates. It was a monetization of fiscal deficits as well as purchase of toxic assets. The distortions and uncertainties created by this unrestrained money are immense. Debt has been pushed to record level, and asset prices soared at about 23 percent year during 2009–2015. Beneficiaries would enjoy free wealth from this expansion.

Fiat money has been inflationary. Figure 6.2 illustrates an inconvertible money system; inflation has become an irreversible phenomenon in the United Kingdom (UK) and the United States. More specifically, inflation tax has become permanent; it injures the holders of the currency as well as the creditors, pensioners, and workers. The inflation tax is a bonus to debtors, government, and speculators. In 2013, the UK Retail Price Index (RPI) rose to 3,766 (1945 = 100); whereas the US Consumer Price Index (CPI) rose to 1,294 (1945 = 100) (Measuring Wealth n.d.). In contrast, Figure 6.3 illustrates the RPI for the UK and the CPI for the US under the gold and silver system during 1800–1913. In both countries, there was a significant transmission of economic

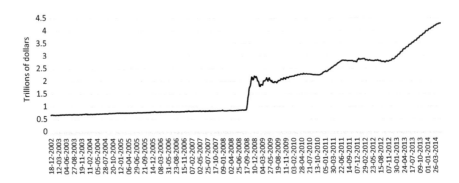

Figure 6.1 The Federal Reserve credit, 2002–2014 (trillions of dollars)

Source: The Federal Reserve

Figure 6.2 The United Kingdom and the United States Annual Price Indices, 1945–2013

Source: Measuring Wealth n.d.

growth in form of long-term trends of price declines. In 1913, the UK RPI fell to 82 (1800 = 100); and the US CPI fell to 79 (1800 = 100) (Measuring Wealth n.d.). To the extent that nominal wages were slightly increasing, workers had shared greatly in the fruits of growth. Such sharing has been reduced under fiat paper in almost every country where this money is in effect.

The nature of paper money is illustrated in Table 6.2 and 6.3. Ostensibly, base money may expand at 7 percent/year as well as 244 percent/year. Similarly, broad money may expand by 8 percent/year as well as by 231 percent/year, outpacing real GDP growth. Evidently, gold could not expand at such fantastic rates. McKinnon (1973) and Shaw (1973) showed that money

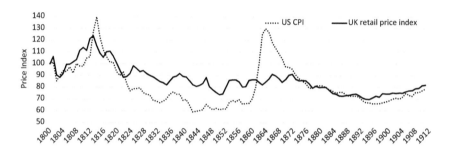

Figure 6.3 The United Kingdom and the United States Annual Price Indices, 1800–1913

Source: Measuring Wealth n.d.

Table 6.2 Money data, 1960–2014 (annual averages, in percentages)

Country	Money Base	Broad Money
France	6.7	. . .
Italy	10.5	12.3
Japan	10.7	10.2
Norway	8.1	9.6
United Kingdom	10.4	10.8
United States	9.1	7.6
Bangladesh	16.0	17.0
India	13.3	16.5
Indonesia	19.4	25.0
Malaysia	10.4	13.5
Turkey	15.7	43.9
Mauritania	10.5	15.2
Morocco	11.4	11.8
Tunisia	39.2	12.8
Uganda	241.1	38.8
Argentina	244.5	149.9
Brazil	26.4	231.3
Mexico	12.9	27.4

Source: IMF, IFS

Table 6.3 Commodity price inflation, 1960–2014

	Gold	Crude oil	Rice	Soybean oil	Wheat
Average Annual price increase (%) 1960–2014	10.3	14.5	6.5	5.6	5.1

Source: IMF, IFS

inflation reduced significantly financial intermediation. Inflation, measured by the consumer price index (CPI) may range between 3.1 percent/year and 344.8 percent/year. The real purchasing power of one money–unit in 1960 would require a large multiple of money units in 2014. Inflation measured by the stock price index may exceed the CPI inflation. Measured by commodity prices, inflation ranged between 5.1 percent/year and 14.5 percent/year. In relation to gold, inconvertible paper fell by 10.3 percent/year. The redistribution effects of inflation are considerable, a form of outrageous injustice imposed by the state. Inconvertible paper cannot be a standard of value. The apostles of inconvertible money believe that paper is real wealth, the more paper that is issued, the more real wealth is generated; that the economy is constantly short of money; and that it has to be permanently fueled with paper.

6. The debate: Locke versus Lowndes

The Locke-Lowndes debate constitutes, till today, a main controversy on the nature of money. It opposed two fundamentally different beliefs: sound money versus inflationism. It took place during 1692–1696 when Great Britain considered recoining its clipped silver coins: it consisted of the views of John Locke (1632–1704) versus those of William Lowndes (1652–1724), who was the Secretary of Treasury. Locke proposed a re-coinage at an unchanged mint-parity of 62 pennies/ounce of silver. Lowndes proposed a re-coinage at a new mint price of 75 pennies/ounce of silver, a devaluation of the currency by 20 percent. Hence, Locke wanted to keep the silver content of a unit of account unaltered, and Lowndes wanted to diminish it by 20 percent. The latter observed rightly that the market price of silver bullion, at 75 pennies/ounce of silver, was significantly above the mint price of 62 pennies, which created arbitrage opportunities, and discouraged traders from bringing silver to the mints. Locke stated that money of account was a convention fixed by law as a physical quantity of silver; he rejected Lowndes's view that a unit of account was a nominal unit of value with no physical reference. Locke maintained that clipped coins lost about 30-40 percent in silver and could not be exchanged for bullion at face value. He dismissed the money illusion. It was natural that an ounce of silver could be exchanged only for another ounce of silver; hence, if all coins were clipped and lost 50 percent of their silver weight, an ounce of silver would exchange for one ounce of silver, which meant twice the number of clipped coins. This never meant that silver bullion's market price had risen above the mint price.

Not admitting the clipped coin fact, Lowndes (1695) attributed the high price of silver bullion over the mint price to silver metal becoming dearer, in particular, due to external trade imbalance. Lowndes was not truly oblivious to the deterioration of the coin; his devaluation plan was to ease a war-strained treasury and defend the interest of debtors and merchants. Locke, wary of this plan's purpose, wanted to defend the class of landlords and creditors. Locke prevailed in 1696; however, Lowndes prevailed in modern times with the dismantlement of gold after 1931 and the triumph of nominal standard of money, which considers money as a unit of value, and not a commodity. All countries nowadays operate with money as an inconvertible paper with no physical support, a form of IOU emitted by the state in a discretionary way.

Locke insisted on the preservation of the monetary standard. Monetary policy must strengthen faith because altering the standard of value will weaken, if not totally destroy, the public faith when all who have trusted the public in their contracts shall be defrauded of 20 percent. Locke assigned the value of any coin to the silver it contained (by weight and fineness), not to the denomination stamped on it. Money is the measure of commerce; it measures the price of every commodity, and therefore ought to be preserved, as all other measures, as steady and invariable as might be.

Locke recognized that coins have several values: intrinsic, extrinsic, and exchange value. The intrinsic value of a unit of currency is the value of that unit's raw material when not used as currency. In the case of specie, the intrinsic value of a coin is the market value of that coin's metallic content as bullion. The currency's extrinsic "value" is its denomination (e.g., shilling, guinea, pence, etc.) as determined by the stamp placed on it by the monetary authority. The currency's exchange value is its purchasing power in terms of other commodities.

Locke stated against Lowndes that the monetary names were not names of definite quantities of *value*, but of definite quantities of silver. Locke (1691) argued that silver by its quantity, and not denomination, is the standard of value; it is by the weight of the silver in it and not the name of the coin that traders estimate commodity prices (P. 144). Merely increasing the quantity of denominations was chimerical. Wealth can only be increased by increasing the quantity of goods and services available. Money, after all, was only valuable as a means to secure real wealth.

The exchange value of coins was tied to their intrinsic value. The price of bullion proves nothing but that the quantity of silver in money governs the value of it, and not the denomination; as appears when clipped money is brought to buy bullion. Market efficiency will assert that 20 shillings of lighter new money will buy no more of any commodity than 19 shillings would before. For it is not the denomination but the quantity of silver, that determines the value of any coin, 19 grains of silver, however denominated or marked, will no more be worth, or buy so much of any other commodity as 20 grains of silver will. For it is silver and not the names that pay debts and purchase commodities. The contract was made for *silver*, not for denominations and nominal *values*.

The relation between silver and shilling is that of law, not of value. Shilling is the name of a particular amount of silver, and silver is the standard of price. Clipping, then, explained the high nominal price of bullion in England. Bullion cost more in terms of nominal units because the nominal units had come to represent less silver. Locke defined the function of the mint: to maintain the currency as purely a standard of the weight of silver; any debasement, any change of standards, would be as arbitrary, fraudulent, and unjust as the government's changing the definition of a foot or a yard.

Lowndes (1695) stressed an obvious fact that the market price of silver was consistently higher than the mint-parity for a period of time. He intended to show that this fact was the consequence of another fact, which was the rise in the value of silver. Seemingly, to account for the two facts observed, Lowndes introduced the theoretical principle that the unit of money is a unit of value. On the theoretical principle that a monetary name is the name of a definite quantity of exchange value (and not of silver) Lowndes concluded that the purchasing power of money remained constant as long as the monetary names of the values of the commodities remained constant. From this principle, Lowndes intended to show that a reduction in the silver content of the coins regulated by the excess of the market price of silver over the mint-parity would not involve any redistribution of wealth. All prices remain unchanged, no inflation occurred; only coins become lighter in terms of silver. For him, traders considered only the denomination of the coin and not its silver content; a loan of £100 is fully paid at maturity by a money equal to £100 regardless of the silver content at the time the loan was disbursed and the time it was repaid.[11] He was an early projector of today's inconvertible paper money, where the intrinsic value of money is zero. He argued that a devaluation of 20 percent will only realign the mint price with the bullion price and will have no inflationary or redistributive effect. The measure will only increase the quantity of money in the economy and make money plentiful. It will have a stimulating effect. Locke did not deny the stimulus effect of devaluation; however, he was against its redistributive and unjust effects, and the perturbation to the standard of measure.[12]

7. Theories of optimum money

Theories of optimum quantity of money addressed the quantity as well as the cost of money. How much money should an economy have? What is the cost of money? Views have been diverse since the sixteenth century. There were the mercantilists who viewed gold and silver as wealth and should be prevented from being exported. The more a country accumulated gold and silver, the better it was. This doctrine was exploded by Hume (1752), Smith (1776), and Ricardo (1817), showing that money was an international commodity and was distributed among countries in such a manner as that no country could have a surplus or a shortage of it. Prohibition of exports of gold and silver were futile. Hume established the monetary approach to the balance of payments, the price-specie flow mechanism, and the law of one-price. Gold and silver will leave countries where they are cheaper to countries where they are more expensive. Smith contended that if an economy requires a given quantity of money to circulate its produce, then any additional money will flow to other countries.

Smith and Ricardo's views on gold were based on the principle of economizing on this money essentially with the use of paper money. Both viewed gold and silver as expensive commodities absorbing labor and capital in mining which could be diverted to socially more useful industries if replaced by costless paper money. Smith pretended that paper money would not exceed the quantity of metal it displaced. Smith thought that banknotes of reputable bankers would be less costly than gold. He also seemed to approve the credit bills of the American colonies that reduced significantly the need for gold. Ricardo initiated the gold–exchange standard claiming that a perfect currency is attained when paper replaces specie. Both Smith and Ricardo maintained the convertibility of paper; however, Ricardo wanted it to be restricted to bullion, not coin, at a minimum of 20 ounces of gold. Carroll (1850) virulently attacked Smith's money theory. He stated that a cheap currency is the most costly and wasteful machinery a nation can possess; the history of the world shows it to be uniformly unprofitable or disastrous. There was never a greater mistake in any science, and never one so fatal to the stability of property and the well-being of society.

Prior to Smith and Ricardo, costless paper appealed to many projectors who proposed landed banks that would monetize real estate property based on mortgage loans. The doctrine underlying these schemes, plainly stated by John Law (1705), is identical to unorthodox policy of today's US Federal Reserve. Law noted that plenty of resources in land and labor were idle; only money was lacking. If land banks supplied an abundance of costless paper, interest rates would be negligible, and great wealth would be created as idle resources are put in action. John Law managed to establish such scheme in France during 1716–1720; although it created a tremendous speculative boom, it collapsed in a disastrous ruin. This delusion dominates policymakers continuously.

Many theories of optimal inconvertible money were propounded. Keynesians and adepts of the Phillips curve urged a rate of inflation that reduced unemployment. This policy has been implemented in many advanced countries that use money policy to create employment instead of removing structural rigidities impeding employment. Mises and Rothbard exploded these theories which ruled out flexible wages, and led to unjust redistribution of wealth, recurrent financial crises, and total money and fiscal disorders as fully established by the conditions of the United States, Japan, and other countries since 1930s.

A theory of optimal policy addressed the welfare cost of inflation. Bailey (1956), based on Cagan's analysis of hyperinflation, showed that inflation caused a social welfare loss, because it increased the cost of holding real money and reduced the holding of real money. As money neared its death, and barter re-emerged, transaction cost became high. By definition, there is a conflicting effect of money printing: gains to government in seigniorage revenues, and simultaneous loss to money holders in form of inflation tax on their real balances. An optimum money can only maximize one effect at the sacrifice of the other. Friedman (1969) proposed an optimum money for costless paper which required setting the opportunity cost of money, measured by the nominal interest rate, equal to the marginal cost of paper, i.e., zero. To make the nominal interest rate zero, the government has to engineer a deflation until the rate of deflation is equal to real rate of interest. Phelps (1973) criticized Friedman's rule on the grounds that it ignores considerations related to taxation. Phelps pointed out that inflation is a source of tax revenue for the government and that if inflation were reduced other taxes would have to be increased in order to replace the lost revenue. He also argued that some inflation would be desirable if distortions associated with inflation taxes were less costly than distortions associated with other taxes to which the government might resort; and, therefore, the nominal interest rate has to be positive. Based on statism and costless paper, both Friedman's and Phelps's doctrine were fallacious. In a commodity money, the economy decides on optimum money without perturbations in price levels; moreover, the state would need no inflation tax if it restricted its domain and undertook mostly productive expenditure.

Last, but not least, a theory of optimum costless paper addressed stabilization of the price level at a desired rate of inflation ranging from zero upward. Many modern central banks increase money supply to achieve an inflation rate that may vary between 2 percent and 15 percent. However, Fisher (1936) and Simons (1948) proposed an optimum money which yields zero inflation. In the event of deflation, the central bank injects money via purchasing bonds. In the event of inflation, the central bank withdraws money through selling bonds. Graham (1944) advocated commodity price stabilization, with money issued by a commodity storage bank. When commodity prices trend downward, the bank issues money, buys and stores commodities to maintain stable prices. In reverse, if prices trend upward, the bank dumps commodities to chock off price increases.

Bastiat (2011) noted that it is irrelevant whether there be much or little money in the world. If there is much, much is required; if there is little, little is wanted for each transaction: a simple application of the quantity theory of money. Mises (1953) and Rothbard (1962) maintained that once a commodity has been established as money and considered to be in sufficient supply to be so, there is no social benefit from increasing its quantity. Hence, there is a benefit to increase the supply of wheat, oil, fruits, etc. since every addition of these goods enhances consumers' living standard; an increase in money has no benefit since by definition no consumer consumes money; it only dilutes the purchasing power of money. The issue of the optimal quantity of money is dismissed as the economy adjusts to any nominal quantity of money, as illustrated by Hume (1752). The latter claimed that if four-fifths of the United Kingdom's money were destroyed overnight, the economy would simply adjust to a new money supply equal to one-fifth of the initial stock.[13] Moreover, under high inflation or hyperinflation, the economy adjusts to an ever-rising money supply and develops deep-rooted inflationary expectations. The real quantity of money is an endogenous variable.

8. Sharia money

Sharia stands against all forms of fraud and injustice by rulers or individuals as explicitly stated by the Quranic verses stated above. The origin of money as a valuable and borderless commodity in the exchange against other valuable commodities, based on free choice, cannot be altered. Locke stated that:

> It is the interest of every country that the standard of its money, once settled, should be inviolably and immutably kept to perpetuity. For whenever that is altered, upon whatever pretense so ever, the public will lose by it. Men in their bargains contract, not for denominations or sounds, but for the intrinsic value.
>
> (P. 144)

The state should not spread financial and economic disorders through costless paper creation. Gold and silver money were not superseded throughout centuries and never vanished as money. Costless inconvertible paper was not chosen freely by the market as a better money than gold and silver, and often died in ruins. It is inflationary and constantly defrauds victims of price inflation. Gouge (1833) maintained that paper is paper, and money is money. He rejected the notion of government issuing paper money as it would provide incentives to extravagance in public expenditures in even the best of times; moreover, it would prevent fiscal stability and would cause various evils.

In Sharia, money is what it was at the time of the Prophet PUH; namely, gold and silver coins, common to all countries, a medium of exchange and store of value, and not a means of taxation.[14] It was distributed among countries via trade. In a free trade, money departs from those countries where its amount is beyond what their trade and industry require to those countries where it is in shortage. No country can be deprived of its just proportion of the precious metals. A government that undertakes productive spending has no need for inflation tax. Money is not a discretionary policy tool to overcome government rigid laws such as minimum wage laws, impediments to trade, and control of the foreign exchange market. The government may emit gold and silver money if it owns these metals from mining deposits or buying them with other minerals such as oil.

The government has a regulatory duty in asserting the quality of coins. It should have no impediments to gold and silver trade and free minting of coins according to established standards.[15] Sharia allows a convertible paper money to be issued by a monetary agency with 100 percent gold backing. It allows non-interest money substitutes such as clearing operations, credit, bills of exchange, and credit cards; these substitutes are Sharia-compliant.

Sharia requires a just government to observe financial discipline and to restore fully gold and silver as lawful money. A government observing financial discipline never needs inconvertible paper. Sharia refutes the idea of money as a policy tool. Statists believe money is a policy tool.[16] General people are ignorant about the deficiencies of inconvertible money and think there is no better system to it. Gouge asserted that some policymakers, who have never considered a more improved system of money and banking, firmly believe that it cannot exist; they consent to the injurious evils of the prevailing system, and comfort themselves for their existence by admitting that they could not possibly be otherwise.

In a modern economy, money is emitted by the central bank and the credit money is emitted by the banking system. To the extent that credit money is based on interest-based debt, it is Sharia-non-compliant. There is no interest paid on gold and silver money. However, debt money pays interest to the banking system. In managing the money supply in the economy, the central bank is often compelled to create liquidity and make interest-based advances to the banking system in order to prevent a contraction in credit, deflation, and bankruptcy. The central bank allows banks to lend a capital to the economy which itself did not possess. Such policy of the central bank may not be Sharia compatible. To the extent that central banking and the banking system's money is based on interest-based debt, it may be in contradiction with Sharia. In contrast, a 100 percent reserve banking combined with a risk-sharing, non-interest-based investment banking is fully Sharia compatible.

9. Conclusions

Money as an inconvertible paper is the culmination of inflationism, which confuses money and wealth, and considers printing money paper ex-nihilo as creating wealth. For instance, in a poor country, the central bank may print tons of money paper, but it can add not one gram of wheat or one drop of oil. This confusion dominates policymakers who consider money as a policy tool; accordingly, they print unlimited quantities of it and set interest rates at near-zero. All money printed is a confiscation of an existing wealth in favor of a group of beneficiaries at the expense of a group of losers, a zero-sum game. The Locke-Lowndes debate opposed views of sound versus inflated money. Statists maintain that the government has an absolute right over money; the state has a sovereignty over money, and is free to print as much money as it wishes as clearly stated by John Law, and later by his adepts. Locke, in line with Oresme and Copernicus, condemned the alteration of the mint price and the standard of measure as a sheer violation of property rights which should not be committed by a government trusted by the public to preserve property and justice. The dismantlement of gold standard was due to government bankruptcy. The experiences of hyperinflation show how governments may keep printing money to finance fiscal deficits until money dies.

Sharia considers money as a commodity, determined by the market, and attributes to the state a regulatory mission similar to any regulation aimed at preventing fraud. Table 6.1 showed that paper can disappear within few months. This would never happen with gold. Table 6.2 showed that government money is purely discretionary, inflation over many decades may range between 4 percent/year and 345 percent/year and money supply may rise by 8 percent/year to 250 percent/year. Sharia does not agree with this inherent feature of paper money. Only a commodity money is immune from discretion and obeys market laws.

Modern central bank and banking system's money as well as liquidity management by the central bank are based on interest transactions. Both central bank and the banks earn their income from interest. Their debt-based money is not Sharia compatible. However, currency emitted by banks as counterparts to deposits and foreign exchange purchase or deposits is fully Sharia-compliant.

Notes

1 Starvation became widespread during the German hyperinflation (Bresciani-Turroni 1931). Starvation occurred also in France during the assignat hyperinflation.
2 The US Constitution was explicit that gold and silver were money. Article 1, Section 8 of the Constitution stipulated that the Congress shall have the power: (i) to borrow money on the credit of the United States; (ii) to coin money, regulate the value thereof, and of foreign coin, and fix the standards of weights and measures; (iii) to provide for the punishment of counterfeiting of securities and current coin of the United States.
3 These channels may include credit to the government and the banking sector and purchase of foreign exchange.
4 Some writers include money substitutes under money since they fulfill the same functions as money.
5 Gouge (1833): "Their only misfortune was, being ignorant of the principles of currency, and having rulers as ignorant as themselves. . . . Thousands were reduced to poverty, and scores rose to wealth on the ruin of their neighbors" (P. 227). In fact, the restoration of the gold standard in the United Kingdom (UK) in 1925 at the prewar parity, instead at a market rate, showed an example of conflict in money policy. Had the UK government used the market rate of the pound, the gold standard would have most likely remained in effect.
6 Hjalmar Schacht (1967), President of the Reichsbank, said the price of one egg in 1923 would have bought 500 billion eggs in 1913. Frank Graham (1930) reported that nominal mortgages were 1/6 of Germany's wealth in 1913; they were less than one US cent in 1923, meaning that one US cent in 1923 was more than enough to pay off all 1913 nominal mortgages.
7 In a barter economy of 100 commodities there are 4,950 exchange ratios. If one commodity is chosen as money, there will be only a 99 exchange ratio yield in the price of each commodity in terms of the money commodity.
8 The indexing of contracts, as a standard of value, was used in rent contracts in England where part of the rent was indexed to corn prices. Today, many contracts, such as wage contracts, are indexed to price indices.
9 Mises (1953) stressed that medium of exchange and store of value functions of money were inseparable.
10 In England, a silver pound was initially coined into 20 shillings, then later into 66 shillings.
11 The German hyperinflation (1919–1923) showed that nominal values of debt caused a huge real wealth redistribution from creditors to debtors.

12 Steuart (1767) stressed that every variation upon the intrinsic value of the money-unit has the effect of benefiting the class of creditors, at the expense of debtors, or vice versa. By "intrinsic value of the money-unit" Steuart meant the quantity of precious metal contained by law in the money-unit. He rejected Lowndes neutrality theory, noting that: "Lowndes replied that silver was augmented 20 per cent in its value, and that therefore the pound sterling, though reduced 20 per cent in its weight of pure silver, was still as valuable as before. This proposition Mr. Locke exploded with the most solid reasoning, and indeed nothing could be more absurd, than to affirm, that silver had risen in value with respect to itself" (Chapter 6, P. 328).

13 What matters for the economy is real money balances. The nominal money is determined by the central bank. However, market participants determine real money by way of changes in the price level. In fact, if prices and wages adjust downward, the economy is able to create larger real money balances for its needs. In contrast, inflation creates a money shortage; real money was in dire shortage during the German hyperinflation (1922–1923).

14 Today all countries use inconvertible paper as money. While gold and silver are fully Sharia-compliant, the Sharia compliance of inconvertible paper has to be addressed. We have not studied scholars' views on this topic.

15 Voltaire called the decree restricting the legal possession of metal coin the most unjust edict ever rendered and the final limit of tyrannical absurdity.

16 Mises (1953) rejected money as a policy tool such as to achieve full employment. He stressed this objective should be attained by dismantling all legislations hampering competitiveness in labor and goods markets.

References

Bailey, M., 1956, "The Welfare Cost of Inflationary Finance," *Journal of Political Economy*, 64(2): 93–110.

Bastiat, F., 2011. *The Bastiat Collection*, Auburn, AL: Ludwig von Mises Institute.

Bresciani-Turroni, C., 1931, *The Economics of Inflation*, Northampton, Great Britain: John Dickens & Co Ltd.

Cagan, P., 1956, "The Monetary Dynamics of Hyperinflation," in Friedman, M. (ed.). *Studies in the Quantity Theory of Money*, Chicago: University of Chicago Press.

Carroll, C. H., 1965, *Organization of Debt Into Currency and Other Papers*, Edited with an Introduction by Edward C. Simmons, D. Van Nostrand Company, Inc. Princeton, NJ.

Einaudi, L., 1936, "The Theory of Imaginary Money From Charlemagne to the French Revolution," in Lane, F.C. and Riemersma, J.C. (eds.). *Enterprise and Secular Change*, Homewood, IL: Richard D. Irwin, 1953.

Fisher, I., 1936, *100% Money*, New York: Palgrave Macmillan.

Friedman, M., 1969, "The Optimum Quantity of Money," in *The Optimum Quantity of Money and Other Essays*, Chicago: Aldine Publishing Company.

Gouge, W., 1833, *A Short History of Paper Money & Banking*, New York: Augustus M. Kelley Publishers.

Graham, B., 1944, *World Commodities and World Currency*, New York: McGraw-Hill.

Graham, F., 1930, *Exchange, Prices, and Production in Hyperinflation: Germany, 1920–1923*. New York: Russell & Russell.

Hume, D., 1752, *Political Discourses*, Edinburgh: Printed by R. Fleming, for A. Kincaid and A. Donaldson.

Law, J., 1705, *Money and Trade Considered, With a Proposal for Supplying a Nation With Money*, Glasgow: R. & A. Foulis.

Liverpool, L., and Jenkinson, C., 1805, *A Treatise on the Coins of the Realm*, London: Effingham Wilson, Royal Exchange, 1880.

Locke, J., 1691, *Some Considerations on the Consequences of the Lowering of Interest and the Raising of the Value of Money*, The Works of John Locke, 1824, London: C. Balwin, Printer.

Lowndes, W., 1695, *A Report Containing an Essay for the Amendment of the Silver Coins*, London: Charles Bill.

McKinnon, R., 1973, *Money and Capital in Economic Development*, Washington, DC: Brookings Institution.

Measuring Wealth. (n.d.), www.measuringworth.com/uscompare/

Menger, C., 1892, *Principles of Economics*, Glencoe, IL: Free Press, 1950.

Oresme, N. (Late 14th century), *De Moneta*, London: Thomas Nelson and Sons Ltd, 1956.

Phelps, E. S., 1973, "Inflation in the Theory of Public Finance," *The Swedish Journal of Economics*, 75(1): 67–82.

Ricardo, D., 1821, *On the Principles of Political Economy and Taxation*, 3rd edition, London: John Murray.

Rothbard, M., 1962, *Man, Economy, and State, With Power and Market*, Auburn, AL: Ludwig von Mises Institute.

Schacht, H., 1967, *The Magic Money*, London: Oldbourne.

Shaw, E., 1973, *Financial Deepening in Economic Development*, Oxford: Oxford University Press.

Simons, H., 1947, *Economic Policy for a Free Society*, Chicago, The University of Chicago Press.

Smith, Adam, 1776, *An Inquiry Into the Nature and Causes of the Wealth of Nations*, London: Methuen and Co., Ltd., ed. Edwin Cannan, 1904, Fifth edition.

Steuart, Sir James Denham, 1767, *An Inquiry Into the Principles of Political Economy*, London: A. Millar, and T. Cadell.

Von Mises, L., 1953, *The Theory of Money and Credit*, New Haven: Yale University Press.

Walker, A., 1873, *The Science of Wealth*, Philadelphia: J. B. Lippincott.

7 On the nature of inflationary financing

1. Introduction

Inflationary financing is defined as printing money out of thin air by the government or as unbacked credit by banks. In both cases, there is inflation.[1] Unbacked bank credit often ends in a financial crisis and a depression. Sharia has no place for money creation out of thin air by the government or banks. Moreover, Sharia is incompatible with any form of injustice; particularly with inflation which originates from government inflationary financing.[2] Money creation ex-nihilo is a costless mean of taxation and free wealth redistribution from victims to beneficiaries. Only oppressive governments practice it. Just governments never impose inflation.

Inflation has become a secular and an endless phenomenon. Practically, there is no country where prices are declining or even stable. A dollar in 2016 is worth less than one cent in 1913; a Tunisian dinar in 2016 is worth less than 0.02 dinar in 1958, simply because both monies are a costless paper which enabled governments to inflate endlessly the money supply.

This chapter covers the following topics:

- Seigniorage, a centuries-old tax on money
- Historical hyper-inflationary financing
- Illustration of inflationary financing
- The welfare cost of inflation

2. Seigniorage, a centuries-old tax on money

Money creation is one potential source of revenue for a government. Seigniorage – government revenue received through money creation – is a relatively inexpensive means of raising funds. The problem is that although paper money may be cheap to produce, the social costs of money creation, distortions, and wealth redistribution could be overbearing. Money creation may cause high inflation.[3] Thus, faster money creation costs the society by eroding the purchasing power of money already in circulation, which is the inflation tax. Though tempted by low money printing costs, governments must balance the benefits with social costs when deciding how much to rely on seigniorage.

In fact, there are two sources for governments to raise their revenues: taxation and seigniorage.[4] Both sources of revenue cause deadweight social losses; moreover, inflation also brings some other social costs, such as reducing the purchasing power of consumers. Government resorts to seigniorage when taxation reaches its limit and becomes unpopular. In turn, money printing, through inflation tax, may become too unpopular and may cause unrest.

With the demise of the gold standard in 1931, almost all nations abandoned gold backing for their currencies and adopted a fiat money standard under which the paper issued is backed by nothing more than faith and confidence in the issuer. Under this system, the cost of issuance declines to close to zero and there is no longer any limit on the quantity of money that can be issued. Money keeps increasing in most countries at more than 5 percent/year, and often at two-digit annual rates. Under a fiat money system, seigniorage revenue is given by the product of the inflation rate and the inflation tax base. This inflation tax base reflects the purchasing power of the public's money holdings and is the level of real money balances (nominal money holdings divided by the price level). Undertaking more rapid monetary expansion causes the inflation rate to rise, but the revenue effects are partially offset as individuals attempt to quickly spend the extra money before it depreciates further. If people spend money faster than it is being printed, the rate of price increase exceeds the rate of money issuance.[5]

A government that is unable to fund its expenditures through conventional taxes or bond sales may become dependent on seigniorage revenues to finance its spending. Attempts to raise seigniorage revenues are, however, not only inflationary, but eventually self-defeating. Under circumstances where the decline in real money balances becomes proportionately larger than the rise in the inflation rate, the inflationary policy actually lowers seigniorage revenue. Phillip Cagan's (1956) classic analysis of hyperinflations showed instances where real seigniorage fell sharply when the inflation rates exceeded 50 percent per month.

Sargent and Wallace (1981) pointed to some "unpleasant monetarist arithmetic", which implied that, in the face of continued budget deficits, tighter monetary policy today would necessarily lead to an inflationary policy tomorrow once the limit on bond issuance is reached. Furthermore, the greater the outstanding stock of bonds, the greater the potential governmental gains from inflating away the real value of these obligations through inflation – which, in turn, likely limits the demand for such bonds unless inflation protection is built in. The typical mechanism of inflation finance is for the government to sell bonds to the central bank, which then immediately "monetizes" the debt with new money emissions. This is characterized as money finance rather than true bond finance and provides the government with new funds to spend via excess money creation. Conversely, selling bonds to the public, rather than the central bank, is likely to be far less inflationary and has no direct effect on the money supply.

A common measure of "seigniorage", the resources appropriated by the monetary authority through its capacity to issue zero interest fiat money, is the change in the monetary base, $\Delta M_t = M_t - M_{t-1}$ where M_t and M_{t-1} denote nominal base money outstanding at time t and t-1, respectively. The new money printed, ΔM, is a nominal money. Its purchasing power in real goods is $\Delta M/P$, where P is the price level. Assume the government issues ΔM equals $100 to buy bread. We are interested in the effect of ΔM on two demands: the demand for money and the demand for bread. Let the equilibrium price of bread be $1. Assume bread consumers want to hold more cash. For this purpose, they reduce their demand for bread to increase their cash holdings. They cut down their consumption of bread by 100 breads, the government buys 100 breads. Overall demand for bread remains the same and so does the equilibrium price of bread. Now assume that bread consumers are not willing to demand any additional cash, and not willing to reduce their demand for bread. For a given supply of bread, government demand for bread pushes aggregate demand for bread upward. At new equilibrium price of $2/bread, the government buys only 50 bread. Consumers are forced to consume 50 bread less, called inflation tax, even though they are holding more cash by $100. Now, worse, assume consumers want to reduce their cash balances and buy more bread. Besides government demand for bread, there is a higher demand for bread by consumers. The equilibrium price of bread goes up to $5. The government can buy only 20 breads. There is more nominal cash by $100; however, with far higher prices, real balances are lower than before the issuance of new money. The real seigniorage has been significantly reduced by the decline of demand for cash balances. Eventually, if no one wants to hold government money, real seigniorage goes to zero via a hyperinflation. Hence, real seigniorage is influenced by changes in two demands: change in the demand for money and change in the demand for goods and services. The government can decide on nominal money ΔM, but it cannot decide on $\Delta M/P^6$.

3. Historical hyper-inflationary financing

With costless paper, the government tends to run inflation until the value of money reaches its marginal cost, which is zero. At this point, money vanishes on its own. Perry (1873) stated that there has never been a government yet, of the many which have issued irredeemable paper, which had the wisdom and firmness to resist the strong temptation to overissue. The more the government issues money paper, the greater the real amount of resources it appropriates.

Historical hyperinflations are illustrated by John Law's System (1716–1720), the US continental money (1775–1783), the French Assignats (1790–1796), and the German mark (1919–1923); they established the dangers of inflationary financing. Each hyperinflation ended in disorder and economic decline.

Although history after 1931 is replete with hyperinflations, the interest in historical episodes is to show that inflationism is not a novelty; it is associated with bankruptcy. It was pervasive in the American colonies which emitted bills of credit in unlimited amount to finance their expenditures. Inflationary financing is an inherent aspect of a bankrupt government that wants to use inconvertible paper as a forced money and indulge in excessive, unproductive spending.

3.1 John Law: monetizing the French debt

John Law's landed bank scheme was rejected by the Scottish Parliament in 1707 and was endorsed in France in 1715. Bankrupted by war and overburdened by a debt amounting to 22 times the taxes, France ignored Locke's sound money and embraced Law's finance. The cardinal point of Law's theory (1705) was that money was only a voucher for buying goods. This function can be performed by costless paper instead of costly metal. Since paper cannot circulate without public force, the principle expressed by John Law was that money belonged to the Sovereign (i.e., the State); the latter has the absolute power to legislate in money power. Force of the state is applied to inflate paper money, tax, and repudiate public and private debt. Law founded the "Banque Generale" in France in 1716. Initially, a private bank with a monopoly to issue banknotes, the Banque Generale became a state-owned bank in 1718 under the name "Banque Royale." Its banknotes were fully convertible to silver (ecus) at a fixed parity and were decreed as unlimited legal tender to discharge taxes as well as debt. Law emphasized the convertibility of banknotes into species upon demand. Unfortunately, as his system was collapsing in 1720, Law suspended convertibility.

Immediately, upon the establishment of the Banque Generale, Law emitted banknotes against the government debt, "effets publics," at discounts reaching about 70 percent of the nominal value of debt. All government debt was redeemed through issuing banknotes, which became worthless paper in 1720.[6] To increase demand for banknotes, Law made it the only currency acceptable for purchasing shares on the stock exchange. The higher the share price rose, the higher the demand for banknotes became and the more paper was emitted. The shares of the Mississippi Company were issued initially at 150 livres; at the peak of the speculative delirium, they reached 18,000 livres.

As expected, a brief and powerful boom took place in France; as paper money kept pouring, people felt rich, the word "millionaire" appeared for the first time as many people got rich instantly from speculation.[7] Consumption rose, balance of trade deteriorated dramatically, prices rose at a frantic speed, inflation became fully anticipated, and merchants kept hiking up prices ahead of higher money injection. In 1719–1720, inflation turned into hyperinflation. The government was threatening merchants who increased their prices and called for price controls. Housing prices skyrocketed. At the peak of the bubble, speculators sold out their shares and acquired real assets. The panic took place; the shares rapidly collapsed as no buyers were willing to invest in them anymore. To prevent a flight to gold and silver, the government issued a decree forbidding use of metallic money in trade as well as its possession.[8] The paper money no longer had any value, it became worthless, and the last holders of it were ruined.

There was total money anarchy in France during 1716–1720. The Law's System wanted to build real wealth and employ idle resources; it turned into an unjust and speculative scheme. Some got too wealthy at no cost; others were ruined; there was a purely arbitrary redistribution of wealth with no growth. Today, this system has become cherished. Governments fuel speculation and euphoria, confounding speculative booms and asset prices hyperinflation for real prosperity while only plundering is occurring and long-term growth sacrificed. A long economic decline followed after 1720, and the French people became adamantly against money paper.

3.2 War finance: the American continental currency, 1775–1783

After the American Revolutionary War began in 1775, the Continental Congress decided to issue paper money known as Continental currency, or Continentals, to finance the war. The Continental Congress had no taxation mechanism in place and no taxation power; it had to emit paper money. Continental currency was denominated in dollars from 1/6 of a dollar to $80, including many denominations in between. It had no backing in gold or silver. Continentals were backed by the "anticipation" of tax revenues. It was understood that the money would be redeemed in gold or silver by the states after the war. For the first time in the US, currency's value was derived solely from its purchasing power, as it is today. During 1775–1783, Congress issued $241,552,780 in Continental currency.

At first, the continental bills were accepted at face value. Immediately all hard money disappeared. It was a case of Gresham's law, which states that bad money will drive out good money. No one wanted to spend his gold coins when paper was just as acceptable. The trouble was that paper was not as acceptable and many merchants preferred real money to paper. In fact, this became so frequently the case that Congress had to pass a resolution in 1776 that "whoever should refuse to receive in payment Continental bills, should be declared and treated as an enemy of his country and be excluded from inter-course with its inhabitants." But prices continued to rise, as the printing of the currency proceeded apace.

Moral suasion proved useless against the flood of paper money. The price of common labor in Boston, which was fixed at three shillings a day in 1777, had risen to 60 shillings by mid-1779. In April 1779, Congress attempted to reform the currency by removing the old bills from circulation and issuing new ones, without success. By May 1781, Continentals had become so worthless that they ceased to circulate as money. The depreciation of the currency had, in effect, acted as a tax to pay for the war.

The painful experience of the runaway inflation and collapse of the Continental dollar prompted the delegates to the Constitutional Convention to include the gold and silver clause into the United States Constitution so that the individual states could not issue bills of credit or "make anything but gold and silver coin a tender in payment of debts."

3.3 The French assignats: a revolution of paper money

During the French Revolution in 1789, the newly formed National Assembly faced a severe financial and economic crisis. The people were starving, the public deficit was enormous and the government was virtually bankrupt. Inheriting a financial mess, and worried about invasion from neighboring monarchies, the government responded with a military build-up; it undertook massive public spending on public works and buildings and paid large subsidies on bread consumption. Freed from the royal authority, the people were in no mood to resume paying taxes, much less pay more. Many of them interpreted the Revolution to mean the end of taxes, and the annihilation of the coercive tax administration. Meanwhile, obligations of the national debt in form of interest and principal were accruing and had to be paid. The Assembly rejected debt repudiation because they feared antagonizing the moneylenders.

The Assembly was not able to lay new taxes. Further borrowing was not possible until new taxes could be laid. The remedy for fiscal insolvency was government fiat paper currency. In March 1790, the Assembly authorized the printing of 400 million livres of paper assignats of denomination of 200, 300, and 1,000 livres, bearing 5 percent interest then reduced to 3 percent, and receivable for taxes and the purchase of the national properties. Originally meant as bonds, the assignats evolved into a currency used as legal tender in April 1790. Lacking funds, the government issued 800 million livres, reduced the interest payment to 0 percent, and made them legal tender for all purchases and debts across France. The consequences of the second issue were a depreciation in their value, rising prices, feverish speculation, complaints about a shortage of money, calls for more assignats, the prostration of commerce and industry, inordinate consumption, and declining savings. The fast depreciation of assignats made it unprofitable for farmers to take their crops to market. They stayed home and produced only for themselves or for barter with their neighbors. The government had to send troops into the countryside to confiscate grain and other foodstuffs.

The revolutionary government decided to cure the evils generated by inflation with more inflation. It authorized more issues of assignats. Then came 1793 – the year of *la Terreur*. Having tried inflation and legal coercion, the government forced the population into accepting the crumbling assignats at par. In 1793, the government prohibited the trading (i.e., buying or selling) with specie; it passed the General Maximum, extending price ceilings to all foodstuffs, as well as firewood, coal, and other essentials;[9] it kept issuing massive quantities of assignats until their purchasing power had fallen to almost nothing.

The Directory was done with the assignats, but it was not done with inflation. In February 1796, it issued a new paper currency, the mandat, and made it exchangeable for assignats at the rate of 30 to 1. Following excessive money printing, the mandat had fallen to 3 percent of its face value. In 1796, the Directory discontinued both the assignats and the mandats. Napoleon restored hard money and gold standard in France. As First Consul (1801), he introduced the 20 francs gold piece and insisted that from thenceforth soldiers, contractors, and merchants would be paid only in gold, or its equivalent.

3.4 The Weimar republic hyperinflation, a calamity of inflationary financing

The German hyperinflation was a disastrous tragedy that Germany suffered during 1919–1923.[10] German inflation was already high during the war period 1914–1918. Becoming a taxation instrument on holders of marks in favor of the government, speculators, and debtors, inflation escalated to a hyperinflation during 1922–1923. Its victims were doubly taxed; they paid an inflation tax to the government as well as to the debtors, businessmen, speculators, and all other profiteers of inflation. The taxation paid by the victims of inflation to non-government profiteers far exceeded the taxes paid to the government.

The figures measuring hyperinflation were frightening. By November 15, 1923, the day the inflation was officially ended, the amount of paper money issued by the central Bank, the Reichsbank, was an incredible sum of 92.8 quintillion German marks. Despite this incredible number, Germany had literally no real money. As prices were running ahead, there was shortage of real money. Germany's cost-of-living index, measured at 1 in 1914, reached 1,535 milliards by November of 1923. Prodded by super-money printing the government expanded its expenditure at a high speed; taxes represented only 0.7 percent of expenditure in 1923. All calculations, accounting, and contracts became uncertain. Millions of Germans were suffering food shortage and starvation, middle-class people had their money savings wiped out and became beggars on the streets, and all this resulted in many suicides. A class of profiteers were strong supporters of inflation: these were businessmen, speculators, and borrowers. They enjoyed abundant free wealth and indulged in the most sumptuous consumption and accumulation of jewelry. Practically, borrowers inherited free wealth such as houses, farms, buildings, machinery, etc. In Germany, hyperinflation ended on its own: money died. No farmer and no shop would accept marks anymore. Inflationists solved no problem, they wrecked German economy, and demoralized people for many years. They brought contempt and revolt against the government.

The German government resorted heavily to borrowing to finance the war and built a huge internal debt. It decided, through money printing, to wipe out completely its mark-denominated debt, asserting clearly that any government can wipe out is own currency-denominated debt through money printing. Taxation financed 15 percent of total expenditure during 1914–1918 and about 1 percent during 1922–1923; the rest was financed through money printing. Moreover, the Reichsbank promoted a Keynesian money policy with unorthodox money policy to support economic activity and reduce unemployment.

Most strikingly, the hyperinflation ended instantly on its own in November 1923 with vain attempt of both the central bank and the government to further it; however, it ended in the most catastrophic conditions imaginable.[11] Established in 1871 as a goldmark issued by Reichsbank and redeemable in gold, the German mark was detached from gold in August 1914, and died in November 1923. A new currency, called the Rentenmark, replaced the defunct mark. The Rentenmark was issued by a new bank, the Deutschen Rentenbank, a state-owned monetary authority, founded by a regulation of October 15, 1923. The Rentenmark was nominally pegged to gold, but not redeemable in gold.

The new Rentenbank refused credit to the government and speculators. Discounting of commercial trade bills was allowed, but the issue of rentenmarks was strictly controlled to conform to current commercial and government transactions. Farmers accepted the rentenmark in trade for their crops, and the food crisis was resolved. A new reichsmark anchored to gold replaced the rentenmark. The money reform showed that it took almost no preparation to adopt a gold standard system. The Rentenbank held little gold. The rentenmark was not convertible into gold. No planning was necessary for declaring a gold standard. The only thing that was necessary was a clear policy, namely to maintain the value of the rentenmark equivalent to a prewar goldmark, and a clear strategy to accomplish this policy was to restrict the supply of rentenmark to maintain its value.

Hyperinflation had impoverished the great majority of the German population, especially the middle class. People suffered from food shortages and cold. Inflation caused forced savings in favor not only of the state but also, in the case of a highly developed capital market and banking system economy, in favor of borrowers and speculators. In violation of Say's law of markets, commodities are not traded for commodities. The recipients of new money, in the form of paper money or unbacked credit, acquire real commodities without injecting any new commodities in the economy. Holders of money, creditors, workers, pensioners are forced to save with their saving transferred to the profiteers of inflation. This saving is consumed and/or invested by the inflation beneficiaries.

There was a severe dearth of working capital, in form of subsistence fund, and a consequent great decline in labor efficiency.[12] Part of this was the result of malnutrition brought about by high food prices. Bresciani-Turroni noted that at the peak of inflation Germany was exhausting its resources, building capital goods at the expense of producing much-needed consumer goods such as food and clothing.[13]

In 1923, the government was financing virtually 100 percent of its expenditures by means of note issue (Sargent 1982). The monetary reform stopped government borrowing from the central bank. The management of the Rentenbank strictly limited government borrowing to within the amount decreed. The government moved to balance the budget by taking a series of deliberate and permanent actions to raise taxes and eliminate expenditures. The civil service was downsized by 25 percent. Substantially aiding the fiscal situation, Germany also obtained relief from her reparation obligations. Reparations payments were temporarily suspended, and the Dawes plan assigned Germany a much more manageable schedule of payments.

The rentenmark miracle that ended promptly an astronomical hyperinflation destroyed all modern fatalistic claims that inflation is a stubborn phenomenon that cannot be cured; it is blamed on cost push; if the government cures it, mass-unemployment will occur. All this sophism was nonsense in Germany of 1923. The essential measures that ended hyperinflation in Germany were the creation of an independent central bank that was legally committed to refuse the government's demand for additional credit and a simultaneous drastic fiscal reform. These measures had the effect of binding the government to renounce deficit monetization (Sargent 1982). Once it became widely understood that the government would not rely on the central bank for its finances, the inflation terminated and the exchanges stabilized. Contrary to fatalistic views that consider inflation as an incurable cost push–demand pull phenomena, the German experience showed that inflation was a pure money phenomenon emanating from excessive note issuance that was never retired through taxation and from pyramiding bank credit on an ever-rising money base. Once fiat money was brought under strict control, inflation ended. The accommodative policy of the Reichsbank was suspended; it was replaced by strict quantity limitation. Most interesting, gold standard was not a technical problem. It was implemented by decree despite the hallucinating money inflation that existed in Germany of 1923.

4. Illustration of inflationary financing, 2014

With inconvertible paper money, the money base[14] is at the pure discretion of the central bank. Such was not the case under gold standard. The central bank can allow the government to borrow at its own desire, and banks to extend credit; it can even bail out failing banks. Countries differ in reliance on money creation in financing their fiscal budgets (Table 7.1). There are governments that observe no fiscal responsibility and rely heavily on money creation by the central bank. The ratio of net claims on government to the monetary base may reach 198 percent. Some countries may rely to a large extent on central bank money creation; ratios may vary from 30 percent to 86 percent. There are countries that rely only mildly on the central bank; there are countries that are in balance with no debt to the central bank. There are finally countries with substantial deposits at the central bank and therefore have no need for central bank financing.

Countries vary in respect to the counterparts of their broad money, defined as the sum of currency in circulation plus demand and time deposits at the consolidated banking system. The sources of money supply are the net foreign assets (NFA) and the domestic credit (DC). The NFA represent a true backing of money creation. The currency and demand deposits emitted on NFA have 100 percent backing in terms of purchasing power. The domestic credit, however, may be created through a multiplier effect, and may be restrained only through reducing the central bank's monetary base. If the central bank adopts a cheap money, and allow banks to rediscount their papers with it, then domestic credit may expand at a quick pace and may exceed the real savings in the economy.

Table 7.2 shows that net foreign assets contribute in varying degree to money stock. There are countries where NFA may represent more than 50 percent of the money stock. There are countries where NFA contribute to between 20 percent and 50 percent of money stock. There are also countries where NFA contributes little or negatively to the money stock. In these cases, NFA may vary between –5 percent and 5 percent of money stock.

Domestic credit is a source of money creation: it is called debt money. The money, as a liability of the banking system, is backed by credit. If credit is paid, money declines; if credit is expanded, money expands. We observe that domestic credit may far exceed the money supply; it may range between 100 percent and 279 percent of the money supply. This means that the banking system (i.e., central bank and commercial banks) has non-liquid liabilities in the form of borrowing from the private sector which they use to extend loans to the domestic economy. Net claims on government (NCG) may vary widely in terms of their contribution to money supply. They may exceed the broad money at one extreme and contribute negatively at another, i.e., the government is a net creditor of the banking system. There are varying contributions in between, depending on how much a government wants to borrow and how prudent it is in regard to money creation. Lax governments may rely on borrowing from the

Table 7.1 Central Bank: net government claims in 2014 (in percent of the monetary base)

Bangladesh	-9	Mauritania	24	United States	58
Brazil	76	Mexico	-157	Zimbabwe	198
Chile	-13	Morocco	0	Peru	-58
France	34	Norway	0	Pakistan	86
India	30	Tunisia	8	Argentina	132
Japan	79	Turkey	-4	Australia	-37
Indonesia	30	Uganda	-45	Burundi	74
Malaysia	-2	United Kingdom	111	Chad	31

Source: IFS

Table 7.2 Net Foreign Assets (NFA), Domestic Credit (DC), and Net Claims on Government (NCG) (in percent of broad money)

	NFA	DC	NCG		NFA	DC	NCG
Argentina	28	183	110	Malaysia	21	101	7
Bangladesh	22	106	26	Mauritania	47	111	24
Brazil	33	279	70	Mexico	27	58	6
Burundi	20	127	42	Morocco	22	132	18
Chad	51	75	16	Pakistan	9	117	68
Chile	21	130	-3	Peru	61	58	-23
France	11	173	17	Tunisia	5	121	12
India	20	100	33	Turkey	-5	146	20
Indonesia	27	107	12	Uganda	78	104	14
Japan	16	148	54	United Kingdom	9	122	21
Kenya	21	104	17	United States	-4	158	26

Source: IMF, IFS

banking system; prudent and fiscally responsible government may keep their bank borrowing low, e.g., less than 10 percent of broad money.

5. The welfare cost of inflation

The phenomenon of persistent inflation became familiar only with inconvertible paper money as proven by the emission of this paper by governments. There is a dilemma regarding the definition and measure of inflation. To create a steady rise in prices, there has to be a steady rise in inflation and money supply. Inflation disappears instantly as soon as money supply ceases to rise. Rising prices are therefore the effect of money inflation; it would be important to measure inflation by the rise of the money supply. To eliminate inflation, money supply has to be equal to the real demand for real balances. Friedman (1959) proposed an empirical rule of 2–3 percent money growth in line with real GDP growth which may lead to zero inflation.

Money is considered an asset as any other asset such as land, houses, stocks, bonds, etc. Each asset has a pecuniary yield, an income stream over time. Money is a non-income yield asset. People hold money instead of an income yielding asset such as a stock which brings dividends or a bond which yields interest (Keynes 1936; Friedman 1956; Laidler 1985). The motive for money holding is obvious: money yields a non-pecuniary service in form of saving on the transaction cost and avoiding barter trade. It is a liquid asset; the opportunity cost of holding money is the yield forfeited on stocks or bonds to hold money. Generally, people do not hold money beyond transactions, precaution, and speculation motives. They lend or invest excess money beyond their desired holding. Inflation is considered to increase the opportunity cost of holding money by increasing the nominal yield on real assets which includes capital gains and dividends. As inflation rises, money holders cannot reduce their nominal money; whatever additional money printed by the government has to be held by money holders. Individual money holders may succeed to reduce their nominal money balances; however, the community as a whole has to hold the old and newly printed money. Money becomes like a hot potato which has to be passed around as quickly as possible. The community's attempt to get rid of money drives upward prices of commodities and assets, and increases the velocity of money. As velocity rises, prices may speed up faster than money printing, entailing a decline in real money balances.

Inflation, called public enemy number one, is inherent to costless inconvertible paper and has a social cost. As it kept raging during 1930s and 1949s, it raised concern regarding its social cost. Friedman (1953) and Bailey (1956) regarded inflation as a tax levied on real money balances. The tax base is the money stock (M) deflated by a price level index (P), i.e., (M/P). Bailey dealt with inflation tax as any other excise tax on commodities. Two analytical tools are necessary to assess the welfare cost of an excise tax on a commodity. The demand function of the commodity in terms of its price, and the excise tax rate on the commodity. In accordance, Bailey used Cagan's (1956) model which formulated the demand for real balances in terms of the expected inflation rate. He considered the tax rate to be equal to the inflation rate. As in the study of any tax, he determined the tax revenue from the tax rate, and the welfare loss, or the deadweight burden, associated with this tax rate. The tax base shrinks with each rise of the tax rate, i.e., the demand for the commodity declines as the tax rate rises. The welfare loss rises monotonically with the inflation rate; however, government revenue, as any excise tax, obeys a Laffer curve: it rises with the tax rate and falls beyond a certain tax rate, i.e., the tax becomes regressive.[15] As in the case of any tax, tax revenue is maximized when the elasticity of commodity with respect to the tax rate is equal to unity. Bailey showed that when inflation revenue is equal to 18 percent of real national income, the welfare loss is 7 percent of real national income. The ratio of welfare loss to tax revenue is called collection cost per dollar of revenue. If this ratio is higher for inflation tax than for other conventional taxes, then inflation tax has to be renounced.

What is the nature of the welfare cost associated with inflation tax? Similar to losing electricity through a power outage, losing the services of money creates inconveniences to both consumers and producers. These inconveniences are numerous. Bailey considered the cost arising from the changes in payment procedures and habits which take place during hyperinflations; these changes consist of the adoption of barter or people's rushing to make purchases as soon as they receive payment for anything. As rates of price inflation became too alarming, firms pay their workers more and more frequently: first weekly, then daily, and then sometimes twice a day or more. Having received payment, the workers or their wives rushed to purchase consumer goods, foreign currencies, or other assets. Shopkeepers tended to close early or even to close after making a few sales, in order to exchange their newly acquired cash at once for more inventories. Outside the cities, trade quickly went on a barter basis.

Kessel and Alchian (1962) stated that an increase in the cost of holding money induces a community to divert some resources to the production of money substitutes. Consequently, a paper that is nearly costless to society is in part supplanted by goods that have greater costs. These costs constitute the efficiency losses, or the welfare effects, of anticipated inflation. The use of money substitutes that are infinitely elastic in supply in the short run, such as foreign currencies, increases very rapidly. The substitution of real resources for money, and the corresponding welfare loss caused by any given rate of change of prices, is greater in the long run than the short run. In the long run, by definition, the supply conditions of money substitutes are more elastic. Hence more resources will flow into the production of money substitutes in the long than in the short run. The more a community shifts from money to money substitutes the greater the welfare loss and the smaller the real tax receipts attributable to any given rate of change of prices.

Bailey asked why, then, has inflationary finance been employed at such tremendous cost in some cases and at definitely excessive cost in most others? The reason appears to be that the costs are at first largely hidden, whereas the costs of other forms of taxation – the costs of administration and compliance – are obvious. Where a country has a serious problem of reconstruction and therefore wishes to channel a large share of the national income through the government budget and where, on the other hand, the costs of administration are especially high because of war damage and other factors, the temptation to use the apparently almost costless method of printing money has evidently been irresistible. Most such countries might very well agree in retrospect that the temptation should have been resisted.

Inflation is the worst economic injustice inflicted by a government on its people. It is an incurable disease of inconvertible paper. Severe inflation has entailed a decline in the rate of economic growth and even drastic drop of national income. During 1989–2000, the Democratic Republic of Congo (ex-Zaire) lost 63 percent of its real GDP due to inflation. Zimbabwe lost 33 percent of its GDP during 1999–2004. Inflation inflicts a loss of real incomes on workers and pensioners. If prices rise by 5 percent/year and wages by 2 percent/year, then workers lose 50 percent in real terms in 20 years. Inflation causes an impoverishment and drastic drop in consumption. As seen in historical inflations, there was severe shortage of commodities. If government imposes price controls, the shortage will be too severe. Inflation inflates prices and deflates output.[16] Inflationary expectations accelerate the rate of inflation. By withholding commodities, merchants hike up prices tremendously and make far more receipts with lesser commodities.

Inflation begets inflation; as prices race ahead, nominal cash becomes insufficient for circulating goods. More nominal money is required to buy fewer goods. The central bank and banks validate each price rise, and accommodate more inflation by providing more and more money. Paradoxically, real money was too scarce under hyperinflation and plentiful under metallic money. In

Germany's hyperinflation, there was severe shortage of real money.[17] At the end of the hyperinflation in 1923, there was practically no real money; in contrast, before 1914, under the gold standard, real money was plentiful in Germany. Inflation distorts the production structure and allocation of resources. The demand for real assets such as housing, factories, increases, and labor is redirected toward the production of assets that provide a hedge against inflation. Understanding the gains from inflation, borrowers increase tremendously their bank debt and invest in real estate, plants, land, etc. Luxury consumption reaches its zenith. Speculation is too rife. Bresciani-Turroni (1931) documented these distortions; there was considerable mal-investment which became useless after the hyperinflation. Labor had to be redirected to the production of needed goods such as food, clothes, shoes, and milk instead of over-capacity in real estate and capital goods industries.

The notorious injustice of inflation is a free redistribution of wealth from one group of the population to another group. The inflation tax brings revenues not only to the government, but also to other beneficiaries. Foremost, as noted by Locke (1691), debtors gain at the expense of creditors. This phenomenon was stressed by Bresciani-Turroni (1931) and Graham (1930) in the case of German hyperinflation. All financial saving dissipated in Germany in 1923. Many people, finding that their lifetime savings would buy not even a tramway ticket, committed suicide. Price of assets rose considerably during inflation. There were capital gains to holders of these assets. This capital gain was a transfer of wealth from money holders and fixed income classes in favor of holders of non-monetary assets and entrepreneurs who derive their incomes from profits.

6. Conclusions

Governments outlawed gold and silver to possess monopoly over costless inconvertible paper. By its very nature, this money is defective; it is inflationary, redistributive, and alters the value of contracts. The government is now able to set the interest rate at near-zero and print monumental money. Since paper is costless, every government would tend to draw free resources and steadily depreciate paper until the money value reaches the cost of paper, which is zero as illustrated by hyperinflations. Sharia does not endorse government paper money; it does not approve of inflation tax. Often, paper money is issued as a monetization of interest-based debt, and may violate the Sharia interdiction of interest. Sharia considers money as a market commodity which obeys the laws of value, and there cannot be an outside money issued at the discretion of a government. Sharia allows no inflationary financing. This financing often turns out to be hyper-inflationary, entails large economic loss, impoverishment, transfers property unjustly to beneficiaries of inflation, destroys money, and distorts the production structure. It causes many competitive devaluations of currencies and deranges trade. Workers and pensioners suffer steadily decline in real incomes. An inflation tax is an unjust tax and cannot be permitted by Sharia which restricts the taxation power of the government to Sharia-compliant taxes; inflation is no substitute to taxes.

Historical inflations showed that inflationary financing originated in bankruptcy and had the same consequences now and then. It showed that paper money may disappear within months, ruining its holders; in contrast to gold and silver which never disappeared over the centuries, and never caused any ruin to their holders. Inflationists contended that gold and silver were not in elastic supply with growing trade; this was a fallacy: paper money makes real money in severe shortage, which reduces trade and employment. Many countries are suffering inflation and money disorders caused by inflationary finance of unproductive spending. Costless paper has become a serious source of economic and social disorders. When banks recklessly expand credit, they end up in ruin and cause an economic depression.

Since John Law's time until nowadays, there have been scholars and policymakers who believe that poverty can be abolished by the issue of printed money paper. Today, the top brass of central bankers as well as Nobel Prize winners in economics hold that unlimited money printing and near-zero interest rates are the panacea for unemployment and poverty. They try to push more debt on the top of already defaulted debt. Consequently, paper inflation is afflicting many countries: inflation has become inextricable and is steadily eroding the value of currency.

Hyperinflations showed the dangerous nature of paper money and the fallacy of growing on money. Money is not real capital. Doubling the stock of money adds no social utility. Doubling the output of wheat increases tremendously social utility. Printing money does not create real capital. A dollar or a euro note is not a commodity. Printing dollars does not create crude oil, wheat, cars, etc.; money only circulates commodities and is a purchasing power in commodities. Printing money out of thin air amounts simply to a redistribution of wealth from a group in favor of another group. The delusion that money can increase real wealth and achieve full employment is so deep-rooted in the United States and other leading countries that it led to highly expansionary fiscal and money policies after 2008. Each government is firmly convinced that it will succeed where John Law failed. Leading scholars brand gold as barbaric and a fetter, and consider money as an unrestrained policy tool. Certainly, economies were liberated from the fetters of gold; they fell into worse fetters in the form of severe rigidities of labor markets, hyperinflation, consumption of capital, redistribution of wealth in favor of inflation profiteers, and distorted economic calculations.

Notes

1 Two definitions of inflation apply; an increase in the money supply or a general price level increase.

2   Maurice Allais (1999) wrote: "In essence, the present creation of money, out of nothing, by the banking system is, I do not hesitate to say it in order to make people clearly realize what is at stake here, similar to the creation of money by counterfeiters, so rightly condemned by law. In concrete terms, it leads to the same results."

3   Price inflation includes all types of prices, such as asset prices, commodities, food, energy, etc. Limiting inflation measure to selected items has been considered as a deluded view (Kindleberger 1995).

4   Debt is a form of deferred tax to be paid by future taxes, money printing, or default. Seigniorage may be redeemed if the government decides to retire created money through budget surpluses from cutting spending or higher taxes.

5   The tax base is the amount of fiat money, M emitted by the government or banks and held by residents or foreigners. Let P, the price level, the amount of real seigniorage is $\Delta M/P$, where ΔM is the new fiat money emitted by the government. The expression $\Delta M/P$ may be re-written as $\dfrac{\Delta M}{P} = \dfrac{\Delta M}{M}\dfrac{M}{P} = \mu\dfrac{M}{P}$, where μ is the rate of expansion of money supply per period of time, and M/P is the amount of real balances. We note the identity:
$$\Delta\left(\frac{M}{P}\right) = \frac{\Delta M}{P} - \frac{\Delta P}{P}\left(\frac{M}{P}\right),$$
which may be re-written as $\dfrac{\Delta M}{P} = \Delta\left(\dfrac{M}{P}\right) + \dfrac{\Delta P}{P}\left(\dfrac{M}{P}\right).$
Hence, total seigniorage $\dfrac{\Delta M}{P}$ may be decomposed into a change in real money balances and a loss of purchasing power on existing stock of money due to price inflation $\dfrac{\Delta P}{P}$.
The term $\dfrac{\Delta P}{P}\left(\dfrac{M}{P}\right)$ is inflation tax; the holders of money suffer a capital loss when prices rise.

6   Gleeson (1999) and Minton (1975) provided very good narration of the banking and speculative experience of John Law.

7   See Janet Gleeson (1999).

8   Voltaire called the decree restricting the legal possession of metal coin the most unjust edict ever rendered and the final limit of tyrannical absurdity.

9   The extension of the "maximum" to all commodities only increased the confusion. Trade was paralyzed and all manufacturing establishments were closed down. Attempts by the Convention to increase the value of the assignats were of no avail. Too many causes operated in their depreciation: the enormous issue, the uncertainty as to their value if the Revolution should fail, the relation they bore to both specie and commodities, which retained their value and refused to be exchanged for a money of constantly diminishing purchasing power.

10   Constantino Bresciani-Turroni's (1931) book, *The Economics of Inflation*, was among best documented books on Weimar Republic hyperinflation. The author was an outstanding economist who worked in Germany during 1919–1937. Not only he lived the conditions of Germany during and after the hyperinflation, but he had substantive illustrative data.

11   All trade ceased, shops were closed, unemployment among unionized workers was 30 percent in November 1923, people were starving in the cities, and no farm produce was brought to the cities. The very meager trade was based on dollars, gold, and silver coins, or direct barter. Here, we have the opposite of Gresham's law; namely, the good money drove out the bad money.

12   The interest rates were kept at 5 percent by the Reichsbank until late stage of the hyperinflation and could not reflect the scarcity of capital. In real terms, interest rates were overly negative.

13 Jacques Rueff (1964) maintained that inflation may cause starvation by destroying the working capital. To stave off general famine, Germany was provided loans in the Dawn Plan which were used practically for food imports.
14 Defined as the sum of currency in circulation outside the banking system and banks' reserves at the central bank.
15 Often, when the tax rate is high, smuggling develops, a parallel market emerges, and government loses most of the tax revenue. This is the case for petroleum products, and many other products facing high tax rates.
16 If an orange price is 5 cents, a trader has to sell 20 oranges to earn a dollar. If the price is $1, a trader sells one orange to earn a dollar. Carroll (1850) called it price without value.
17 Besides its printing presses, Reischbank contracted 133 additional printing firms with 1,783 machines to print marks, and more than 30 paper manufacturers worked at full capacity solely to provide paper for the Reichsbank notes. It authorized the provinces and municipalities to print and put into circulation their own emergency money notes, and gave the assurance that it would redeem these notes exactly as if they were Reichsbank own banknotes. This illustrates how severe real money shortage was.

References

Allais, M., 1999, *La Crise Mondiale D'Aujourd'hui*, Paris: Clément Juglar.
Bailey, M., 1956, "The Welfare Cost of Inflationary Finance," *Journal of Political Economy*, 64(2): 93–110.
Bresciani-Turroni, C., 1931, *The Economics of Inflation*, Northampton, Great Britain: John Dickens & Co Ltd.
Cagan, P., 1956, "The Monetary Dynamics of Hyperinflation," in Friedman, M. (ed.). *Studies in the Quantity Theory of Money*, Chicago: University of Chicago Press.
Carroll, C. H., 1965, *Organization of Debt Into Currency and Other Papers*, Edited With an Introduction by Edward C. Simmons, D. Van Nostrand Company, Inc. Princeton, NJ.
Friedman, M., 1953, "Discussion of the Inflationary Gap", in his *Essays in Positive Economics*, Chicago: University of Chicago Press, pp. 253–257.
Friedman, M., 1956, "The Quantity Theory of Money – a Restatement," in Friedman, M. (ed.). *Studies in the Quantity Theory of Money*, Chicago: University of Chicago Press.
Friedman, M., 1959, *A Program for Monetary Stability*, New York: Fordham University Press.
Gleeson, J., 1999, *Millionaire*, New York: Simon & Schuster.
Graham, F., 1930, *Exchange, Prices, and Production in Hyperinflation: Germany, 1920–1923*, New York: Russell & Russell.
Kessel, R., and Alchian, A., 1962, "Effects of Inflation," *Journal of Political Economy*, 70(6): 521–537.
Keynes, J. M., 1936, *The General Theory of Employment, Interest, and Money*. Reprinted London: Macmillan for the Royal Economic Society, 1973.
Kindleberger, C., 2009, "Asset Inflation and Monetary Policy," *PSL Quarterly Review*, 62(248–251): 29–50.
Laidler, D., 1985, *The Demand for Money: Theories, Evidence, and Problems*, New York: Harper & Row.
Locke, J., 1691, *Some Considerations on the Consequences of the Lowering of Interest and the Raising of the Value of Money*, The Works of John Locke, 1824, London: C. Balwin, Printer.
Minton, R., 1975, *John Law, the Father of Paper Money*, New York: Association Press.
Perry, A. L., 1873, *Elements of Political Economy*, New York: Charles Scribner's Sons.

Rueff, J., 1964, *The Age of Inflation*, Gateway Editions, Chicago: Henry Regnery Company.

Sargent, T., 1982, "The Ends of Four Big Inflations," in Hall, R. E. (ed.). *Inflation*, University of Chicago Press and National Bureau of Economic Research.

Sargent, T., and Wallace, N., 1981, "Some Unpleasant Monetarist Arithmetic," Federal Reserve Bank of Minneapolis, *Quarterly Review*.

8   On the nature of financial repression

1. Introduction

McKinnon (1973) and Shaw (1973) opposed financial repression, which is defined as the central bank's policy of pegging the interest rate at below the equilibrium rate with a view to hike borrowing and substantially reduce interest payments. This policy distorts the capital markets. In the wake of the 2007–2008 financial crisis, with the aim of increasing employment, the United States, the Eurozone, and some other governments forced interest rates to near zero-bound. As to be expected, the distortionary effects of financial repression followed: debt exceeded GDP in many countries;[1] stock prices rose at an annual average rate of about 19 percent during 2009–2016; and yield differentials between stocks and fixed-income securities ranged between 19 percent for long-term securities and 21 percent for short-term bills and notes. Other fallouts of financial repression were competitive currency depreciations, slow economic recovery, and higher income and wealth inequalities.

McKinnon (1973) and Shaw (1973) showed that financial repression damaged economic growth, stifled the financial sector, caused high and chronic inflation and unemployment, conferred large rent and subsidies to beneficiary groups, and disrupted the foreign trade and the foreign exchange sector. Inspired by the earlier work of Henry Simons (1947), they condemned financial repression and called for full financial liberalization, including free market interest and exchange rates, wages, prices, capital flows, and financial deepening and the dismantling of trade tariffs and licensing. In countries characterized by wage and price rigidity, financial repression aimed at achieving full employment and inflationary economic growth. Some countries had to rely on foreign aid or foreign borrowing to survive the effects of financial repression.

Financial repression may end in a financial crisis (e.g., 1929 and 2008), or costly hyperinflation (Cagan 1956). Its beneficiaries are either accumulating free wealth (e.g., borrowers, speculators, etc.), or consuming capital (e.g., transfer recipients), and will defend it as a power group. Its advocates argue that the state has the mandate of full employment and economic prosperity, and there is practically no other means to achieve these laudable ends except through near-zero administered interest rates, money printing, and government spend-ing.[2] With debt at record levels in many countries, it is difficult to end financial repression and allow interest rates to rise to market-clearing rates as this would increase the likelihood of debt default, falling asset prices, and financial sector bankruptcies (Fisher 1933). Financial repression, by disconnecting the financial and the real sectors, has severed the relation between the market rate and the available return on the best physical projects.

Sharia model opposes price setting by the government as well as inflation-ary policies, all are unjust and distortive; it has a risk-sharing equity banking where interest is ruled out. In a Sharia model, the rate of return on capital is determined by the free competitive mechanism and is related directly to the marginal product of capital and the time preference of savers. Hence, a Sharia model is immune to financial repression, its unjust redistribution of wealth, and destabilizing consequences. The chapter covers:

- The classical and Keynesian interest rate models
- The theory of two Rates of interest: natural rate versus market rate of interest
- Sharia model of rate of return determination
- McKinnon and Shaw Doctrine against financial repression
- Unorthodox monetary policy and financial repression
- The futility of financial repression

2. The classical and Keynesian interest rate models

To illustrate the nature of financial repression, we begin with the theory of interest rates, whose administered fixing by the government is a main instru-ment of financial repression. Prices of assets such as securities, foreign currency, land, and housing are determined by the rate of interest in the money mar-kets. Manipulation of the interest rate, as in Japan during 1985–1989 and in the United States during 2002–2006, may destabilize the economy for a long period. The relation between the price of an asset V, which provides a net cash flow CF per unit of time and has a maturity T, and the nominal interest rate i is provided by the following formula:

$$V = CF + \frac{CF}{(1+i)^1} + \frac{CF}{(1+i)^2} \ldots + \frac{CF}{(1+i)^T} \sim \frac{CF}{i} \text{ when } T \to \infty \quad (1)$$

With $\Delta V / \Delta i < 0$. The price of money is measured by the opportunity cost of holding it, which is the return to the best available physical investment project in an economy. When i is low, say at 1 percent, investors hold on to their cash, because an increase in interest rate will result in a decline in asset prices. The rate of interest is a key price; repressive policy has attempted to either lower it or to put a ceiling on it as discussed by McKinnon (1973) and Shaw (1973).

The classical interest model of Bohm-Bawerk (1888) and Fisher (1907) stipulated that the interest rate observed in the banking sector was determined by thrift and productivity and cannot be altered by changes in the money supply. Money savings, S, is an increasing function, $S(i)$, of the interest rate, i.e., $\Delta S / \Delta i > 0$; and investment, $I(i)$ is a decreasing function, i.e., $\Delta I / \Delta i < 0$. The equilibrium interest rate equalizes savings and investment: $S(i) = I(i)$. Influenced by Adam Smith, Ricardo (1817) stated that money does not affect the interest rate, which is determined by real forces only.[3]

The loanable funds theory of interest rate, essentially attributed to Thornton (1802) and Wicksell (1898), is a monetary version of the classical theory of interest based on thrift and productivity. The interest rate is determined in the market for loanable funds. The demand for loanable funds (i.e., supply of securities) $L_d(i)$ is a demand for investment (i) and hoarding money balances (ΔH). The supply of loanable funds $L_s(i)$ originates from money savings, S, dishoarding of money balances, (ΔZ), and an increase in the money supply (ΔM); banks create new money (ΔM) in form of deposits, which can be drawn by borrowers. The equilibrium interest rate equalizes the supply and demand of loanable funds: $L_s(i) = L_d(i)$.

Keynes (1936) dismissed savings and investment from the interest rate determination. In Keynes's theory, saving is influenced by income Y; namely, $S = S(Y)$; for any interest rate, saving can be made equal to a given investment by changes in income. According to Keynes, the rate of interest depends largely on demand for money (M) and securities (B); i.e., the rate is determined by the liquidity preference. Other things remaining unchanged, the desired ratio between money and securities holding tends to rise with a fall in the interest rate, and the equilibrium interest rate is the one where the desired ratio of money to securities corresponds to the actual ratio. Accordingly, money demand is expressed as $(M / B)^d = \ell(i)$, with $\Delta \ell(i) / \Delta i < 0$, and money and securities supply is exogenous at given $\bar{M}$ and $\bar{B}$. At a given instant of time, the equilibrium interest rate equates $(M / B)^d = \dfrac{\bar{M}}{\bar{B}}$. From this, it follows that any monetary or banking policy which increases the actual quantity of money relative to the actual quantity of securities will reduce the interest rate at which the money market is in equilibrium. Thus, an arbitrary increase in the quantity of money or an increase in the quantity of money through a limited and temporary purchase of securities by the central bank will reduce the equilibrium interest rate in Keynes' system.

Hicks (1937) attempted to reconcile the classical and Keynesian theories through the IS and LM diagram (ISLM model) whereby the equilibrium interest rate results from interaction of real (IS) and monetary (LM) forces. A notable reconciliation was due to Metzler (1951). He assumed that the capital market was subject to three main influences: (1) the influence of current saving and investment, as in the classical theory; (2) the influence of decisions concerning the holding of cash or securities, as in Keynes's liquidity preference theory; and

(3) the influence of wealth (W) on current saving, with saving reformulated as, $S = S(i, W)$ with $\partial S / \partial W < 0$. Assuming perfect price and wage flexibility, he showed that the equilibrium rate of interest was determined by the interplay of these three influences and was, therefore, affected by real and monetary factors.

3. The theory of two rates of interest: natural rate versus market rate of interest

Thornton (1802) and Wicksell (1898) elaborated the theories of two interest rates, viz. the market rate of interest and the natural rate of interest, which is the expected yield or the marginal rate of profit on new capital projects. Entrepreneurs compare the two rates and borrow money when the expected yield or rate of profit surpasses the market rate. Thornton noted that the two rates were distinct concepts; the money rate was observed in the market for loanable funds, whereas the natural rate was determined by the rate of profit. Thornton established a relation between the two interest rates and inflation; namely inflation arises from a difference between the two rates. If the money rate is below the natural rate, there will be an expansion of bank credit due to a high demand for loans. Prices are bid up; inflation would persist for as long as the market rate is below the expected rate of profit.

In line with Thornton's thesis, Wicksell distinguished between the market rate (i) and the natural or equilibrium rate of interest (r). The former is market money rate or the cost of money. The latter has been defined in many equivalent ways: (i) it is the marginal efficiency of capital, i.e., the expected marginal yield or internal rate of return of investment; (ii) it is also the rate which equates planned investment to desired saving at the full employment output; or (iii) equivalently, the rate that equates aggregate demand with full employment output. When equilibrium prevails in the goods' market, the natural interest rate is associated with price stability. Hence, if the market rate hits the natural rate, price stability would obtain.

Wicksell observed that planned investment I and planned savings S may differ; in this condition, a gap $E = 1-S$ emerges. This gap may be formulated in terms of the two interest rates as follows:

$$I - S = \mu(r - i), \; \mu > 0 \tag{2}$$

Wicksell noted that the excess of investment over saving causes banks to expand credit, which fuels all sorts of speculation and bids up the price level P. Formally, the rate of inflation $\dfrac{dP}{Pdt}$ may be expressed in terms of the wedge between the two rates as follows:

$$\frac{dP}{Pdt} = \varphi(I - S) = \varphi\mu(r - i), \; \varphi > 0 \tag{3}$$

We note that price inflation and the credit expansion that causes it both arise from the wedge between the natural rate and the loan rate of interest. As inflation accelerates, banks respond by jerking up the interest rates; in doing so, the money rate rises toward the natural rate. Eventually, the two rates may become equal, and prices stabilize. By forcing financial repression, the government eliminates the market mechanism and sets the interest rate i far below the equilibrium rate r in order to increase credit and make it cheap for borrowers. The central bank has to increase the money base to keep interest rates depressed and allow for inflation to evolve as a result of money creation.[4] The real interest rate defined as $q = i - \Delta P / P$ may become significantly negative, with debtors earning a substantial real income equal to r-q, and leverage becomes ominous resulting in the accumulation of wealth through cheap borrowing.

4. Sharia model of rate of return determination

Sharia rules out interest-bearing assets; all financial assets are risky, with contingent payoffs. Simons (1947) stated that the best investment banking is the one that has no fixed money contracts at all:

> What arrangements as to the financial structure would be conducive to lesser or minimum amplitude of industrial fluctuations? An approximate ideal condition is fairly obvious – and unattainable. The danger of pervasive, synchronous, cumulative maladjustments would be minimized if there were no fixed money contracts at all – if all property were held in residual equity or common stock form. With such a financial structure, no one would be in a position either to create effective money substitutes (whether for circulation or for hoarding) or to force enterprises into wholesale efforts of liquidation.
>
> (P. 165)

The prohibition of interest makes the returns to financial assets primarily determined by the returns to the real sector. In a Sharia model, the rate of return is no longer an interest rate on loans and bonds, but a rate of return on common shares that depends on marginal product of capital and thrift in the economy as well as on portfolio balance.[5] The Sharia model has two sectors: a real sector and a financial sector, and therefore two prices, which are the price level for output P, and the rate of return on capital r (Metzler 1951; Mirakhor 1993; Askari et al. 2014). The financial sector has two assets: money and equities. As in a general equilibrium framework, excess demand in one market is related to excess demand or supply in the other market, and the price in one market influences the price in the other market. The forces of demand and supply operate freely to equilibrate each market. A general equilibrium is defined by a rate of return on equity and a price level that equilibrate simultaneously assets and commodities markets. The condition of equilibrium in the commodities market is aggregate demand for goods, i.e., consumption and investment, should be equal to the full employment output. This condition is the same as the equality of saving and investment. This was the classical condition for determining the equilibrium interest rate; the latter is determined by time preference and capital productivity independently of the money market. Likewise, the equilibrium condition in the financial market requires that money demand be equal to the fixed nominal money supply, and the demand for securities be equal to the value of existing securities. This condition was called the portfolio balance or the liquidity preference which determines the equilibrium interest rate in the money market, irrespective of the equilibrium of the commodity market, which may be in an under-employment equilibrium.

As in a typical IS-LM, the equilibrium rate of return is attained when the commodities and asset markets are simultaneously in equilibrium. Most importantly, the equilibrium rate of return is not an interest rate. It reflects the marginal product of capital which is at the same time the rate of return on equities. Hence, in a Sharia model, the equilibrium rate of return to capital is neither a purely monetary rate, as in a Keynesian framework, determined in the money market by the demand and supply of money, nor is it solely influenced by the demand and supply of real savings, as in the classical model. Instead, the rate of return to capital is determined by the rate of return to equities and is related to the value of the marginal product of capital as well as to the portfolio balance equilibrium. Since the rate of interest is precluded, there is only a profit rate. Hence, the existence of two rates of return that characterize the conventional model; viz., the interest rate determined in the money market and the natural rate of interest determined by the rate of profit, is excluded. The divergence of these two rates was recognized to be a source of instability as illustrated in the writings of Thornton (1802) and Wicksell (1898).[6]

Sharia allows no financial repression; simply because there is no money interest rate determined in the loanable funds markets, which can be lowered by the government. There are no two rates of return as in Thornton and Wicksell models. There is only one rate of return, which is the return on common stocks, or the rate of profit. For a given profit rate r the nominal price of a share is the present value of its income stream, approximated by the value of marginal product divided by r. The nominal price of a share will tend to be stable, since the real marginal product of capital is stable; in addition, because there is no debt money and no unbacked credit creation, the price level tends to be stable.

5. McKinnon and Shaw doctrine against financial repression

5.1 McKinnon and Shaw's rebuttal of financial repression

McKinnon (1973) and Shaw (1973) opposed policies of financial repression, which they defined as the government policy of low nominal interest rates and inflationary financing of fiscal deficits, with the government extracting resources for its budget through an inflation tax. Some government spending was waste expenditure, which consumed capital that could have enhanced social and economic development. Wherever it was practiced, financial repression was anti-growth, undermined the development of the financial sector, reduced savings and investment, and resulted in high inflation and slow economic growth. Financial repression distorted exchange rates, led to capital flight, undermined exports, enlarged trade deficits, preserved dependence on foreign debt, and penalized employment by cheapening the price of capital (McKinnon 1973; Shaw 1973).

McKinnon and Shaw called for a full liberalization of the financial sector and financial deepening. In contrast to established doctrine of low interest rates favored unanimously by politicians, they emphasized the merit of market-determined interest rates to reflect the rate of return in the real sector. High real interest rates necessarily implied high real economic growth since capital is deployed efficiently into highest return projects (reflecting the opportunity cost of capital). Such was the case of South Korea and Taiwan who implemented Shaw's advice in 1960s. McKinnon endorsed the view of money as wealth; however, he dismissed the notion of the substitution between money and physical assets (called the Tobin Effect in 1956) in favor of complementarity between money and physical assets. Specifically, higher demand for money does not reduce the demand for physical assets at the level of the economy; instead, it enhances the demand for physical assets. In considering money as a conduit for physical capital accumulation, a higher reward of saving deposits would lead to higher accumulation of physical assets. He considered that highly productive investment may involve large indivisibilities, and therefore prior accumulation of large monetary savings may be required before undertaking large-scale and efficient investments. This is the very foundation of capital markets which pool savings from small savers and channel them to large-scale projects. The return of projects involving indivisibilities far exceeded that of small-scale investments. For instance, farming using fertilizers, machinery, and irrigation had a far greater return than small-scale traditional farming.

5.2 The McKinnon-Shaw model: achieving both full-liquidity money and golden growth

With full liberalization of the financial sector, McKinnon-Shaw model showed that a country may achieve two objectives: (i) optimal real money, defined as full-liquidity (Friedman 1969) or satiety in real money balances (m = M/P); and (ii) Golden rule capital (K)/labor (L) ratio ($K = K/L$) which maximizes long-run per capita consumption (Phelps 1965). Full financial liberalization and deepening lead to best m and K. The McKinnon-Shaw model contains two assets, a productive physical capital (K), and real money balances (m), and therefore two markets, the capital market and the money market. Nominal money is assumed as a fiat money, costless to produce. It includes government currency and bank deposits. Each asset has a real rate of return per period of time Δt, and portfolio holders are assumed to change the composition of their portfolio by holding the more remunerative asset. If they expect higher inflation, they would reduce their demand for money in favor of physical assets.

The marginal real return on physical capital is r_k.[7] The real return on real money balances r_m is a composite return, defined as:

$$r_m = d - \dot{P}^* + u \tag{4}$$

d is nominal interest rate paid by banks on bank deposits; $\dot{P}^*$ is the expected rate of inflation which may be estimated from the actual rate of inflation $\dot{P}\left(= \dfrac{\Delta P}{\Delta t}\dfrac{1}{P} \right)$; and u is a convenience yield of money, called also liquidity yield, as it avoids the inconvenience of barter trade. The term u is a non-pecuniary item, not directly observable.[8] It can only be deduced indirectly as the difference between pecuniary yield on physical capital and pecuniary yield on real balances. A condition for portfolio equilibrium is:

$$r_m = r_K \tag{5}$$

Friedman (1969) recommended that $m = M/P$, socially costless to produce, should be expanded in the portfolio of wealth holders until its marginal product, u, falls to zero ($u = 0$). Hence, the optimal strategy for securing full monetary liquidity can be described by the full-liquidity rule:

$$r_m = d - \dot{P}^* + u = d - \dot{P}^* = r_K \tag{6}$$

The central bank may increase real balances by increasing the real return $d - \dot{P}^*$. If d is close to zero, then the central bank may set the money growth rate $\dot{M} = \dfrac{dM}{Mdt}$ so to achieve a steady deflation, i.e., $\dot{p} < 0$. The full-liquidity rule implies that price deflation at rate r_k (the real return to capital) is socially optimal if no formal deposit rate of interest is paid on holdings of cash balances. Alternatively, when the nominal deposit rate d is equal to the money rate of interest (i), there is full-liquidity demand when u is zero and:

$$d = i = r_K + \dot{P}^* \tag{7}$$

For money that is costless to produce, the real deposit rate should be set equal to the real rate of return on physical capital ($r_m = r_k$). The equality of the expected deflation rate with the real rate of return induces demand for money to the limit at which the marginal product of money is zero, $u = 0$. This marginal product at zero is equal to the marginal cost of money, and the income effect of money deepening is maximized.

This ultimate goal of monetary policy can be achieved when the price level is flexible with a constant nominal money stock. Let money demand be $M = aPY$,

$a>0$; we have $\dot{M} = \dot{Y} + \dot{P}$, where $\dot{Y} = \dfrac{dY}{Ydt}$. With $\dot{M} = 0$, we have $\dot{Y} = -\dot{P}$. At the full-liquidity of real money, i.e., $u = 0$ we have:

$$d - \dot{P}^* = r_K \tag{8}$$

$$d = r_K + \dot{P}^* = r_K - \dot{Y} \tag{9}$$

The nominal deposit rate would be dictated by the difference between the rate of return to physical capital and income growth. Along the golden path of growth, with equality between $\dot{Y}$ and r_k, nominal deposit rate could be zero.

Shaw was a strong supporter of Friedman's fixed rule of money, which consisted of pegging nominal money growth at a fixed rate approximated by long-term real GDP growth rate (Simons 1947). He contended that the assumption of downward price-level flexibility may be discarded; he noted that price deflation involves a social welfare loss in the short-run instability of income and employment and is not acceptable. There is no reason for deviating from the target of full-liquidity. Given money-income elasticity at unity,[9] the central bank may set $\dot{M}$ equal to $\dot{Y}$ to preserve price-level stability, $\dot{P}^* = 0$, and fix the nominal deposit rate equal to r_k. With the rate of growth in nominal money and the deposit rate under the control of the central bank, downward price-level rigidity implies no sacrifice of social welfare. The central bank may distribute its seigniorage to money holders in form of remuneration of deposits or higher purchasing power of money.

Along the path of the Golden Rule, long-run consumption per capita is maximized; real output, real capital stock, and labor all grow at the same rate δ; the capital-labor ratio becomes a constant. Moreover, the marginal rate of return (real rate of interest) is equal to the rate of real GDP growth:[10]

$$r_K = \dot{Y} = \frac{\Delta Y}{Y} \tag{10}$$

In Keynesian theory, money was wealth; its accumulation competes with physical investment. Savings are destined to become physical investment as well as to the increment in real money (Tobin 1965). In this event, the full-liquidity rule becomes a dilemma. A large accumulation of money would reduce physical investment. Hence, the Keynesian paradox of saving, whereby an increment in real cash balances depresses investment and leads to unemployment. In turn, lower income leads to lower saving. The underlying assumption for this paradox is that wages and prices are rigid and cannot change to clear markets. In the tradition of the classics, and assuming downward flexibility of wages and prices, Pigou (1943) refuted the Keynesian saving paradox.[11] He maintained that price deflation would not reduce nominal income provided nominal money supply remains unchanged. Price deflation will be offset by higher output stemming from higher employment of labor in such a way to maintain nominal income unchanged.[12] Price deflation increases wealth, spending, and employment.

Shaw considered the debt–intermediation view of money. Savings, through debt–intermediation, are redeployed from surplus to deficit units via banking and capital markets; there are therefore no idle savings. The greater the financial intermediation, the greater is the level of physical assets. Money hoarding rarely existed as an economic problem; even if it did, it would not have impaired physical investment. It would have simply lowered prices and conferred greater well-being for consumers or stimulated exports. For Pigou (1943), Patinkin (1948), Metzler (1951), higher money demand induces a real balance effect via price and wage flexibility and greater aggregate demand for output. According to McKinnon and Shaw, the government has a costless solution for the dilemma that money satiation is achieved at the expense of capital accumulation. An economy can enjoy full-liquidity and optimal capital too – the best m and K. The key to optimal money is a real deposit rate that sets the marginal product u of money to zero. The key to the best K and r is the physical-savings propensity. If K lies below the Golden rule target, the government may save more of its revenues or impose additional taxes with a view to hike up investment. In contrast, if k is too high, the government may increase its current consumption or lower taxes. Actions affecting d and k through monetary and fiscal policies, respectively, are socially costless and may be used to solve the optimality dilemma which implied a tradeoff between the Golden rule and the full-liquidity rule. Indeed, let the Golden rule of fiscal policy be implemented by setting the real rate of interest equal to the real output growth, and the nominal interest rate on deposit to zero, full-liquidity monetary policy would simply maintain the nominal stock of money fixed, so that price deflation rate is equal to real output growth rate. Considered together, the two optimization rules require:

$$\dot{Y} = d - \dot{P}^* = r_K, \text{ with } \dot{M} = 0 \text{ if } d = 0 \tag{11}$$

The two rules prevent financial repression as envisaged by McKinnon and Shaw. The McKinnon and Shaw theory stressed positive real return on money and deposits and restricted the nominal money supply; therefore, it stood in contrast with policies of financial repression which reduced the interest rate, stepped up inflation, and inflicted negative return on money balances. Financial deepening, along with full liberalization of capital, labor, and commodities markets, was essential for sustained growth. In contrast, policymakers who emphasized money creation and near-zero interest rates, McKinnon and Shaw stressed market-determined real interest and exchange rates. For them, highly developed banking and capital markets would mobilize enormous savings, finance efficient projects, reduce risk, and enhance economic growth.

Before McKinnon and Shaw, Tobin (1969) and Keynes (1936) had noted the policy-induced deviation of interest rates from the true opportunity cost of financial resources. Tobin argued that monetary policy had the ability to force a deviation between market valuation of capital and its replacement cost. His fundamental valuation efficiency concept, interpreted as allocative efficiency, would establish the opportunity cost of financial resources requiring that they be directed to their best uses. In a market where prices were not allowed to reflect their opportunity cost, repression ruled. This was the McKinnon-Shaw argument for the liberalization of the financial sector of developing countries. Financial repression, the deviation of "administered" interest rate from the "market" interest rate, led to market distortions, and discouraged saving, investment, and economic growth.

6. Unorthodox monetary policy and financial repression

During the nineteenth century, the response of markets to financial crises was a significant rise of nominal interest rates and a sharp drop of nominal wage rates, simply because a financial crisis resulted from a drying up of real circulating capital (wage funds) and a misallocation of capital and labor; it caused massive unemployment (Labordere 1908). Savings in the form of wage goods became too low to support investment. The economic depression was brief, savings were rebuilt, and the economy recovered to a higher level of employment and income than in the pre-crisis period (Juglar 1862). In contrast, during 2009–2016, the US government decided to socialize the losses of the crisis; it adopted a repressive financial policy which dragged the recovery process over many years.[13] Decidedly, the US Federal Reserve (Fed) forced interest rates to a near-zero level and expanded the money supply with a multiple purpose: to achieve full employment of the labor force, to re-inflate stock and housing prices, and to finance record government deficits. The federal funds rate was kept at 0.1 percent, while the Fed credit, through quantitative easing, was expanded from $0.839 trillion in April 2008 to $4.449 trillion in April 2015 at an average annual rate of increase of 27 percent (Figure 8.1). This represented money creation out of thin air: about $2.5 trillion of Fed's assets were US

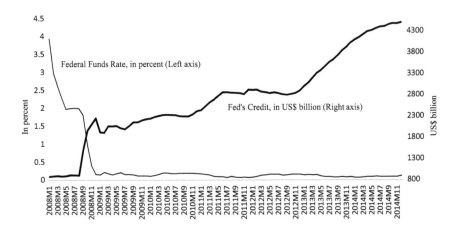

Figure 8.1 United States financial policy, 2008–2015

Treasury bonds. The holding of government bonds by the Fed represented a retirement of US public debt by paying private holders directly with *ex-nihilo* money and inscribing it as an asset on the Fed's balance sheet. The interest paid by the Treasury on Fed's bond holding will be refunded as Fed's income to the Treasury (Tolley 1957). At the same time, the government expanded its debt at a fast rate, from $10 trillion in 2008 (64 percent of GDP) to $18.2 trillion in 2014 (102 percent of GDP), or by about 10–11 percent per year. At such a high level, public debt becomes unsustainable. A rise in interest rates would afflict the budget and may be opposed by the government.

Despite low interest rates, US private, domestic credit rose at only 4–5 percent average annual rate during 2009–2015, as compared to 9–10 percent annual rate during 2001–2008. Banks became swamped with excess reserves averaging about $2,700 billion in 2015 compared to $8 billion during 2000–2008 (Figure 8.2). As predicted by the McKinnon-Shaw model, the near-zero interest rate reduced bank intermediation. Since the cost of borrowing from the Fed is near-zero, banks pay no interest on demand deposits and have no incentive for competing for deposits.

As experienced in the 1929 stock market crash, in the 1992 Japanese crisis, and in a number of other speculative episodes, low repressed interest rates lead to stock speculation and excessive leverage. Figure 8.3 illustrates the effect of financial repression on US stock prices: the S&P 500 stock index broke records, climbing constantly at about 19 percent per year during 2009M1–2015M5, and tripling from 700 to 2,100, in spite of low economic growth. Unlike dividends, which are paid from profits, capital gains are paid as an inflation tax to speculators and stockholders, a form of wealth redistribution. As predicted by McKinnon and Shaw, low interest rates displace finance to the "curb market" and lead to high market returns in this market. In search for high returns, investors and speculators divert their investment to assets and commodities markets.[14] Speculators make large gains from securities compared to tangible assets, such

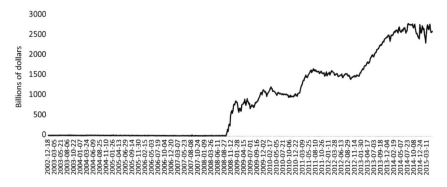

Figure 8.2 Reserve balances with the Federal Reserve Banks, 2002–2015

as housing, with the transaction cost of buying and selling securities small in comparison to that of real estate.

Some asset prices may become largely overvalued either in relation to their intrinsic value, as measured by company earnings, or in relation to goods and factors whose price or wage are slow to adjust. When securities are compared to labor cost, it would appear that they are overvalued. Labor wages have risen at a very moderate rate, while S&P 500 index was rising at 19 percent per year during 2009–2015. This implies that labor cannot save enough for retirement; its saving would buy a far-reduced quantity of real capital for retirement, and hence, its retirement income will be far smaller in real terms. A measure of overvaluation is the price/earnings ratio (P/E) (Figure 8.4). This ratio shows that it costs $27 in 2015M5 to buy a stream of $1 of earnings compared to $13 in 2009M3, implying a far lower earning rate in 2015 compared to 2009.

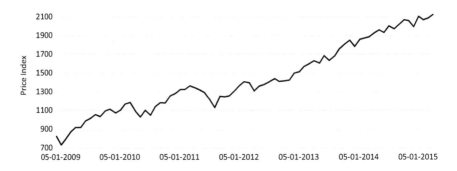

Figure 8.3 Monthly S&P 500 Stock Price Index, 2009M1–2015M5

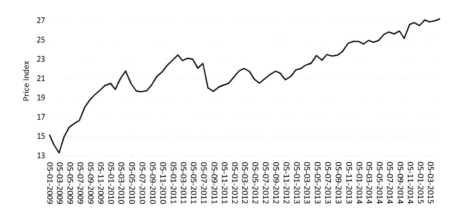

Figure 8.4 United States: price/earning ratio, 2009M1–2015M5

The fixing of interest rates by a central bank has been the most effective mean for distorting asset returns, particularly returns from fixed income securities and stocks. Return to stocks has two components: dividend and capital gain. Figure 8.5 compares yields from stocks with 10-year bond interest rate during 2009M1–2015M5. It shows that dividends were often substantially lower than interest rates. Figure 8.6 compares total returns of stocks to 10-year bond interest rate. Total stock returns exceeded the 10-year bond rate by a substantial spread, stemming from stock prices rising rapidly at about 19 percent

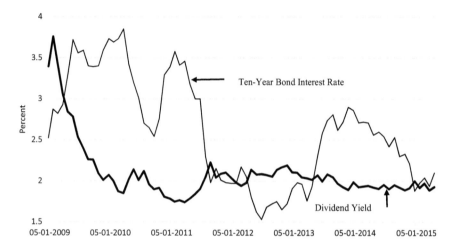

Figure 8.5 United States: stock dividend yield and 10-year bond interest rate, 2009M1–2015M5

Source: Yahoo Finance

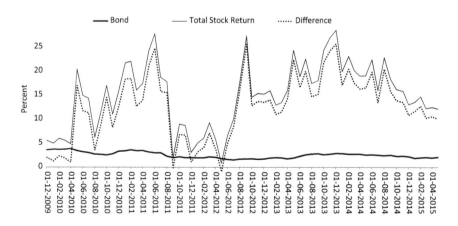

Figure 8.6 United States: stock returns versus 10-year bond interest rate, 2009M12–2015M5

a year during 2009–2015. Such distortion has penalized creditors. Assuming a creditor bought a 10-year bond with a face value of $100; a stock at $100 would rise at 19 percent per year to $569, implying a loss of value on the bond of 82 percent in real terms.

7. The futility of financial repression

McKinnon and Shaw attributed financial repression to government bureaucracy that resists relinquishing power over managing economy and exercising administrative controls. Financial repression arises from the pressure of power groups that oppose free market mechanisms and want to secure subsidies and rent; and it arises from fiscal pressure due to excessive government expenditures, which makes further taxation politically infeasible.[15] Hence, financial repression becomes the most appealing policy for governments, when all that is required is printing money and spending it (Cagan 1956).

A main foundation of financial repression is the full employment mandate of the central bank. The principle is that the higher the financial repression, the closer to full employment, and the greater prosperity. Government interference in labor markets leads to a freezing of a vital force for growth and to impoverishment. The labor market should be the market with utmost flexibility. Instead, modern governments oppose downward price and wage adjustment called deflation, regardless of the level of unemployment. Pigou argued that all markets adjust rapidly; unemployment would be short-lived if wages were to adjust in relation to the size of the unemployment. Robbins (1934) and von Mises (1953) claimed that employment opportunities were too large because there were huge human needs that were not yet satisfied in food, housing, clothing, medical, education, etc. All what was needed for fuller employment was wage flexibility.

Mises contended that increasing the debt of borrowers may not achieve the equilibrium in the labor market. Higher debt may mean forced saving, which means borrowers' demands crowding out non-borrowers' demands, leading to a negligible effect on output and employment. As in any market, the latter may be attained with wage flexibility and labor mobility. Anderson (1945) meticulously documented that recovery and full employment were very fast without government money creation and were slow with government intervention. Government interference with the labor market prevents mobility and retraining, and may undermine work ethics and efficiency. It inflicts two types of social losses: there is the forgone output that is lost when labor refuses employment at less than the government set wage, and there is the cost of unemployment benefits that are supplemented with other welfare payments. Hence, only money printing remains a way for economic adjustment. Inflation lowers real wages and encourages employers to hire at the government dictated wage.

Henry Simons (1947), maintained that sound money and price stability were essential for growth and employment. In their absence, there is little scope for sound planning and calculations, and thus an investor faces high uncertainty in respect to stocks prices, commodities prices, and exchange rates. With interest rates forced at near-zero bound, savings will be consumed, and more forced saving is needed to support investment. With distorted capital markets, low return projects will be selected and mal-investment will increase. Eventually, capital consumption in leading countries will depress world economic growth. The stock prices will continue to climb, fueled by liquidity, and stock returns will continue to far exceed fixed income securities by a significant margin. Eventually, as in previous stock booms, stock prices may reach a tipping point at which they crash, causing disastrous financial disorders.

8. Conclusions

Financial repression in form of near-zero interest rates has been enforced since 2008 by the US Federal Reserve, the European Central Bank, the Bank of Japan, etc. with a view to increase debt and restore full employment and prosperity. This policy seems to be endless. It showered massive free wealth to a group of beneficiaries at the expense of a group of losers. Becoming rich through enterprise is fully legitimate: becoming rich through financial repression is a form of government's injustice. Sharia opposes such injustice; it opposes using inflationary policy and money as a policy tool, the government blocking competition in labor and capital markets, and setting prices in these vital markets. Government-blocking free markets violates the natural attribution of a government and inflicts losses to the economy.

Supporters of financial repression oppose market-determined interest rates, wages, and prices, and oppose market adjustment through deflation or high interest rates. The interest rate is a crucial price in the economic system, and forcing it below its equilibrium rate has introduced costly distortions into the markets and played havoc with the economy as in a number of earlier episodes. Financial liberalization in the 1990s in the United States did not free the most important financial variable, the interest rate; it continued to be administered as opposed to market set, resulting in the misallocation of valuable resources away from physical projects with the highest return. Financial repression has caused distortions in asset returns and in income and wealth distribution. It has transferred wealth to speculators and borrowers. With near-zero interest rates, capital is consumed and low-return projects appear profitable, resources are misallocated, savings are consumed, and the growth of world economy suffers: these are all fallouts that are manifestations of governments' repressive policies. Earlier episodes during 1980–1982 and pre-twentieth century demonstrated that high interest rates of 20–25 percent pulled the economy quickly from stagnation and ushered a period of high growth. McKinnon and Shaw condemned financial repression and endorsed Friedman's rule of optimum money either through remuneration of deposits or holding money supply unchanged. At levels exceeding sustainable ratios, public and private debt in major countries will require more inflation and financial repression. While economists have focused on the difference between money "market" rates and "administered" rates as the measure of financial repression, the much higher return on the best available physical investments is the appropriate measure of the opportunity cost of capital (not the money market rate) with a much larger attendant cost associated with repression.

Notes

1 McKinsey Global Institute, March 23, 2015.
2 This mandate is based on Keynes's theory which rejected Say's law of markets; the latter postulated that the economy had full automatism to re-establish full employment of labor and rejected general over-production, i.e., demand failure; Keynes denied such automatism, postulated demand failure, and urged government intervention to attain full employment of labor.
3 Ricardo maintained: "The interest rate on money is not regulated by the rate at which the bank will lend, whether 5, 4, or 3 percent, but by the rate of profit, which can be made by the employment of capital, and which is totally independent of the quantity or of the value of money. Whether a bank lent one million, ten million, or a hundred millions, they would not permanently alter the market rate of interest; they would alter only the value of money, which they thus issued. In one case, ten or twenty times more money might be required to carry on the same business than what might be required in the other" (P. 246).
4 If the monetary base remains fixed, interest rates may explode as they did during 1979–1982 when the US Federal Reserve (Fed) was controlling the reserves of the banking system.
5 In conventional finance, the rate of return on stocks is influenced by speculative loans as shown in stock booms. For instance, the marginal product of capital may be 4 percent per year; however, the return on stocks may be 22 percent per year. Speculation sustained by low interest rates and abundant credit weakens the relation between equity returns and marginal product of capital (Holden 1907). Speculators gain enormously from abundant credit. In a Sharia model, equity returns cannot be distorted by credit and interest rates, and therefore equity markets instability becomes unlikely.
6 When the money rate falls below the profit rate, banks considerably expand debt, triggering inflation. When real savings becomes insufficient, prices of materials becomes too high; the profit rate falls below the money rate and debt default and bankruptcy result (Carroll 1965).
7 The output of physical capital in terms of a homogenous commodity is denoted by Y. The marginal rate of return of capital is computed as $r_K = \Delta Y / \Delta K$.
8 Undoubtedly, money yields non-pecuniary services, not directly observable, in the form of simplifying the transaction cost, and providing liquidity and security against unforeseen emergency needs. An economy without money may collapse. While returns on physical capital and financial assets such as stocks and bonds are directly observable from market data, services of money are intangible, and cannot be measured directly. The liquidity preference approach measured marginal return on money by its opportunity cost, which was the nominal money interest rate i.
9 In a steady-state growth with money-income elasticity $\varepsilon_{my} = \dfrac{\Delta m / m}{\Delta Y / Y}$ equal to 1, where Y is real income, the rates of nominal money supply and real income growth would be equal to maintain a constant price level.
10 Phelps (1965) stated that "If there exists a golden-age growth path on which the social net rate of return to investment equals the rate of growth (hence, in one class of models, the fraction of output saved equals the capital elasticity of output) or, in market terms,

a golden-age path on which the competitive interest rate equals the growth rate and hence gross investment equals the gross competitive earnings of capital-then this golden age produces a path of consumption which is uniformly higher than the consumption path associated with any other golden age" (P. 793).

11 Pigou's argument is not shared by views that oppose deflation which may cause fall in profits and debt failure.

12 In Pigou's theory, assume that 100 workers are employed at a wage rate of $10. The wage bill is $1,000. Let the wage rate drop to $8. The number of employed workers rises to 125, and the nominal wage bill remains at $1,000 as long as money supply is not reduced.

13 Chodorov (1954) stressed that pre-1913 financial crises in the United States were short-lived because the Federal Government had no constitutional power to interfere in the economy. The Great Depression 1929–1939 was too long-lived because the Federal Government acquired power to interfere in the economy.

14 Reinhart et al. (2011) showed that "hot" money sought investment in emerging capital markets, leading many countries to re-introduce capital controls and prevent an appreciation of their respective currencies.

15 Had government spending being productive, economic growth would be very high. However, the excessive unproductive spending was often coupled with economic stagnation.

References

Anderson, B., 1945, "The Road Back to Full Employment," in Homan, P. and Machlup, F. (eds.). *Financing American Prosperity*, New York: Twentieth Century Fund, pp. 25–28.

Askari, H., Krichene, N., and Mirakhor, A., 2014, "On the Stability of an Islamic Financial System," *PSL Quarterly Review*, 67 (269): 131–67.

Bohm-Bawerk, E., 1888, *The Positive Theory of Capital*, London: Palgrave Macmillan.

Cagan, P., 1956, "The Monetary Dynamics of Hyperinflation," in Friedman, M. (ed.). *Studies in the Quantity Theory of Money*, Chicago: University of Chicago Press.

Carroll, C. H., 1965, *Organization of Debt Into Currency and Other Papers*, Princeton, NJ: D. Van Nostrand.

Chodorov, F., 1954, *The Income Tax: Root of All Evil*, New York: The Devin-Adair Company.

Fisher, F., 1907, *The Rate of Interest, Its Nature, Determination, and Relation to Economic Phenomena*, New York: Palgrave Macmillan.

Fisher, F., 1933, "The Debt-Deflation Theory of Great Depressions," *Econometrica*, 1(4): 337–357.

Friedman, M., 1969, "The Optimum Quantity of Money," in Friedman, M. (ed.). *The Optimum Quantity of Money and Other Essays*, Chicago: Aldine Publishing Company.

Hicks, J. R., 1937, "Mr. Keynes and the Classics"; A Suggested Interpretation," *Econometrica*, 5(2): 147–159.

Holden, E. H., 1907, *Lecture on the Depreciation of Securities in Relation to Gold*, London: Blades, East & Blades.

Juglar, C., 1862, *Des Crises Commerciales et leur Retour Periodique en France, en Angleterre, et aux Etats Unis*, Paris: Guillaumin.

Keynes, J. M., 1936, *The General Theory of Employment, Interest and Money*, London: Palgrave Macmillan.

Labordere, M., 1908, "Autour de la Crise Americaine de 1907," *La Revue de Paris*, Paris: Paul Brodard.

Locke, John, 1691, *Some Considerations on the Consequences of the Lowering of Interest and the Raising of the Value of Money*, The Works of John Locke, 1824, London: C. Balwin, Printer.

McKinnon, R., 1973, *Money and Capital in Economic Development*, Washington, DC: Brookings Institution.

Metzler, L., 1951, "Wealth, Saving, and the Rate of Interest," *Journal of Political Economy*, 59(2), 93–116.

Mirakhor, A., 1993, "Equilibrium in a Non-Interest Open Economy," *Journal of King Abdulaziz University: Islamic Economics*, 5(1): 3–23.

Patinkin, D., 1948, "Price Flexibility and Full Employment," *American Economic Review*, XXXVIII: 543–564.

Phelps, E., 1965, "Second Essay on the Golden Rule of Accumulation," *The American Economic Review*, 55(4): 793–814.

Pigou, A. C., 1943, "The Classical Stationary State," *Economic Journal*, LIII: 342–351.

Reinhart, C. M., Kirkegaard, J. F., Sbrancia, M. B., 2011, *Financial Repression Redux*, Finance and Development, June.

Ricardo, D., 1817, *On the Principles of Political Economy and Taxation*, London: John Murray.

Robbins, L., 1934, *The Great Depression*, New York: Books for Library Press.

Shaw, E., 1973, *Financial Deepening in Economic Development*, Oxford: Oxford University Press.

Simons, H., 1947, *Economic Policy for a Free Society*, Chicago: The University of Chicago Press.

Smith, A., 1776, *An Inquiry Into the Nature and Causes of the Wealth of Nations*, London: Methuen and Co., Ltd., ed. Edwin Cannan, 1904, Fifth Edition.

Thornton, H., 1802, *An Inquiry Into the Nature and Effect of Paper Credit in Great Britain*, New York: Augustus M. Kelley.

Tobin, J., 1965, "Money and Economic Growth," *Econometrica*, 33(4): 671–684.

Tobin, J., 1969, "A General Equilibrium Approach to Monetary Theory," *Journal of Money, Credit, and Banking,* 1(1): 15–29.

Tolley, G. S., 1957, "Providing for the Growth of the Money Supply," *Journal of Political Economy*, 65(6): 465–485.

Von Mises, L., 1953, *The Theory of Money and Credit*, New Haven: Yale University Press.

Wicksell, K., 1898, *Interest and Prices*, New York: Sentry Press.

9 Sharia banking and capital markets sector

1. Introduction

A Sharia model bans interest (Riba)-based debt; this interdiction has far-reaching implications with respect to the nature of money and banking. More specifically, any form of debt-based money, i.e., money in form of banknotes or deposits issued against an interest-based loan is precluded. The interdiction of interest implies that money cannot be an interest-paying debt; it has necessarily to be a non-interest paying asset. This money was gold and silver; presently, government currency. Paper (i.e., banknotes) or deposits (scriptural money) issued against metallic money are fully Sharia-compliant. The prohibition of interest implies that no individual or government is allowed to contract interest-paying debt. Hence, interest-based debt is prohibited at the level of individuals as well as the government. The government should have neither a local nor a foreign interest-paying debt. A fundamental condition for establishing a stable banking system is the abolishment of fractional reserve banking, i.e., debt money, in favor of 100 percent reserve banking. This latter system was advanced by a number of authors: e.g., David Hume (1752), William Gouge (1833), Amasa Walker (1873), C. H. Carrol (1965), F. Soddy (1934), the authors of the Chicago Plan (1933),[1] I. Fisher (1936), Mises (1953), Rothbard (1962, 2008), Allais (1999), and de Soto (2011). These authors proposed, in parallel to 100 percent depository banks, that investment banks specialize in intermediating between savers and investors.

Sharia model promotes risk-sharing investment banking, which is a regular trade, based on profit, and involves no interest contracts (Askari et al. 2012). This type of banking has many favorable properties. It attracts considerable saving and deepens financial intermediation since the rate of return would be far higher than the interest rate on deposits (Mirakhor 2010). Moreover, the risk of bank failure is minimal since interest-based debt is absent, and values of liabilities are equal to that of assets. Risk-sharing banks attract long-term capital needed for long-term projects in agriculture, industry, and commerce. The development of investment banking has necessarily to be accompanied by a stock market to provide liquidity for investors and to raise capital for investment projects. This chapter covers:

- On the necessity of financial intermediation
- The defects of the fractional reserve banking
- Nature of Islamic banking
- Risk sharing: a main principle of Sharia finance
- Capital markets as a pillar of Islamic finance
- On the stability of conventional and Islamic stock markets
- Toward a regulatory framework conducive to Islamic finance

2. On the necessity of financial intermediation

The development of financial institutions and markets is an inherent pillar for economic growth. Financial institutions fulfill two essential functions: settle payments within and across countries, and mobilize saving to borrowers or investors. The act of saving does not ensure investment. Saving may remain idle if it is not deployed via financial institutions. Generally, savers do not know investors and the type of projects financed by their saving.[2] Financial institutions, by intermediating between savers and investors, pooling small savings into a large reserve, reduce significantly the risk for savers as well as the transactions cost of placing savings, and contribute to increase both the rate of saving and investment in the economy. Financial intermediation, by increasing investible funds, reduces money capital cost for entrepreneurs and therefore raises investment in the economy.

There is an undeniable association between the level of wealth accumulation and the depth of financial intermediation.[3] Nowadays, in developing countries, the financial infrastructure is very shallow; per capita income is still low, and, in some countries, 30–40 percent of the population live below the poverty norm. The development of financial institutions is an essential condition for their economic growth. Governments in most developing countries paid little attention to the development of the financial sector, including capital markets. The lack of financial infrastructure continues to impede growth and employment in these countries.

Financial sector development has lagged in many countries, simply because of the lack of a legislation and regulatory framework that addresses the establishment of financial institutions. In many countries, the regulatory and legislative framework dates back many decades, is restrictive, suffers inertia, and has not been updated to the important financial innovations or the needs of the country. The capital requirements for creating a financial institution could be prohibitive and are not tailored to the local needs of small communities, such as rural and farming villages. In many developing countries, only a few banks were permitted to operate and were allowed special privileges. In these countries, rural communities may be deprived from financial services, unless a bank establishes local subsidiaries that attend to a small community. In the United

States and the United Kingdom, legislation was so easy and flexible that most of the small communities during the 18th–19th centuries had their local banks which served both local creditors and borrowers; some of these banks were called country banks.

3. The defects of the fractional reserve banking

The basic truth about fractional banking was that loans created deposits and not deposits which created loans. This truth has been stressed by eminent bankers such as Thornton (1802) and Holden (1907), and writers such as Gouge (1833), Carroll (1965), and Tobin (1963). When a bank makes a loan, the loan becomes instantly a deposit. A bank did not wait until savers deposited money to issue loans. A bank issued a loan when it deemed the loan was profitable and the credit risk was tolerable.[4] Most of the deposits at a bank came from its loan issuance as well as the loans' issuance of other banks. The expansion of bank credit was far in excess of bank reserves, which led to recurrent bank runs and financial failures.

The typical model of deposit multiplication is that of the credit multiplier. Let a depositor Z make a deposit of $100 in his checking account at Bank A. Let the reserve requirement be 5 percent. Then the fractional reserve banking theoretically increases deposits to $2,000. In case Z draws his money, the money supply implodes. Fractional reserve banking needs a central bank, a last resort lender, to provide liquidity to prevent a drastic drop in money supply and bank failures (Bagehot 1873). Without a central bank and money paper, fractional reserve banking cannot survive on its own. These were nineteenth-century stylized facts of recurrent bank failures.

Table 9.1 portrays the leverage power of fractional reserve banking, it describes the nature of fractional banking. Through loans, the banking system expanded money supply to $20,000 on the basis that reserves equal to $1,000; the credit multiplier is 20.[5] When bank runs occurred, banks had only $1,000 to pay depositors for $20,000. Often, banks had to suspend payments of reserve money.

Fractional reserve banking has defects that contradict Sharia. It is an interest-based banking; it evolved into an inconvertible paper money, and needed the support of a central bank. The latter has to maintain an increasing monetary base to prevent bank failures. A large part of the money supply, i.e., the bank money, has to pay interest to banks. This fact contradicts Sharia where money is

Table 9.1 Balance sheet of fractional reserve banking

Assets		Liabilities	
Reserves	$1,000	Deposits	$20,000
Loans and securities	$19,000		
Total	$20,000	Total	$20,000

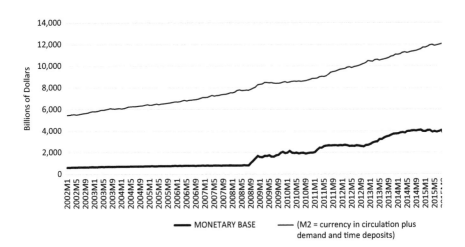

Figure 9.1 United States money creation, 2002M1–2015M9 (in billions of US dollars)

Source: IMF

currency that does not pay interest. Figure 9.1 is valid for any country. It shows that the money base and the money supply are constantly increasing over time. If the money base remains constant or decreases, banks would fail. In almost every country, debt money has been increasing endlessly often at rates that exceed real GDP growth. In many countries, money supply, measured by M2 (currency plus deposits), may rise at two-digit rates. The basis this increase is debt. Simons (1948) stated that:

> We have reached a situation where private-bank credit represents all but a small fraction of our total effective circulation medium. . . . Thus the State has forced the free-enterprise system, almost from the beginning, to live with a monetary system as bad as could well be devised.
>
> (P. 55)

Figure 9.2 shows that inflation is an inherent to fractional reserve banking. Inflation is a tax that unduly penalizes workers, pensioners, and creditors in favor of debtors and speculators.

Sharia is incompatible with fractional reserve banking. This system is inherently unstable; banks have the power to create money out of thin air and earn an income on a real capital that it is not possessed by themselves or by the depositors. Fractional reserve money, called debt money, can only keep rising through credit multiplication to validate new price and wage increases and to pay for the interest rate. It cannot stabilize or decline; in such an event, interest cannot be paid, and the whole banking system collapses. The fractional reserve system cannot survive on its own; it needs a central bank to provide it with

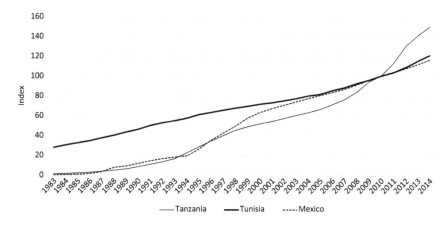

Figure 9.2 Consumer Price Indices in Mexico, Tanzania, and Tunisia, 1983–2014

constant liquidity. Without a central bank, it collapses. It is inflationist; inflation is a form of social injustice and alters the value of contracts and penalizes fixed income recipients.

Gouge (1833) deemed fractional reserve banking as a malum per se. It caused repeated financial crises and had no cure. Debt money caused economies to navigate from booms to recessions (Juglar 1862); it evicted the gold standard.[6] In the pursuit of income from interest on loans, banks kept issuing debt money, in multiple of their reserves, until they reach a financial crisis. By its nature, debt money calls for more debt to provide for rapidly rising prices, replace repaid debt, and pay interest. When debt reaches a high level in relation to income and becomes unsustainable, a severe financial crisis may occur and may cause a debt contraction. Therefore, a drop in debt money is followed by a severe economic and financial disorders.[7] To establish a stable banking system, Simons (1948) recommended to abolish the fractional reserve banking, i.e., debt money, in favor of 100 percent reserve banking:

> Abolition of private deposit banking on the basis of fractional reserves. . . . Legislation requiring that all institutions which maintain deposit liabilities and/or provide checking facilities (or any substitute therefore) shall maintain reserves of 100% in cash and deposits with the Federal Reserve Banks.
>
> (P. 57)

4. Nature of Islamic banking

A fundamental regulation for establishing a Sharia-compliant banking system is to abolish interest, and consequently its corresponding banking, which is the fractional reserve banking. This regulation establishes a two-tier banking system: (i) a 100 percent reserve banking system for safekeeping and payments; and (ii) a non-interest risk-sharing banking system. Simons (1948) stated that:

> The proposals with reference to banking contemplate displacement of existing deposit banks by a least two distinct types of institutions. First, there would be deposits banks which, maintaining 100 per cent reserves, simply could not fail, so far as depositors are concerned, and could not create or destroy money. These institutions would accept deposits just as warehouses accept goods. Their income would be derived exclusively from service charges, perhaps merely from moderate charges for the transfer of funds by check or draft. A second type of institutions, substantially in the form of investment trust, would perform the lending functions of existing banks. Such companies would obtain funds for lending by sale of their own stock; and their ability to make loans would be limited by the amounts of funds so obtained. Various types of agencies, for bringing together would-be borrowers and lenders, would of course appear. In other words, short-term lending would be managed in much the same way as long-term lending; and the creation and destruction of effective circulation medium by private institutions would be impossible.
>
> (PP. 64–65)

In a 100 percent reserve banking system money is not related to debt obligations; a bank cannot create or destroy money.[8] The 100 percent reserve banking has many advantages. In essence, banks collect real savings and make it available to borrowers and investors. There is no unbacked expansion of money supply followed by a contraction detrimental to growth and employment. There are no frequent bank failures and losses suffered by depositors. There is no unjust wealth redistribution via fictitious credit in favor of borrowers and speculators. Last, but not least, debt money has to pay interest; it is therefore costly to use: if interest cannot be paid, debt money falls.

In Islamic finance, money has to be currency and not bank money that pays interest. Banks should not be allowed to create money. Table 9.2 describes the balance sheet of Sharia depository banking.

Risk-sharing investment banking is another main component of Islamic banking. Investment banks do not emit or destroy money. They only collect domestic and foreign savings, which they invest in productive projects or in financial securities such as stocks or capital market funds. Depositors hold investment accounts. The nominal value of the deposits in these accounts is not guaranteed. Depositors share in the profits and losses as well as in capital gains and losses. The investment banking complies with Sharia modes of financing such as *Murabaha, Mudaraba, Ijara, Bai Salam, Lease, Istisna*, or other risk-sharing modes. It finances investments of different maturities such as short-term, medium-term, and long-term investment with funds that match the maturities of assets. Commercial credit could be easily financed through Sharia modes. For

Table 9.2 Balance sheet of Sharia depository banks

Assets		Liabilities	
Reserves	$500	Deposits	$500
Total	$500	Total	$500

Table 9.3 Balance sheet of Islamic investment banking

Assets		Liabilities	
Reserves at depository banks	$500	Investment accounts	$8,000
Cash in vaults	$200		
Investment (equities, *Sukuk, Bai Salam, Istisna, Murabaha, Mudaraba, Ijara, Istisna, Bai Salam, Leasing, etc.*)	$7,300		
Total	$8,000		$8,000

instance, working capital of a company may be financed through a Musharaka mode; the Islamic investment bank provides the working capital based on a predetermined ratio in ex-post profits. Hence, the bank is repaid its money plus a share of the profits at the end of production period. In the same vein, car loans and housing loans could be easily financed through Sharia modes. Table 9.3 describes the balance sheet of investment banking.

A two-tier banking system with 100 percent reserve banking and risk-sharing investment banking was advocated by many writers in the past. Simons (1948) proposed that nothing would be circulated but "pure assets" and "pure money," rather than "near moneys" and other precarious forms of short-term instruments that were responsible for financial crises. Simons advocated non-interest-bearing equity banking. He also opposed the payment of interest on money, demand deposits, and savings.

5. Risk sharing: a main principle of Sharia finance

Interest and interest-based debt have been forbidden in all divine revelations. Quran and Sunna explicitly forbid interest-based transactions. For instance, Quran:Verse 2:275, Allah SWT states that:

> they say that indeed *al-Bay'* [trade] is like *al-Riba* [interest-based debt contract]. But Allah has permitted *al-Bay'* and has forbidden *al-Riba*.

This verse constitutes a pillar of Islamic finance and has many implications on the structure of banking and capital markets. Hence, a capitalist is forbidden to make interest-based loans and earn interest income. Likewise, a borrower cannot contract interest-based debt. A capitalist has to engage in non–interest finance and bear the risk of his investment. He may invest his money jointly with other capitalists and share the risk of the joint investment. A borrower can only contract non–interest debt, or undertake Islamic modes of financing. If a borrower is a corporation, it may issue shares or *sukuks* instead of interest-bearing debt. Entrepreneurs individually or jointly combine their material and human wealth and share the risk of their business. This form of organization is known as risk taking and risk sharing. In a debt contract, the capitalist bears no enterprise risk; the borrower bears the risk of the business. If his business fails, the borrower is still legally obligated to pay his debt.

Risk sharing has been a dominant organization of economic activity whereby associates find it profitable to gather resources, be they entrepreneurial, financial, technical, or other forms of resources, as opposed to operating individually. It constitutes a main foundation of modern corporations, banks, and other financial institutions, which are often joint-stocks organizations. Participants in a risk-sharing enterprise expect that the combination of larger human and material resources would yield higher output and larger profits than operating separately. Capitalism is essentially based on risk sharing. Most firms, be they small, medium, or large, are jointly owned and are founded on the risk-sharing principle. In essence, this principle means that the net income of the enterprise is known only ex-post and is subject to many risks and contingencies. Associates in a business have contractual arrangements that describe their respective contribution, including financing, managerial and technical contributions as well as the distribution of the profits from the business.

The principle of risk sharing is a foundation of Islamic banking. Depositors hold accounts in banks or investment funds and share the risk of the projects in which their saving is invested. The value of their shares is not guaranteed, and the profits or losses from their equity shares are known only ex-post.

6. Capital markets as a pillar of Islamic finance

The development of Islamic finance should emphasize, besides the promotion of investment banking, the development of capital markets. An economy with a banking component only, and without a capital market, would not be able to deepen financial intermediation; its rate of saving and investment would remain constrained by a suboptimal financial intermediation. Banks and capital markets fulfilled different functions, faced different regulations, and contributed differently to financial intermediation. Banks provided essentially short-term credit to business. They offered limited scope for savers, especially high-wealth investors, pension funds, and insurance companies, in terms of risks and placement opportunities. In view of the frequent bank failures, savers had little incentive to place their savings with banks and tended to acquire financial assets secured by real property where the risk of loss is mitigated compared to loss of deposits. Banks offered a limited scope for entrepreneurs in raising long-term capital.

Large projects with considerable indivisibilities required large money capital to be fixed for a long period. Banks had short-term resources and faced daily large drawings and could not freeze these resources in long-term loans without becoming insolvent. Regulations would prevent them from illiquidity risks. Banks had to be liquid enough to face drawings by borrowers as well as depositors. Capital markets offered both savers and entrepreneurs the appropriate channels for satisfying their respective needs for diversified investment opportunities and for a long-term capital to be fixed in real assets such as buildings, machinery, infrastructure, etc. Large projects required fixed capital and had to be financed through the capital markets. Moreover, equity financing and risk sharing may be more appealing to entrepreneurs in relation to debt, where interest cost starts upon signing the loans or issuing the bonds while the projects starts to generate cash flow only after several years. However, in equity financing, the project does not incur any interest cost during its gestation period which could last several years. Moreover, dividends are residual, depending on the profitability of the project while interest payments are obligatory.

6.1 Stock market: a risk sharing and intermediation institution

Stock markets, a main component of capital markets, essentially involve non-interest-based financing and should constitute a priority area in a strategy for developing Islamic finance. They offer the most sophisticated market-based risk-sharing mechanism (Brav et al. 2002). These markets were fully advantageous for governments and corporations seeking external funding. For savers, especially high net worth savers such as pension funds, in search for investment outlets with different risk profile, they offered less risk compared to the high risk of losing bank deposits. Their main functions were to mobilize savings, finance large-scale and long-term investment, provide liquidity for securities' holders, allocate risk among risk averters and risk-takers, and diversify portfolios. Banks were not able to extend loans to large projects in process of formation such as a railroad project. These projects exceeded their capacity to lend. Moreover, these long-term projects generated no cash flow during their construction period which extended over many years and could not pay interest cost during this period. This aspect would not satisfy a bank loan which had to generate interest immediately after its signing. Hence, for large-scale projects that fell outside of bank financing, it was necessary to resort to direct financing through the stock markets where new issues of stocks could be floated. Hence, a stock market was a historical necessity to finance large-scale projects involving considerable indivisibilities and requiring a long period for their gestation; these projects were not qualified for financing by commercial banks. Stock markets relieved the financing constraint for entrepreneurs who needed long-term money capital and could not pay interest during the project construction. Their development enabled corporations to mobilize saving, invest in large projects that featured considerable indivisibilities, and thus increase capital and growth.

Countries that adopted a laissez-faire policy in regard to their securities markets and allowed an unrestrained development of these markets that benefited considerably in terms of capital accumulation and economic growth. The industrialization of the United Kingdom, the United States, France, etc. since early seventeenth century would not have been possible without supporting stock markets. There was a close relation between economic growth and the size of stock markets. Countries with growing and advancing stock markets were also countries that were advancing in industrialization, infrastructure, and economic growth. Stock markets financed large projects in agriculture, mining, industry, commerce, utilities, transport, and contributed significantly to capital accumulation and growth.

Countries that lagged in the development of capital markets were not able to industrialize and advance in economic development. Their finance infrastructure remained too shallow. Their banking sector was too small, confined essentially to short-term financing, and therefore long-term capital mobilization was not helped by supportive stock markets.

Stock markets evolved over time in terms of their size, diversity, institutions, regulation, information technology, settlement, and recording of transactions. Nowadays, stock markets are highly advanced; they offer investment opportunities to a highly varied class of investors, encompassing households, banks, corporations, pension funds, insurance companies, Trust companies, wealth management funds, etc. New issues are floated by corporations in different fields such as mining, industry, real estate, and commerce.

Stock markets fulfill many important functions; they raise sizeable equity capital for long-term projects, allocate risks, and provide liquidity for securities holders. They have some advantages in relation to holding real assets such as commodities or real estate, since the cost of holding stocks is almost negligible, while commodities require storage cost and real estate requires a maintenance cost. The transaction costs for selling and buying stocks is very low compared to transaction costs in commodities and real estate. Promotors of important projects such as maritime fleet, industrial projects, infrastructure, and utilities were able to raise long-term capital for their projects through shares' subscriptions. Contrary to debt, stocks have no maturity and no redemption obligation; they are residual claims on a corporation net income, i.e., they have no contractual positive rate of return. Promotors of large projects would be severely restrained by lack of financing in the absence of stock markets. Very few entrepreneurs, if any, could mount with their own money capital or even bank borrowing, corporations in maritime building and shipping, airline industry, car manufacturing, steel making, etc. These corporations had to be mounted as joint-stock companies with shares subscribed directly by shareholders or floated on the stock markets.

Stock markets allow an allocation of risk and portfolio diversification. Buyers of stocks belong to different risk classes and face different portfolio diversification opportunities. Some buyers have small portfolios and are interested in safe returns; they prefer to hold blue-chip securities of long-established and solid corporations. Other buyers, such as private equity funds and venture capital funds, hedge funds, unit trust funds, wealth management companies may have important funds, and may diversify their portfolio by buying riskier securities that promise high payoffs or even providing venture capital for start-up companies which could be later sold on the stock markets.

One of the most attractive feature of stocks markets is their provision of liquidity for shareholders. Holders of financial assets place considerable value on being able to convert those assets into cash in a short period of time without substantial reduction in price solely because of the need to sell and with a small transaction cost. The stock market makes it possible for the holder of securities to have liquidity based on marketability, while it enables issuers to sell financial liabilities of a long maturity, effectively infinite, for shares. In other words, the market intermediates between the desires of asset holders for liquidity and of issuers for fixed long-term funds. Although securities are often property titles to fixed long-term capital, the holder of this security may always sell it at any time for cash to an anonymous buyer via a brokerage firm. Holders of securities may be temporary holders who invest their surplus cash in stocks until they need it for their own business operations. Often, investors in stocks try to hold stocks which they can liquidate without a loss in price and with a minimum transaction cost. Securities of ailing enterprises become illiquid and could be easily lost. The selling and buying of stocks does not affect the corporation that has issued these stocks. The operation amount to ceding of ownership from one shareholder to another. Stock markets could attract considerable liquidity and become too speculative. In such circumstances, stocks are bid up, and holders of securities could reap considerable capital gains when they sell their stocks for cash. Brokers and speculators afford considerable liquidity for the stock market; a seller in need of liquidity can always sell his stocks to these two categories of agents, however at a market price that clear the demand and supply for the shares to be sold. In order to promote liquidity, stock market regulation may put ceiling on brokerage fees in order to reduce transaction costs and increase turnovers. Most government policies aim at improving liquidity and reducing the risk and cost of transactions in the secondary market.

Highly developed and vibrant stock markets are essential for the financial infrastructure development. Not only individuals and firms benefit from a well-organized stock market that offers risk sharing opportunities, but countries too can benefit from risk sharing with one another. Hence, in international risk sharing, there are gains to be made by countries when they trade in each other's securities. Such was a mode of financing in the nineteenth century when American companies floated shares in the United Kingdom capital markets. With an advanced stock market, venture capitalists can recover their capital investment in a project through initial public offering thus enabling quicker rollover of venture capital to finance more frequently other productive real sector projects.

While vibrant stock markets are recommended, stock markets may be characterized by low investor participation. Low participation of the general public may stem from lack of trust in stock markets (Guiso et al. 2005). In addition, high transaction costs – namely search and information costs as well as high contract enforcement cost – are key factors hindering stock market participation. Conditions for wider participation in the stock market have been analyzed in the literature. Allen and Gale (2007) deemed that a deep and active stock market requires that enforcement and information costs be significantly reduced to promote fuller participation in the market. Lucas (1990) proposed the elimination of capital gains tax as a way to promote investment through stock markets stating that neither capital gains nor any of the income from capital should be taxed at all.

6.2 Islamic funds, key capital market institutions

Asset management funds are a key component of capital markets. Funds are entities that intermediate between savers and investors. They collect savings and invest them in financial or real assets. They are managed by fund managers. Islamic funds have risen in number and size and have become a conduit for mobilizing savings and providing capital for mortgages, corporations, and governments. This rise owes to a deliberate strategy of governments in many countries to develop Islamic finance. Accordingly, the regulatory framework has been strengthened to regulate Islamic investment funds, protect investors, and ensure their Sharia compliance. In addition, Islamic products are Sharia-compliant and attract both Muslim and non-Muslim investors, essentially because of their risk-return profile. More specifically, Islamic products are not interest based; they are asset based and are backed by ownership of income yielding real and financial assets. In this respect, Islamic investment funds own income-generating securities and share in risk; they do not hold interest-based securities.

Islamic investment funds have risen in terms of demand and supply. On the supply side, large financial institutions in Islamic markets such as Deutsche Bank, Citigroup, HSBC, UBS, and Standard Chartered have adapted their existing asset management services to the needs of Muslim and non-Muslim investors. Accordingly, financial institutions have stressed marketability, innovation, and adaptation of asset management funds to both liquidity needs and risk-return preferences of investors. Banks and investment companies in many countries have been active in establishing Islamic funds. They have targeted classes of investors, promoted marketability and trust in their funds. The increasing rise of Islamic funds has been supported by an increasing supply of Sharia-compliant securities. In the *sukuks'* market, governments, corporations, and mortgage institutions emit *sukuks*, instead of bonds, for financing investment, housing and infrastructure projects. Consequently, sukuk issuance has risen in number and volume. In the equity markets, Sharia-compliant stocks are identified separately from other stocks. The cost and fees of Islamic funds have been reduced to competitive levels.

On the demand side, small investors, institutional investors, and sovereign funds have increasing demand for Sharia-compliant finance. Hence, savings have been diverted from conventional banking and funds to Islamic funds. The latter Islamic funds satisfy investors' retirement planning, liquidity needs, risk-return profiles, and tax concerns. Investors may participate in standardized funds, such as Islamic mutual funds, which are long funds, as well as in funds adapted to their specific needs, such as hedge funds, which are speculative long/short funds. Small investors interested in retirement savings may participate in safer and longer-term mutual funds. Investors interested in high return and risky securities may hold shares in private equity and venture capital funds or hedge funds. Treasurers who want to place cash temporarily may be satisfied by Islamic money market funds.[9]

6.3 Private equity and venture capital funds

Private equity (PE) funds and venture capital (VC) funds are important intermediation institutions of capital markets. The principle of these funds is the same: each fund raises risk capital and invests it in risky projects with the expectation of obtaining return from their investment. Some funds have an exit mechanism to sell the project when the project becomes a profitable business.

Private equity fund, owned by a private equity firm, is defined as a fund that raises capital from savers, institutional investors, sovereign wealth funds, and other shareholders of the fund, both domestically and internationally, which funds are destined to launch new companies, or buy shares in existing companies. For instance, the Islamic Development Bank, in cooperation with the government of Indonesia, has launched a private equity fund to finance projects in infrastructure. An important function of a private equity fund is to provide money capital for new projects. Funds in an equity fund are committed for a period between three to ten years, and become illiquid during this time period. Investors recoup their funds, not necessarily at face value, once the company in which they were invested is sold or is made public through selling its shares on the stock exchange.

Venture capital funds are entities that raise money capital from different sources, such as pension funds, insurance companies, etc., and provide seed capital to new projects. A large number of companies were initially financed with venture capital. Microsoft, Apple, Google, are only a few among a great number of companies that were formed with seed capital from venture capital funds.

Private equity and venture capital funds are Sharia-compliant: they involve no loans and therefore no interest-based debt, and they promote investment on a risk-sharing basis. They operate on financing modes of Mudharaba, Musharaka, or Wakala. In view of the importance of succeeding and making gains for the fund shareholders, private and venture capital funds are meticulous about their investment strategies and tend to select projects where the potential of profitability is high.

7. On the stability of conventional and Islamic stock markets

Ever since their establishment, conventional stock markets have been highly speculative; they may experience an extended bubble which could be followed by a crash detrimental to the real economy. Speculation is fueled by cheapness of monetary policy. Low interest rates support borrowing for stocks' speculation (Mises 1953). The unorthodox monetary policy of the US Federal Reserve since 2009, in the form of near-zero interest rates and excessive money creation, has led to record breaking speculation in the stock market.[10]

Tobin (1984) discussed the efficiency of stock markets; more specifically the fundamental-valuation efficiency, the full-insurance efficiency, and the functional efficiency. The first relates to the accuracy with which market prices reflect fundamentals. The fundamentals for a stock are the expected future dividends. As illustrated by Figure 9.3, stock prices, as measured by the S&P 500 index, have been rising at 16 percent per year during 2009–2016 despite sluggish real economic growth. This shows that a conventional stock market may have a vague relation to the real economy and may be driven by cheap money policy and speculation. The US consumer price index was rising at 1.7 percent per year during 2009–2016. If a share bought one bundle of consumer goods in 2009, the same share would buy 2.8 bundles of consumer goods in 2017. Likewise, stock prices have considerably appreciated in respect to gold, crude oil, food, and metals. If we assume a dividend rate of 2 percent per year, total return on stocks, i.e., dividends (2 percent) plus stock price increase (16 percent), would be 18 percent per year, far exceeding long-term interest rates at about 1.8 percent per year. The wide detachment of stocks from fundamentals led Keynes (1936) to think of the stock market as a casino. Although stock

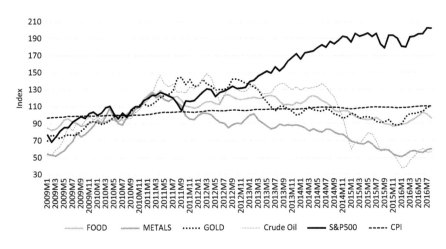

Figure 9.3 S&P 500 Index versus commodity prices, 2009–2016

markets provide liquidity for investors, Keynes considered this liquidity as a mixed benediction. Keynes wished the purchase of a stock to be permanent and indissoluble; however, he estimated that illiquidity would be the worse evil, because it would force savers toward hoarding of money.

Regarding full-insurance efficiency, Tobin observed that new options and futures contracts served mainly to allow greater leverage to short-term speculators and arbitrageurs, and to limit losses in one direction or the other. Hedging instruments increased the cost of stocks' trade. Regarding functional efficiency, he noted that stock markets contributed little to finance new investment. In line with Keynes, he hinted that regulation should discourage transient holdings of financial instruments and encourage long-term investors.

Maurice Allais (1999) considered stock markets as true casinos where big poker games were being played. For him, the stock market system was essentially non-economic, inefficient, and unfavorable to the smooth functioning of the economy. It was advantageous only to a small minority of speculators. The wide changes in stock prices ended in economic crises. Accordingly, he proposed radical reforms such as the interdiction of hedge funds and institutional intermediaries, other than brokers, whose activity consisted only of trading in shares. He proposed the interdiction of debt financing of stock transactions and the imposition of high margins for forward operations, to be paid in cash and not through borrowing.

Stock markets, embedded in Islamic finance, are theoretically stable. In a similar manner to the theoretical stability of banks that operate on the basis of Sharia precepts, Islamic stock markets are free from two major sources of instability, namely interest rates and unbacked money creation. High degrees of instability make a stock market inefficient, requiring large resources for trading and hedging risk, and dissuade savers from participation in the markets. Stock market crashes following stock market booms have often ruined household savings and caused economic disorders. A high degree of stability will encourage savers to participate in stock markets, and enable stock markets to achieve maximum efficiency in financial intermediation, reduce trading costs, and increase levels of participation.

In the absence of speculation arising from interest-based leveraging, equity prices would tend to show less volatility. Essentially dividends and real savings would drive demand for equity shares. Such demand cannot be fuelled by fictitious credit. The supply of equity shares would be determined by real investment plans. The demand and supply of equity shares are influenced by real variables in the absence of interest rates and debt, and equity prices would tend to display a stationary pattern. Asset prices in Islamic finance would feature a low correlation with the market portfolio and would be more influenced by idiosyncratic risks. In Islamic finance, the pool of real savings would determine asset demand, not credit. Since interest-debt financing of investment is forbidden, private entrepreneurs and the government would issue shares for their planned investment. Hence, the supply of stocks would be higher than in conventional finance, creating less tensions on prices. Hence, demand for and supply of shares would tend to be stable. The rate of return would essentially comprise dividends, with very small changes in equity prices. Equity share prices would be stationary variables, with no persistent upward or downward trend.

Because interest-based credit does not exist, Islamic finance is inherently stable. Based on 100 percent reserve banking, the money supply tends to be stable which leads to the stability of the price level. Asset prices are not influenced by intense speculation and are not as volatile as in conventional finance. There are no loans for leveraging large positions in securities or in futures markets.

8. Toward a regulatory framework conducive to Islamic finance

The development of Islamic finance requires an institutional and regulatory framework propitious to establish Islamic banks and support their expansion, enhance foreign participation in the financial sector, protect investors, and insure the safety of the financial intermediaries. In the banking sector, regulation should aim at the safety of the banking institutions by compelling banks to observe prudential guidelines. Regulations play a crucial factor in the development of Islamic banks. They may be an impeding factor or a propitious one, depending on how much conducive to business they are. Regulations encompass a wide array of topics, such as the licensing legislation, the legal system and efficiency of the law in reinforcing contracts, the protection of depositors, the tax code, the labor legislation, the safety and soundness of banks, the banking legislation, and the prudential standards. In finance, there are two regulatory bodies appointed by the judiciary system: an authority that regulates and supervises the banking industry, and another authority which regulates and supervises the capital markets such as the stock markets, the brokers, mutual funds, insurance companies, and finance companies.

A country that aims to develop Islamic finance has to address energetically the legal and institutional framework, i.e., the institutions that supervise Islamic banks and capital markets and the laws that govern banks and markets. The objective of the legislation is to fully liberalize the financial sector, deepen financial intermediation, ease the creation of financial intermediaries and expand fully their geographic coverage to small rural communities, increase competitiveness and innovation among financial intermediaries, impose full information and disclosure obligations, reduce transaction cost, and increase considerably the saving and investment in the country. Regulations should insure the protection of depositors that the latter are fully informed of the nature of their accounts and that banks, funds, and listed corporations provide full disclosure of their financial statements.

An Islamic bank should be licensed to perform only one banking function. It has to be either a 100 percent reserve bank specialized in deposit-taking and in domestic and international payments, or an investment bank, an intermediary between savers and investors. An investment bank should be like the World

Bank or the Islamic Development Bank. It should have no checking facility, and should hold its accounts at a depository institution. It should have no ability to create or destroy money. This legislation is a natural consequence of removing interest and a fundamental one to remove the money power creation from banks.

The capital requirement of an Islamic financial institution should be fully flexible. A bank, be it a depository or investment bank, may intend to serve a small community, a city, or a nation, or be cross-border bank. There should be full flexibility regarding its initial subscribed capital. A bank that plans to serve a small rural community should not be subjected to a large capital. Small communities in many developing countries are deprived of financial intermediation. Legislation, by requiring a very high amount of initial capital, makes it difficult to establish small banks fit for their needs. In these communities, there may be savers looking for placing their money and investors offering investment opportunities in agriculture, trade, and industry. However, the necessary bank intermediation between local supply and demand of investible funds is missing. The absence of a local financial intermediation severely constrains the economic growth of small communities and rural areas.

Islamic banks may be founded as joint-stock companies with initial capital subscribed privately by founding members of the bank or publicly if subscription is open for the public. It is important to secure against swindle schemes. A guarantee fund should be deposited by the founders of the bank at the central bank or the Treasury. The amount of this fund should be proportional to the initial capital of the bank and serve to pay depositors in case of bank failure.

Corporate income tax has to be reduced: after tax dividends should be exempt from any tax (Lucas 1990). The judicial system has to be highly efficient, easily accessible, and capable of reinforcing contracts without delays. This aspect is very important for banking development. In many countries, the judicial system is very weak and banks are unable to reinforce contracts and lose considerable money to delinquent customers. This has prevented banks from going beyond commercial operations with reputable and solid companies.

Islamic banks have to be subjected to supervision and regulatory role of the central bank, observe the accounting standards of the central bank, observe the prudential ratios such as the Basel III standards, communicate periodically their balance sheet data, and disclose information about their activities and financial operations. Clearing operations in the Islamic banking sector should be centralized at the central bank.

Investment banks need long-term resources to invest in highly productive projects that may have a long gestation period. Regulations have to address this aspect of Islamic investment banks. They have to strengthen the link between Islamic banks and capital markets and enable Islamic banks to mobilize long-term resources via these markets and to enhance the liquidity of these resources via deep secondary markets. More specifically, regulation should allow an Islamic bank to float *sukuks* according to models used by the Islamic Development Bank.

Besides *sukuks*, an Islamic bank should be allowed to raise money on the stock markets through special issuance of tradable securities in order to meet their long-term resource requirement, especially when they contemplate financing long-term investment in infrastructure, industry, agriculture, etc. Dividends from these securities should be exempt from taxes. This issuance would attract institutional investors such as pension funds, insurance companies, and sovereign funds. Rates of return of securities would be determined by the profit rates of the projects where funds are invested and no longer by the rate of interest of conventional banks. These rates would be far higher than the present return on Murabaha transactions.

Islamic funds have to be regulated and supervised by the capital market authority. Regulation and supervision have to submit these funds to strict safety guidelines and subject them to licensing requirement, full disclosure and data reporting obligations. They have to encourage the establishment of these funds for their immense role in finance deepening and promoting financial inclusiveness.

To further deepen finance and address inclusiveness, the regulatory authorities should promote an equity crowdfunding (ECF) framework with a view to allow easier access to money capital for the small entrepreneurs who lack financing. Private businesses companies that are approved under an ECF framework may offer shares to investors. The introduction of ECF aims at enhancing inclusiveness so small businesses and entrepreneurs would enjoy greater access to money capital.

Stock markets should not be restricted only to trading old issues of highly prominent companies. They should be allowed an active role in new issues of new companies as well as new venture companies. Otherwise, stock markets will not attain their full potential for mobilizing saving and financing investment. Hence, reforms of the stock market should aim at enhancing savers' participation as well as a broad access for project promoters. Stock markets will allow initial floating of shares for start-up projects; they will also allow the formation of a class of entrepreneurs who may launch profitable projects.

The central bank should apply international standards in banking safety to insure the stability of the banking system. More specifically, it should compel banks to implement the Basel III regulations in areas of capital adequacy, liquidity management, and stability of funding. In terms of risk-based capital standards, financial institutions that assume greater risk have to hold higher levels of capital.[11] Bank's assets are not treated uniformly, and poorly rated assets are weighted heavily and would require either higher capital or reduced exposure to these assets.

9. Conclusions

Sharia model prohibits interest-based money and conceives the banking sector as a two-tier banking, 100 percent reserve banking, and risk-sharing investment banking. The merit of 100 percent banking has long been recognized, with

Hume praising the Bank of Amsterdam for being a pure deposit and payment institution and not confounding the payments with the loan function as the Bank of England did. Writers, in the face of continuing crises caused by bank failures and loss of capital, urged the separation of money from debt. This separation was strongly urged by the Gouge, Carrol, Walker, Chicago Plan authors, Fisher, and Soddy. A Sharia model ensures such separation and makes the banking system immune to crises.

Numerous developing countries have been unable to promote risk-sharing equity markets capable of mobilizing domestic and foreign financial resources to encourage development while many advanced countries continue to be plagued by recurring financial crises. McKinnon (1973) and Shaw (1973) deplored the failure of financial markets to promote growth in developing countries and called for the full liberalization of capital markets. However, their work did not analyze a non-interest model, which is fully liberalized and would deepen significantly the financial sector.

Sharia model postulates risk sharing as a foundational principle of finance. Stock markets were seen to promote risk sharing among investors within and across countries; shares are contingent claims whose payoff depends on the state of the world. To develop long-term investment and venture capital financing, both investment banking and a vibrant stock market are advocated. Developing financial markets require private resources for its operation and government resources for its regulation, monitoring, and supervision. In order to develop an Islamic stock market, there is a need for both types of resources, and especially the active role of government in building the institutional and regulatory framework for capital markets to flourish. An Islamic stock market would provide investment opportunities for investors in a non-interest economy. The role of this market is to promote long-term real investment and at the same time afford liquidity for investors.

A major concern with conventional stock market since Keynes (1936) dubbed them casinos was the predominance of speculative and liquidity considerations and the limited emphasis on their role in allocating resources towards productive long-term investments. Most long-term investments seemed to be financed through retained earnings or debt. The volume of new issues destined for long-term investment was low. An Islamic stock market has to avoid the main shortcomings of conventional stock markets, insure financing of long-term investment, and mitigate speculation. Its regulatory framework must be designed to prevent the excesses of conventional stock markets, ruinous crashes, large transactions costs, and protect the interest of investors against the vagaries of modern stock markets. An efficient Islamic market would enable the mobilization of savings, promote risk sharing, and generate attractive returns for investors, provided that Sharia-compliant regulations and institutions are in place.

The nature of Islamic banking, in form of 100 percent reserve banks and risk-sharing banks, dissociates money from debt, and makes an Islamic stock market inherently stable and less exposed to systemic risks that have periodically undermined the stability of conventional stocks markets and their economies.

This stability derives from the institutional structure prescribed by Sharia that includes the prohibition of interest. Stability is essential for enhancing participation in stock markets and risk sharing. The role of central banks in stock market instability should not be minimized. Bubbles have been fueled by low interest rates and abundant credit. Stability of stock markets cannot be disassociated from the stability of monetary policy.

Notes

1 The authors of the Chicago Plan were: Henry Simons, Frank Knight, Aaron Director, Garfield Cox, Lloyd Mints, Henry Schultz, Paul Douglas, and A. G. Hart. Irving Fisher of Yale University fully endorsed the Plan in his book, *100% Money* (1936).
2 Saving, if not invested, will cause a drop in prices and wages, and therefore higher consumer purchasing power. If prices and wages are rigid, saving, if not invested, will cause unemployment and a fall in GDP (Machlup 1940).
3 During the 19th century, the number of banks were in hundreds in the United States and in the United Kingdom.
4 An example of high leverage was the Bank of England. Founded in 1964 with a paid-in capital of $72,000, it made a loan of $1,200,000 to the British government at a rate of 8 percent per year (Carroll 1850s).
5 The credit multiplier is defined as the inverse of reserve requirement ratio. If the central bank increases this ratio, then the credit multiplier declines.
6 Eminent writers noted that debt money and gold were like water and fire; debt money evicted gold: David Hume (1752), Lord Liverpool (1805), William Gouge (1833), Charles Holt Carroll (1850s), and Amasa Walker (1873).
7 Fisher (1936) noted that US money fell by 35 percent during 1929–1933 following the collapse of debt money. He recommended 100 percent reserve money to remove the banks' power in creating and destroying money.
8 Examples of depository banks were the Bank of Amsterdam 1609 and Bank of Hamburg 1619.
9 Examples of Islamic funds that are important in terms of size and number may be as follows: Islamic Mutual Funds, *Murabaha* Funds, *Mudaraba* Funds, *Ijara* Funds, Unit Trust Funds, Islamic Equity Funds, Sukuk Funds, Islamic Real Estate Investment Trusts (REITs), Islamic Exchange-Traded Funds (ETFs), Islamic Private Equity and Venture Capital Funds, Islamic Hedge Funds, Islamic Commodity Funds, and Islamic Money Market Funds.
10 Mises (1953) deplored the fictive wealth created by stock price inflation which leads to capital consumption.
11 The Islamic Financial Services Board (IFSB) provides a detailed description of the application of Basel standards to Islamic Bank, including risk weights. See Note IFSB-15, Revised Capital Adequacy Standard, December 2013.

References

Allais, Maurice, 1999, *La Crise Mondiale D'Aujourd'hui*, Paris: Clément Juglar.
Allen, F., and Gale, D., 2007, *Understanding Financial Crises*, Oxford: Oxford University Press.
Askari, H., Iqbal, Z., Krichene, N., and Mirakhor, A., 2012, *Risk Sharing in Finance: The Islamic Finance Alternative*, Singapore: Wiley and Sons.
Bagehot, W., 1873, *Lombard Street: A Description of the Money Market*, London: Henry S. King.
Brav, A., Constantinides, G. M., and Geczy, C. C., 2002, "Asset Pricing With Heterogeneous Consumers and Limited Participation: Empirical Evidence," *Journal of Political Economy*, 110(4): 793–824.

Carroll, C. H., 1965, *Organization of Debt Into Currency and Other Papers*, Edited with an Introduction by Edward C. Simmons, D.Van Nostrand Company, Inc. Princeton, NJ.

de Soto, J. H., 2011, *Money, Bank Credit, and Economic Cycles*, Auburn, AL: Ludwig von Mises Institute.

Fisher, I., 1936, *100% Money*, New York: Palgrave Macmillan.

Gouge, W., 1833, *A Short History of Paper Money & Banking*, New York: Augustus M. Kelley Publishers.

Guiso, L., Sapienza, P., and Zingales, L. 2005, "Trusting the Stock Market," NBER Working Paper no. 11648. Cambridge, MA: National Bureau of Economic Research.

Holden, E. H., 1907, *Lecture on the Depreciation of Securities in Relation to Gold*, London: Blades, East & Blades.

Hume, D., 1752, *Political Discourses*, Edinburgh: Printed by R. Fleming, for A. Kincaid and A. Donaldson.

Juglar, C., 1862, *Des Crises Commerciales et leur Retour Periodique en France, en Angleterre, et aux Etats Unis*, Paris: Guillaumin.

Keynes, J. M., 1936, *The General Theory of Employment, Interest and Money*, London: Palgrave Macmillan.

Liverpool, L., and Jenkinson, C., 1805, *A Treatise on the Coins of the Realm*, London: Effingham Wilson, Royal Exchange, 1880.

Lucas, R. E., 1990, "Supply-Side Economics: An Analytical Review," *Oxford Economic Papers*, 42: 293–316.

Machlup, F., 1940, *The Stock Market, Credit and Capital Formation*, London: William Hodge and Company, Ltd.

McKinnon, R., 1973, *Money and Capital in Economic Development*, Washington, DC: Brookings Institution.

Mirakhor, A., 2010, "Whither Islamic Finance? Risk Sharing in an Age of Crises," Paper presented at the Inaugural Securities Commission Malaysia (SC) – Oxford Centre for Islamic Studies (OCIS) Roundtable "*Developing a Scientific Methodology on Sharia Governance for Positioning Islamic Finance Globally*."

Rothbard, M. N., 1962, "The Case for a 100 Percent Gold Dollar," in Yeager, L. (ed.). *In Search of a Monetary Constitution*, Cambridge, MA: Harvard University Press, pp. 94–136. Reprinted as *The Case for a 100 Percent Gold Dollar*, Washington, DC: Libertarian Review Press, 1974, and Auburn, AL: Mises Institute, 1991, 2005.

Rothbard, M. N., 2008, *The Mystery of Banking*, Auburn, AL: Ludwig von Mises Institute.

Shaw, E., 1973, *Financial Deepening in Economic Development*, Oxford: Oxford University Press.

Simons, H., 1948, *Economic Policy for a Free Society*, Chicago, IL: University of Chicago Press.

Soddy, F., 1934, *The Role of Money*, London: George Routledge and Sons Ltd.

Thornton, H., 1802, *An Inquiry Into the Nature and Effect of Paper Credit in Great Britain*, New York: Augustus M. Kelley.

Tobin, J., 1963, "Commercial Banks as Creators of Money", in D. Carson (ed.). *Banking and Monetary Studies*, Homewood, IL: Richard D. Irwin, pp. 408–419.

Tobin, J. 1984, "On the Efficiency of the Financial System," *Lloyds Bank Review*, 153(15).

Von Mises, L., 1953, *The Theory of Money and Credit*, New Haven: Yale University Press.

Walker, A., 1873, *The Science of Wealth*, Philadelphia: J. B. Lippincott.

10 A fully liberalized labor market

1. Introduction

While in pre-1929 recessions, US unemployment reverted within a very short period to 2–3 percent, during 1930s, unemployment remained above 18–19 percent (Anderson 1945). The only explanation was that the government never intervened in pre-1929 recessions to block the market adjustment mechanism; after 1929 until present times, the government prevented market adjustment (Anderson 1945).

With inconvertible paper money, and powerful unions, a government may oppose downward wage adjustment to clear labor markets.[1] In early 1930s, industrial countries had abolished the gold standard so they could inflate money and create jobs with inflation. Poor countries with powerful unions have suffered economic setbacks. Unions control the government administration, police, and the formal private sector, and impose overburdening wages and salaries that eat up capital and force enterprises to shut down instead of lowering their wage cost. Because of high union salaries, many governments are heavily indebted, and neglected education, hospitals, and infrastructure.

Employment is a natural, biological, and survival need. A human being cannot afford to be unemployed except if he is supported by his family or by the government. Otherwise, a person has to seek employment. The labor market is the area of big failure of modern governments. Unemployment rates at 25 percent in advanced countries show the extent of government blocking the competitive functioning of the labor market. Governments have invariably used inflation to counteract rigidities of labor markets.

The structure of the labor market changes continuously with new technologies and scientific advances which are totally outside the government control. Moreover, employment is a free choice of a worker and an employer, and not a state responsibility. By discarding the price-wage mechanism, the government quest for full employment is purely redistributive, and not growth oriented. Simons (1948) disapproved of large interference of government in the economy; he noted that competition in the private industry makes possible a minimizing of the responsibilities of the sovereign state. It frees the state from the obligation of adjudicating endless and bitter disputes among participants in different industries and among owners of different kinds of productive services. In a word, it makes possible a political policy of laissez-faire. He added that the great enemy of democracy is monopoly, in all its forms: corporations, trade associations, trade-unions, or, in general, organization and concentration of power in functional classes.

The chapter covers:

- Nature of unions
- Nature of minimum wage laws
- Nature of unemployment and poverty
- The full employment act
- Employment strategies: absorbing labor surplus with capital formation and flexible wages
- Labor markets in Sharia
- Dismal unemployment rates

2. Nature of unions

In their early apparition in the United States, unions mounted strikes that paralyzed corporations in mining, industry, transportation, farming, and other industries. The labor unions may have emerged or are supported by ideologies such as communism and socialism that consider the capitalist system as exploitive of workers and denies them their full share of the cake, and therefore should be abolished as happened in many communist revolutions. Union strikes may turn violent as illustrated by the Chicago Haymarket incident in 1886, when a strike against a corporation, McCormick Harvesting Machine Company, escalated to violence and deaths.

Newcomb (1877) showed that unions oppose free market. He stated:

> The same law which gives the workmen of a railroad the right to leave it when they are dissatisfied with their wages gives the owners of the railroad the right to employ whom they please to run it; and if you abolish this law, you will soon find that it will be the laborers, and not the railroad owners, who will suffer.
>
> (P. 8)

Newcomb stressed an inherent flaw in unions' ideology, which considered capital as enemy of workers. It is the capitalist that takes the risk for building factories, the hard work for setting up a working project and creating jobs for workers. Workers face no risk; they are paid fully their wages whether the capitalists make profits or losses. He noted the fallacy of the oppression of labor by the capitalists, and of antagonism between these two agencies. Diminish or injure capital, and the power of everybody, the laborer included, to get clothes, food, and shelter will be diminished. He maintained that all accumulated capital is for the advantage of the laborer or the non-capitalist as well as the rich. If the capitalist invests his money in building a factory, that factory is making clothing for the poor as well as for the rich: probably more for the poor than for the rich, because the former will derive the greatest advantages from the cheapening of clothing thus produced. Thus, all actions by laborers to diminish or interfere with the development of capital amount to nothing but actions to reduce the productive potential of the nation.

Newcomb observed that unions prevented any downward wage flexibility. He noted that the receipts of nearly every railway in the country had greatly diminished. It was impossible to run the trains without cutting down the wages. The railway companies should be free to hire non-union workers at reduced wages. The action of the unions to oppose wage cuts or hiring non-union workers was absurd.

Unions at the time of Newcomb were still in ascendancy. Quickly, they gained control of the legislative and political institutions as unionists were elected Presidents and Congressmen; unionism became deeply rooted in popular thinking enjoying strong support among grass-root masses. Labor and socialist parties control many industrial and developing countries. In the United States, much of the task of coercion has been assumed on the unions' behalf by the government. This was the essence of the Wagner Act, the law of the land since 1935. The crucial provisions of this act are as follows: (i) to coerce all workers in a certain production unit into being represented by a union in bargaining with an employer, if a majority of workers agree; (ii) to prohibit the employer from refusing to hire union members or union organizers; and (iii) to compel the employer to bargain with unions. Thus, unions have been invested with governmental authority, and the strong arm of the government uses coercion to force workers and employers alike to deal with the unions.

Di Lorenzo (2012) showed that unionism was founded on a fallacious ideology as plainly illustrated by economic facts and historical experiences such as wage-price inflationary spirals. Neither unions nor employers would be able to contravene the market forces and wage equilibrium. Mises (1949) noted that the main ideological foundation of labor unionism, and of government labor policy, was the myth that employers exploit workers. In labor markets, competition among entrepreneurs assures that there is a close association between worker compensation and the marginal productivity of labor. More precisely, compensation is determined by the workers' marginal revenue product. Workers become more valuable to employers if their marginal productivity increases. Capital investment by employers makes labor more productive and hence more valuable.

If an employer attempts to exploit some or all of his employees, in a competitive, capitalistic labor market he will merely create a profit opportunity for his rivals, thereby harming his own business. If an employee's marginal revenue product is say, $500 per week, but the pay is only $200 per week, then it will pay competing entrepreneurs to hire that worker away for $300, then for $400, or higher, because they will still be earning a profit by doing so. There will be employers eager to take advantage of the margin between the prevailing wage rate and the marginal productivity of labor. Their demand for labor will bring wage rates back to the value of labor marginal productivity.

Unions can never force an increase of wages beyond true productivity without leading to the disappearance of the enterprise. Employers also cannot force a wage other than the equilibrium in the market. Lewis (1954) showed that as long as redundant labor persists, the wage rate will be near the subsistence level. However, as capital accumulation absorbed redundant labor, enterprises had to bid up for labor and offer higher wages in conformity with higher marginal products. Everywhere unions have been a handicap to the economy. They never benefited workers. The high incomes enjoyed by workers, the reduced work hours, health coverage, and many other amenities, all arose from capitalism, entrepreneurs' investment, technical advancement, capital accumulation, and sustained economic growth. Practically, unions have no influence on the factors that contribute to improve the workers' income and increase their leisure time.

3. Nature of minimum wage laws

Government cannot maintain high nominal wages without maintaining low or even negative real interest rates. Sound money and market-determined interest rates cannot exist when the government deploys unorthodox money policy to influence the labor market. Minimum wage laws, by definition, force wages above the marginal productivity of workers and above the market-clearing wages. They are based on fallacies that such laws would protect the interest of workers. The government makes it a crime to pay less than the minimum wage; yet, all that the government does is to erode the real wage of workers through low interest rates and inflation. The minimum wage law encourages unemployment. It causes a double loss for the economy: a loss in the form of forgone output which could have been produced had unemployed workers been employed, and a loss in form of unemployment subsidy which is a tax on the economy and a depletion of investment. If the government does not interfere, the labor market adjusts quickly to full employment; the economy will gain in output, investment, and growth. Statists know surely that minimum wage laws reduce employment. Hence, they try to circumvent them through inflation and money printing to reduce real wages in line with real marginal productivity. Rothbard (1962) argued that the minimum wage is compulsory unemployment; the minimum wage law provides no jobs, it only outlaws them.

The standard of living is not raised by decrees imposing higher wage rates, but by the rise in the productivity of labor, which increases the supply of goods relative to the supply of labor and thus reduces prices relative to wage rates. Labor unions and politicians ignore the essential role played by falling prices in achieving rising real wages. Their main indicator is only the rise in money wages. A rise of real wages throughout the economic system is achieved by a fall in prices relative to wages, resulting from an increase in production per worker. More production per worker – a higher productivity of labor – serves to increase the supply of goods and services produced relative to the supply of labor that produces them. In this way, it reduces prices relative to wages and thereby raises real wages and the general standard of living.

The government and unions can together hike nominal wages as high as they wish. What matters is the real wage: this variable is not under their control, nor the employers' control. Short of shutting down, a firm has immediately to hike its prices, since non-labor cost is as incompressible as the labor cost. There surges a spiral of wage-price inflation which maintains continuously the profits margin and the equilibrium between nominal wages and prices. The relationship between product prices and wages is usually described in a simplistic fashion using the notion of markup.[3] Namely, the price level can be formulated as:

$$p = \frac{1}{d}(1+m)w$$

where d stands for average labor productivity, m denotes the markup, and w denotes the average nominal wage in the economy. In this relationship, an improvement in productivity would lower product prices; however, an increase in the nominal wage rate would be passed through to prices unless offset by higher labor productivity. Wage distortions which make prevailing wages much above equilibrium wages could be a serious source of loss in external competitiveness.

4. Nature of unemployment and poverty

To combat poverty, there is a need to create productive employment. Classical economists, such as Smith (1776), have elaborated the labor value theory; every commodity incorporates labor time, and its value is determined by its labor content. Labor alone creates wealth, and material wealth cannot be created without labor. No house can be built without labor: no car, computer, airplane can be made without labor, and no food can be grown without labor. Hence, labor is the ultimate source of growth. Paradoxically, labor surplus countries suffer acute poverty, and could not grow rich with their labor; they are rich in labor and poor in capital. Wealth cannot be created without labor, yet abundant labor is contributing to no wealth creation; instead capital is being consumed and poverty rising. Many developing countries have an abundance in labor; yet hordes of labor are crossing the seas, at the risk of drowning, in emigration adventure to industrial countries. Some countries tend to stagnate in a subsistence equilibrium. Adam Smith (1776) attributed this poverty to the abundance of unproductive labor, either sitting idle, or being employed in a nonproductive manner such as the army, in bureaucracy, etc. It is consuming capital and not being able to invest and produce tangible products such as food, clothing, and shelter. Lewis (1954), in line with Ricardo (1817), elaborated his theory of labor surplus absorption based on income distribution skewed in favor of profits, sustained capital accumulation, and the formation of a class of entrepreneurs.

Decades after Lewis (1954), labor surplus persists in many countries; moreover, industrial countries, although considered as non-labor surplus countries, suffer prolonged structural unemployment, attaining 27 percent in some cases. Hence, considerable unemployment, especially among the young, often exceeding 15 percent of the labor force, characterize many countries. Such human factor could be a source of considerable economic growth if governments succeed to put in place market-oriented employment policies capable of redeploying this idle human wealth into the economy. The state has to remove every single obstacle against full employment, be it unions, labor laws, unemployment compensation, or theft and larceny. Unemployment is a serious economic disequilibrium. It means a large loss in output and deterioration in poverty. The loss of output is estimated according to Okun's law as:

$$y - y^e = \beta\left(u^n - u\right)$$

Where y is observed real gross domestic product (GDP), y^e is full employment real GDP, u the prevailing unemployment rate as a percent of the labor force, u^n is the natural rate or frictional unemployment, generally estimated at 2–3 percent of the labor force, and β is a technological parameter. In view of the high unemployment rate, it can be inferred that the prevailing wage rate w is far above an equilibrium wage rate w^e that would bring unemployment to a natural rate at 2 percent of the labor force. Firms face therefore a cost disadvantage of the order $w-w^e$. Achieving full employment is an overriding objective of an Islamic economic model and is thought to be the best strategy for reducing poverty and achieving social equity.

Unemployment is a luxury phenomenon. A worker cannot be unemployed except if he has wealth, or family or government support. Under-employment and preponderance of the informal sector could be attributed to low capital accumulation arising from low savings, exodus from rural to urban zones, mismatch between education and skills required by the economy, distorted consumer preferences that favor industrial products from developed countries and therefore encourage imports at the expense of traditional industries. In many countries, excessive government controls of investment, marketing, and prices, combined with heavy taxes, have stifled the private sector and accentuated unemployment.

Some Asian labor surplus countries managed to develop by relying fully on their labor resources and steadily absorbing their labor surpluses. These economies followed a market model and export-oriented growth, emphasized labor-intensive technologies, and removed major distortions in their economies. In contrast, many developing countries followed a dualistic economic model which failed to enhance labor employment, with a small modern sector using capital-intensive technologies paralleled with a large informal sector using very little capital. These economies relied on foreign debt to finance the modern sector development as well as sustain the consumption patterns of industrial countries. Many development economists in the 1950s feared that foreign aid could accentuate technological dependence on industrialized countries and called for trade instead of aid.

While major reforms for liberalizing the economy and promoting private sector development are essential for an employment strategy, important distortions relating to the labor market itself have to be removed. Full employment has to prevail in any country as long as there are large human needs in food, housing, clothing, trade, transport, etc. which are unfulfilled inside or outside a given country (Mises 1949). A fully competitive labor market freed from distortionary laws is a prerequisite for absorbing unemployment. Many poor countries have inherited industrial countries' labor laws, which have seriously hampered employment creation and undermined their economic development. These laws prescribe minimum wages far above marginal productivity, prohibit firing, limit the working hours, and impose excessive taxes on employers. In view of the very high cost of labor, legislative constraints, low-skill and poorly disciplined labor force, firms in many poor countries have pushed for an outright use of capital-intensive production methods (use of machinery in agriculture, industry, and construction) thus reducing the use of labor and displacing a large number of employment opportunities.

5. The full employment act

Under the impulse of Keynesian economists, and with a view to prevent the recurrence of the 1930s' mass-unemployment, the US Congress voted the Full Employment Bill of 1945, which declared:

> All Americans able to work and seeking work have the right to useful, remunerative, regular, and full-time employment, and it is the policy of the United States to assure the existence at all times of sufficient employment opportunities to enable all Americans who have finished their schooling and who do not have full-time housekeeping responsibilities to freely exercise this right.

This bill underwent numerous revisions and became the Employment Act of 1946, which mandated the federal government to do everything in its authority to achieve full employment, which was established as a right guaranteed to the American people.

With the dismantlement of gold standard in 1971, The US economy experienced high inflation and unemployment, which led the government to intervene more in the economy as bad policies begot bad or even worse policies. In 1977, the Federal Reserve Act was amended to instruct this institution to pursue three goals: stable prices, maximum employment, and moderate long-term interest rates. In 1978, the Full Employment and Balanced Growth Act, known as the Humphrey-Hawkins Act, amended the 1946 Employment Act and became law. The Act set up four goals for the federal government: full employment, economic growth, balanced budget, and elimination of inflation. It stated that the government preferred private investment to accomplish these goals, but if it was not forthcoming, then the government could invest to spur demand and, if necessary, create make-work jobs along the lines of the New Deal. The Humphrey-Hawkins Act contained numerous objectives. Among them, unemployment should not exceed 3 percent for people 20 years or older, and inflation should be reduced to 3 percent or less, provided that its reduction would not interfere with the employment goal.

In classical economics, the government should not interfere in the labor market; the latter is vital for the economy and has a natural, self-regulating mechanism. If an economy was in a boom supported by a huge expansion of bank money then went into a depression because of debt defaults (Fisher 1933), it is able to recover in a few months to full employment, mal-investment is corrected or liquidated, real circulating capital is rebuilt, and labor and capital are redirected into most productive sectors. Because of a deflation of bank money, the general level of prices has to adjust downward; in similar fashion, wages have to adjust downward. Workers in the nineteenth century were used to flexible nominal wages, and mass-unemployment was only very brief. Thanks to government rigid wage legislation, workers became unfamiliar with nominal wage adjustment; only inflation is the adjustment mechanism.

6. Employment strategies: absorbing labor surplus with capital formation and flexible wages

The classical macroeconomic model did not allow for unemployment, simply because during the 18th and 19th centuries labor unions did not exist, and government labor legislation was also inexistent. Hence, labor markets were always in equilibrium and full employment was maintained throughout. The classical model is based on the assumption of full flexibility of wages and prices. Models proposed by David Ricardo (1817) and Arthur Lewis (1954) showed that the wage rate was at the marginal product level; consequently, saving out of profits and capital accumulation proceeded. In such a model, the demand for labor by firms is determined by the marginal product. The labor supply curve is related to the real wage rate. The labor market clears at a wage rate that ensures full employment. The volume of employment will in turn determine real GDP.

Countries with pro-labor laws cannot compete with countries where labor is freely competitive. For instance, firms in industrial countries have significantly lost their domestic and international markets. Many firms had to relocate to countries where there are no pro-labor laws to realign their costs with international costs and be able to remain in the market. Wage rates in countries with free labor markets determine fully the labor costs in internationally tradable goods. No country with higher wage rates can compete with these lower wage countries. Hence, wage rates in Bangladesh, China, and India determine the labor cost in many tradable goods such as clothing, appliances, etc.

In contrast, Keynes's model assumes the presence of powerful labor unions, as the case was in the United Kingdom, which will preclude downward adjustment of the nominal wage rate to absorb mass-unemployment. Hence, there will be involuntary unemployment, and the economy will settle in under-employment equilibrium. The model requires a "Big Government" that steps up spending through fiscal deficits financed by money printing to achieve full employment. This model, despite its failure in the 1930s and great disorders after 2008, appealed to statists, and was widely applied in most countries. Held in high esteem, it constituted the ideology of the US Federal Reserve's mandate of full employment.

In many countries, wages are predetermined both in the private and public sectors and are considered as a fixed cost. However, sales or sale prices may decline and firms may incur operating losses. Firms have to fully absorb the losses and cannot transfer part of them to labor through flexible downward wage adjustment. Similarly, the government may incur a severe drop in taxes or royalties; however, the wage bill is predetermined, and the government cannot adjust it in relation to loss in revenues and is forced to run a fiscal deficit. Wage rigidity has led to considerable economizing on labor use and has become a source of inflation.

The pervasiveness of unemployment in many countries provides evidence of labor redundancy and therefore very low marginal labor productivity. When the value of marginal labor productivity in agriculture, industry, and construction is compared to the actual average wage in these sectors, a major distortion appears. Such distortion will stand against the short-term full employment of the labor force.

Opting for an economic model that fully uses the labor force is the most recommended strategy, not only for reducing poverty and social inequity but essentially to restore a durable, balanced, and export-oriented economic growth. In order to compete in exports, the state should not allow policies that distort wages in relation to international competitiveness. Besides investing in education and developing the skills of manpower in various occupational fields, the most efficient way to absorb labor surplus is to remove all types of price and institutional distortions and encourage the implementation of a competitive wage structure that reflects the true productivity of labor. Realigning wages in line with productivity growth will encourage the demand for labor in sectors that are traditionally large employers of manpower such as agriculture, industry, construction and services. Undistorted wages will allow savings to increase rapidly and capital accumulation to proceed faster. They will help to support exports and remove a source of overvaluation of the exchange rate. Competitive wages in agriculture will help increase agricultural surplus and will therefore mitigate pressure on food prices.

Maintaining a highly distorted wage structure will play havoc with the development process and exacerbate the unemployment situation. It will lead to both migration to urban zones and immigration in a bid to find employment. Rigidities in laying off workers should be removed. Vocational training which increases productivity and teaches workers new skills that increase their inter-occupation mobility would be recommended. Only when wages are in line with productivity and legal constraints are eliminated would private enterprises find it profitable to invest in vocational training. High unemployment is extremely costly as millions of people have to be fed and provided with necessary amenities without contributing to real GDP, leading to a drain of saving and higher foreign financing. Furthermore, poverty and deterioration of standards of living become pervasive. Income inequality becomes very high. Such high unemployment has become a cause of alarming crime rates and social insecurity. Because of strong unions and burdening government regulations, unemployment has become structural and politically intractable in many economies. Strong political forces will stand in the way of reforms in the labor market. Labor strikes in key sectors, such as public transport, paralyze economic activity, inflict financial losses, and discourage employment. The failure of many countries to overcome the unemployment problem plainly demonstrates that wrong government policies can only aggravate unemployment and spread misery.

7. Labor markets in Sharia

The Sharia model has no interest rate and no interest-debt borrowing. The Sharia model has no cyclical mass-unemployment, since credit expansion and contraction by banks are the only cause for cycles. The labor market has to equilibrate, as any other market, according to supply and demand. In a Sharia model, the labor market tends to be in equilibrium since there is no government obstruction to the competitive functioning of this market.

The state should not contribute to worsen unemployment through its wasteful spending, consumption of capital, and protection of labor unions. A main purpose of a Sharia model is to eliminate distortions in labor markets with a view to maximize employment and promote exports. It aims at establishing perfect wage flexibility capable of equilibrating labor markets. Policies that interfere with labor market adjustments such as payment of unemployment benefits to unemployed workers may be accommodated in a Sharia model; The rate of unemployment, which should be low at its natural rate of 2 percent, has reached disturbing levels in many countries. The high unemployment rates cannot be explained by unavailability of productive employment opportunities.

Wages are prices, and as any price should be determined by the market mechanism. The more the government interferes in areas that are not under its attribution, the more lawyers, police, and jails are needed (Mises 1949). To fix a minimum price above the equilibrium price, the government has to subsidize the surplus of labor or any commodity whose price is above equilibrium.[4]

8. Dismal unemployment rates

Many countries suffer high unemployment rates and consequently high poverty and deteriorating social conditions (Table 10.1).

It is important to reach full employment in every country, as demonstrated by many countries whose unemployment rate is very low, less than 2–3 percent. In

Table 10.1 Examples of high unemployment rates (2015)

Country	Rate	Country	Rate	Country	Rate
South Africa	24.9	Ethiopia	17.5	Tunisia	15.4
Cameroun	30	Greece	27.9	Ghana	11
Mali	30	Chad	22	Mozambique	21

Source: The World Bank

order to achieve this objective, high unemployment countries have to remove all obstacles to employment and ensure full flexibility of the labor markets. It often happens that high unemployment countries suffer paradoxically acute labor shortage due to powerful unions, the lack of flexibility, mobility, and poor work ethics. An oversized government may be an obstacle to the private sector where the bulk of employment is to be found. High unemployment rates undermine economic growth and social stability and have to be addressed with utmost priority to a view to implement deep reforms that enhance investment, flexibility, mobility, and security.

9. Conclusions

Labor markets are the areas of failures of many countries. In some countries, unemployment rates remained un-tractable at 25 percent. Unorthodox policies create a boom and may reduce unemployment significantly. However, they contribute to a massive debt build-up by the government and the private sector which cannot be repaid without creating a systemic default. Over-indebtedness culminates in general default: mass-unemployment recurs again, with a repeat of bailouts, more cheap money, and over-expansionary fiscal policies.

Notes

1 Most of the countries celebrate a Labor Day as a national holiday. In these countries, downward wage flexibility may not be politically feasible.
2 The cost structure of a firm obeys technical relations in which wages are only a component among other components such as raw materials, utilities, office stationary, etc. If a firm is forced by unions to increase wages, it will not be able to cover the rest of costs and may have to increase its product price or shut down its operation.
3 In the short run, the real cost structure of a firm is rigid. The share of a given cost component in firm's receipts cannot be increased at the expense of other components without disrupting the firm's operation, unless the product price is increased through a markup coefficient.
4 Assume the government fixes the price of fish above the equilibrium price. The government has to buy any surplus fish and dump it back into the sea. Moreover, there is a loss of welfare in terms of increased consumption of fish if government did not interfere.

References

Anderson, B., 1945, "The Road Back to Full Employment," in Homan, P. and Machlup, F. (eds.). *Financing American Prosperity*, New York: Twentieth Century Fund, pp. 25–28.

Di Lorenzo, T. J., 2012, *Organized Crime, the Unvarnished Truth About Government*, Auburn, AL: Mises Institute.

Fisher, F., 1933, "The Debt-Deflation Theory of Great Depressions," *Econometrica*, 1(4): 337–357.

Hayek, F. A., 1944, *The Road to Serfdom*, New York: Routledge.

Keynes, J. M., 1936, *The General Theory of Employment, Interest, and Money*, London: Palgrave Macmillan, St. Martin's Press, 1970.

Lewis, W. A., 1954, "Economic Development With Unlimited Supplies of Labor," *The Manchester School*, 22(2): 139–191.

Newcomb, S., 1877, *The ABC of Finance: or, the Money and Labor Questions Familiarly Explained to Common People in Short and Easy Lessons*, New York: Harper and Bros.

Nock, A. J., 1935, *Our Enemy, the State*, Caldwell, ID: The Caxton Printers Ltd.

Ricardo, D., 1817, *On the Principles of Political Economy and Taxation*, London: John Murray.

Rothbard, M., 1962, *Man, Economy, and State, With Power and Market*, Auburn, AL: Ludwig von Mises Institute.

Simons, H., 1947, *Economic Policy for a Free Society*, Chicago: The University of Chicago Press.

Smith, A., 1776, *An Inquiry Into the Nature and Causes of the Wealth of Nations*, London: Methuen and Co., Ltd., ed. Edwin Cannan, 1904, Fifth Edition.

Von Mises, L., 1949, *Human Action*, Auburn, AL: Ludwig von Mises Institute.

Weidenbaum, Murray, 1996, "The Employment Act of 1946: A half century of presidential policymaking," *Presidential Studies Quarterly*, 26(3): 880–885.

11 Sharia free trade and foreign exchange policy

1. Introduction

Free international trade is essential for economic growth. It expands the markets of an economy beyond its territory through exports and imports. Mercantilism, defined as the government restriction of imports to protect local producers and employment, and to accumulate trade surplus, is harmful to trade and growth. An example of trade restriction was the Corn-Laws (Mill 1821; Spooner 1886). The classics, namely Adam Smith (1776), David Ricardo (1817), James Mill (1821), and J.B. Say (1803) exploded the fallacies of mercantilism based on Say's principle that commodities are exchanged for commodities; namely, a country cannot export without importing. Moreover, mercantilism deprived countries from efficiency gains arising from trade. The classics showed that trade, within a country or across countries, was beneficial to each trading party in all cases of absolute or comparative advantage; it leads to greater production and consumption than in autarky,[1] simply because the exported product (e.g., wheat in the United States) is cheaper (in terms of cloth) than in the United Kingdom (UK) and the imported product (e.g., cloth from the UK) is cheaper (in terms of wheat) in the UK than the United States; even though both wheat and cloth may be less costly in terms of man hours in the United States than in the UK. Ricardo superbly established the principle of trade along the comparative cost advantage even though a country may be more efficient in all goods.

Opposing mercantilism's accumulation of gold and silver, Hume (1752) showed that persistent trade surplus or deficit accumulation was not possible since there was a self-correcting mechanism, called the price-specie flow mechanism, which eliminated trade imbalances between countries; it was therefore inopportune to forbid gold and silver exports. The Hume mechanism became known as the monetary approach to the balance of payments adjustment. The balance of payments is the cumulated balance of trade and capital operations. An excess supply of money in relation to money demand will cause a balance of payments deficit, and vice versa.

Today, mercantilism, in form of protectionism, still dominates trade policy; exchange rate depreciation continues to be relied upon to stimulate exports and restrict imports in opposition to price deflation implied by the Hume's wage-price flexibility mechanism. Many developing countries followed an anti-trade model where the government controlled exports and imports, both subjected to licensing, and imposed the non-convertibility of local currency (McKinnon 1973; Shaw 1973). This model inflicted a huge cost on countries that adhered to it. These countries had to finance their imports through debt and were not able to develop their exports. Moreover, developed countries imposed trade restrictions that narrowed down developing countries' exports essentially to raw materials. They promoted exports to developing countries through debt financing; consequently, many developing countries became debt-stressed and had to default on their debt.

Sharia model is a free trade and foreign exchange model. Trade is a pillar of civilization and no region or country can develop without trade. Any restriction to trade, in the form of taxes, subsidies, or quotas is a violation of Sharia. There is no interest-based debt. Therefore, a country cannot finance its imports with interest-based debt. Sharia model opposes structural impediments to wage and price flexibility, and opposes inflationism and use of exchange rate as a policy instrument to promote exports or alleviate balance of payments deficits. The foreign exchange market should be a fully liberalized market.

This chapter covers:

- Mercantilism
- The genesis of the free trade doctrine
- The Heckscher-Ohlin (H-O) model
- The effects of an import tariff
- The effects of an export subsidy
- The foreign exchange markets
- Sharia free trade and exchange model

2. Mercantilism

Mercantilism is an economic policy aimed at accumulating monetary reserves (e.g., gold or foreign currencies) through encouraging exports and restricting imports (Rothbard 2006). Mercantilists wanted a persistent surplus in the balance of payments. Exports were to be supported by bounties since they stimulated industry and led to an import of the precious metals gold and silver, which mercantilists identified with true wealth. Imports were to be restricted since they reduced the demand for domestic products and drained away gold. The policy advice offered by mercantilists was that exports and local industries should be encouraged by state support and subsidies, while imports should be discouraged by protectionist restrictions. Mercantilist governments during the eighteenth century banned the export of gold and silver, even for payments; forbade trade to be carried in foreign ships; subsidized exports; and restricted domestic consumption through tariff barriers to trade.

3. The genesis of the free trade doctrine

3.1 Hume price-specie flow mechanism

The fallacies of mercantilism were exploded by many writers; it was not a natural system since it erected barriers that only undermined the natural market mechanism. David Hume (1752) attacked the falsehood of trade barriers and the accumulation of trade surpluses. He presented the price-specie mechanism, based on monetary theory, which equilibrated balances of payments and price levels among trade partners. The essence of any trade was an exchange of commodities against commodities; according to Say's law, there was no such thing as one trader or country only selling commodities without buying commodities. Regarding the adjustment mechanism, Hume said:

> Suppose four-fifths of all the money in Great Britain to be annihilated in one night, and the nation reduced to the same condition, with regard to specie, as in the reigns of the Harrys and Edwards, what would be the consequence? Must not the price of all labor and commodities sink in proportion, and everything be sold as cheap as they were in those ages? What nation could then dispute with us in any foreign market, or pretend to navigate or to sell manufactures at the same price, which to us would afford sufficient profit? In how little time, therefore, must this bring back the money which we had lost, and raise us to the level of all the neighboring nations? Where, after we have arrived, we immediately lose the advantage of the cheapness of labor and commodities; and the farther flowing in of money is stopped by our fullness and repletion. Again, suppose, that all the money of Great Britain were multiplied fivefold in a night, must not the contrary effect follow? Must not all labor and commodities rise to such an exorbitant height, that no neighboring nations could afford to buy from us; while their commodities, on the other hand, became comparatively so cheap, that, in spite of all the laws which could be formed, they would be run in upon us, and our money flow out; till we fall to a level with foreigners, and lose that great superiority of riches, which had laid us under such disadvantages?
>
> (P. 53)

Hume applied the quantity theory of money with a simple illustration, indicating that any quantity of money, small (e.g., one-fifth of initial money) or large (five times the initial money), would be adequate to circulate commodities. Based on the quantity theory, an increase in money increases proportionally prices, and vice versa. The price-specie flow mechanism applies the quantity theory to many countries. The rise in money supply in the United Kingdom (UK) will cause its prices to rise;[2] its goods are no longer as competitive compared to other countries. Its exports will therefore decline, and imports of cheaper goods will rise. UK's trade balance will be in deficit, and specie will flow out to settle the deficit. This outflow of specie will cause a sharp contraction of money in the UK, a proportional fall in prices, and a trade surplus. In a free trade model, a self-regulating mechanism equilibrates balances of payments and price levels and prevents persistent inflation in any given country. Hume established the monetary approach to the balance of payments, which related the adjustment of the balance of payments to the demand of money in the country. An increase in demand for money would necessarily reduce prices and increase competitiveness. Inversely, a decrease in demand for money would have the opposite effect.

3.2 Adam Smith's absolute advantage

To oppose mercantilism, Adam Smith elaborated the principle of absolute advantage. A country should produce commodities for which it is most efficient, and then exchange these commodities for goods in which it is least efficient. Trade along the absolute advantage principle would elevate the welfare of each trading country. It is easy to prove that the United Kingdom should not grow tea, but rather produce cars, computers, and medicine, and exchange them for tea grown in Burundi. Let us assume two countries and two commodities. If each country can produce one good cheaper (i.e., with less labor) than it can be produced in the other, each will have an advantage in the production of one commodity and a disadvantage in the production of the other. Free trade makes each country export the commodity in which it has an advantage and import the commodity in which it has a disadvantage.

Table 11.1 shows that wheat can be produced more cheaply in the United States and textile more cheaply in Britain. The United States has an absolute advantage in wheat and an absolute disadvantage in textile. It will export wheat and import textile. Based on labor products in Table 11.1, one yard of textile is worth one bushel of wheat.

3.3 Ricardo's comparative advantage

Ricardo admirably elaborated the law of comparative advantage that trade was mutually profitable even when one of the countries was able to produce every commodity more cheaply (in terms of labor or all resources) than the other country. Let the labor cost of both wheat and textile be less in the United

Table 11.1 Production of one unit of labor

	In US	In UK
Wheat (in bushels)	3	1
Textile (in yards)	1	3

Table 11.2 United States and UK labor input to produce (in labor hours)

	In US	In UK
One unit of wheat	1	3
One unit of textile	2	4

States than in the UK; the theory of comparative cost advantage asserts that the United States would benefit from trade with UK! Suppose the United States produces textile with one-half the labor and wheat with one-third of labor than the UK does (Table 11.2). Then, the United States has a comparative edge in wheat and a comparative disadvantage in textile, in spite of an absolute edge in both goods. By the same token, the UK has a comparative edge in textile. The earnest principle in Ricardo's theory of comparative advantage is that each and every country has definitely an advantage in some industries and a disadvantage in others and trade will spontaneously obey this principle.

Table 11.2 portrays the principle of comparative advantage. In the United States, labor input is one hour for wheat and two hours for textile. In the UK, labor input is three hours for wheat and four hours for textile. Obviously, the United States is far less costly in both wheat and textile. With a remarkable genius, Ricardo showed that the United States and the UK would both benefit if the United States would specialize in wheat, the UK in textile, and the United States would sell wheat against UK's textile. Opponents to free trade in the UK may contend that the United States will undersell UK producers in every commodity: wheat and textile. They may appeal for protection in form of an import tariff or quota to preserve UK employment. Likewise, opponents to free trade in the United States may contend that the UK wages are lower than those of the United States. Consequently, competition of the UK workers would reduce US workers' real wage. If the US workers face competition of the UK workers who have lower real wage, the real wage of the US worker must drastically fall. A protective tariff against cheap imports would preserve US real wage. Brilliantly, Ricardo proved that both contentions were unfounded.

In a free trade regime, workers in the United States and the UK would enjoy higher real wages than in no-trade equilibrium, simply because they would buy the imported goods for fewer hours of labor. Consequently, prohibitive tariffs on either or both sides would diminish real wages in both countries.

Table 11.2 depicts real wages before trade. The real wage of the US worker for an hour of work is one unit of wheat or 0.5 unit of textile, i.e., the price of one unit of wheat = 0.5 unit of textile. Before trade, the UK worker is even less well-off; he is remunerated for an hour of work only 1/3 unit of wheat or 0.25 unit of textile, i.e., the price of one unit of wheat = 0.75 unit of textile. Clearly, the difference in relative labor cost ratios yielded different price ratios of wheat and textile in the two countries. In the United States, textile will be twice dearer than wheat, because it uses twice as much labor. In the UK, textile will only 4/3 times as expensive as wheat.

In free trade regime, arbitrage opportunities become available and arbitrageurs will equalize the relative price of wheat and textile in the US and UK markets. Arbitrageurs buy where goods are cheap and sell where they are expensive. With textile price relatively higher in the United States, they will soon ship textile from the UK to the United States. To counterbalance the flow of textile, they will ship wheat from the United States to the UK markets, where wheat prices are higher than in the United States. The US textile industry will experience a severe price competition; it may lose all its workers to its rival US wheat sector. The opposite will happen in the UK; workers will leave the wheat sector for the textile industry, in which the UK has a comparative cost advantage.

Gains arise from trade. In the United States, each one hour of labor is still paid one unit of wheat it produces. But, with trade, one US unit of wheat is exchanged for more than 0.5 unit of textile. However, it cannot be exchanged for more than 0.75 unit of textile which is the UK's price. In the trade regime, the common wheat price will be somewhere between 0.5 and 0.75 unit of textile. US labor earns more in textile to the extent the wheat price exceeds 0.5 unit of textile. Likewise, the UK labor benefits in selling textile for wheat by any extent the price of wheat is less than 0.75 unit of textile. With trade, in the United States, one hour of labor buys the same wheat; but it buys more imported textile. Hence, labor in the United States is able to consume more of both goods. The same welfare gain is enjoyed by the UK workers who get more of the cheapened imported wheat for an hour of labor. Inasmuch as they receive the same real wage in textile, their budget is also enlarged. It is the increased production of both goods in the United States and UK, which specialization and trade entailed, that makes workers in both countries well off.

The theory of comparative advantage asserts that even if one of two countries is absolutely more competitive in the production of every commodity than the other, if each specializes in the commodity for which it has a comparative edge trade will yield gains to both countries. Real incomes of productive factors increase in both countries. Restricting foreign trade will not favor production factors such as labor; instead, it will diminish their real wages by making imports expensive and by making the commercial countries less productive through forfeiting the efficiency inherent in the specialization along comparative advantage. Ricardo's comparative advantage principle establishes the solid foundation for free trade.

Figure 11.1 illustrates the gains from trade for any country. The triangle OAB shows the production possibilities set of the United States; the line AB has a slope equal to the price of wheat in terms of textile before trade. Without trade, the United States can achieve only allocation H which maximizes its social welfare. With trade, a new set of allocations becomes achievable through trade.

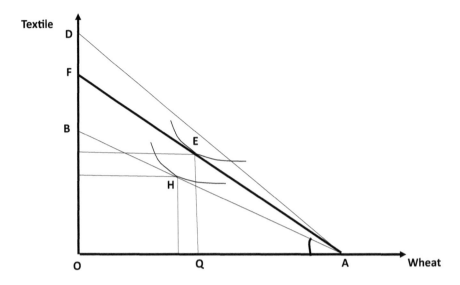

Figure 11.1 Comparative advantage: gains from trade

It is shown by a triangle ABD. The line AD has a slope equal to the price of wheat in terms of textile in the UK before trade. Thanks to trade, the United States can attain an allocation E where it consumes more wheat and textile than before trade. The new price of wheat in terms of textile is shown by the slope of the line AF. At the new equilibrium, the United States produces only wheat, with wheat output equal to OA; it consumes OQ of wheat and exports AQ of wheat to the UK against imports of textile equal to EQ. In a free trade regime, each country must be fully specialized. Before trade, both countries produce some of both goods. The price at which they produce and consume differ. After trade, the price at which both countries produce, consume, and trade must be the same. The common price of wheat in terms of textile will lie between the two pre-trade price ratios and will depend upon the strength of the demand and supply in the two countries for each of the two commodities. If consumers have an intense desire for wheat relative to available supplies of wheat and textile, the price ratio will settle near the upper limit shown by the slope of the line AD; if textile is much demanded in both countries, the final wheat price in terms of textile will settle near the slope of the line AB.

4. The Heckscher–Ohlin (H-O) model

In 1920s, Heckscher and Ohlin (H-O), became interested in explaining the origin of comparative cost advantage through a more encompassing view of the production factors and natural resources of a country. In fact, Ricardo's theory of comparative advantage used a one-factor model in which a country had a relatively higher competitive edge in one sector while the trading partner had a comparative advantage in another sector. According to H-O, there should be differences in the underlying countries' endowments in climatic conditions, land, natural resources, labor skills and ethics, level of technical know-how, entrepreneurship, capital, marketing networks, etc. that explain comparative advantage in labor costs. Hence, although the UK was a producer of corn, in view of climate conditions, the United States would have a comparative advantage in corn production. The essence of H-O theory was that countries were endowed differently in natural resources, climate, factors of production, work skills and ethics, etc.; the differences in underlying resource endowments created comparative advantage by affecting the production costs of goods. For example, an energy-intensive country would have comparative cost advantage in producing and exporting goods that are energy intensive (e.g., petrochemicals, paper, cement, steel, etc.). The H-O model generalizes Ricardo's model to many resources; its theory is that a country will export goods that use its affluent resources intensively against importing commodities that use its scarce resources intensively. In a two-factor case, such as energy and climate, the H-O predicts that an energy-rich economy will sell energy-intensive goods. In contrast, a climate-favored economy will develop tourism.

The H-O model considers two countries, two homogenous factors of production, labor and capital, and two homogenous goods: one is capital intensive (e.g., harvesters) and another is labor intensive (e.g., clothing). The prices are the factors' prices and the goods' prices. Perfect competition is assumed; each country has a free market economy consisting of consumers and competitive firms. An essential hypothesis of the H-O model is that the two countries are identical, except for the difference in factor endowments. More specifically, it stipulates that technologies are identical, but that each commodity uses one of the factors more intensively; it supposes that the social preferences are the same. The relative affluence in capital will cause the capital-rich country to produce the capital-intensive commodity cheaper than the labor-rich country and vice versa. The only channel of exchange between countries is trade in goods; capital and labor are now allowed to move between countries. The H-O model has encompassed four main principles: the H-O theorem, the Stolper-Samuelson Theorem, the factor-price equalization (FPE) theorem, and the Rybczynski theorem.

4.1 The Heckscher-Ohlin theorem

The H-O theorem shows that differences in resource endowments among countries underline the reason for trade to exist. The composition of trade between countries will be influenced by their respective resources and comparative cost advantages. A capital-rich country is one that possesses more capital relative to the other country; equivalently, a labor-rich country has a larger labor force than the partner country. Accordingly, the capital/labor ratio is higher in the capital-rich country than in the labor-rich country. In a pre-trade regime, the capital-rich capital may produce the capital-intensive commodity in excess in relation to its output in labor-intensive commodity; consequently, the price of the capital-intensive commodity in terms of the labor-intensive commodity will be lower in the capital-rich country than in the labor-rich country. Likewise, the former country, being rich in labor, may produce the labor-intensive commodity in excess to its output in capital-intensive commodity; consequently, the price ratio of capital-intensive to labor-intensive commodity would be higher compared to the ratio that prevails in the capital-rich country.

In a free trade regime, arbitrageurs will seize differences in price ratios to make a free gain. Traders will ship the cheaper good to the dearer market; accordingly, capital-intensive commodities will be shipped to the labor-intensive market. Inversely, the labor-intensive commodities will be exported to the capital-intensive market where they fetch higher prices. The trade volumes will increase until the price ratio is equalized in the two markets.

4.2 The Stolper-Samuelson theorem

The Stolper-Samuelson analyzes the relationship between changes in output, output prices, and changes in factor remunerations such as wages and capital rentals (i.e., the interest rate) in the H-O model. The theorem was initially invented to examine how tariffs would modify the capitalist and workers compensations, viz. the income distribution, in a country. The theorem may be applied to study the effects of trade liberalization. The theorem held that a rise in the price of the capital-intensive commodities, for whatever reason, will entail a higher demand for capital; consequently, the capital rental will increase and the labor wage rate will decline. Likewise, an increase in the price of the labor-intensive commodity would entail higher demand for labor; consequently, the wage rate increases and the capital rental declines.

4.3 The Factor-Price Equalization (FPE) theorem

As clearly conveyed by the name of the theorem, in a free trade regime, output prices would be equalized; in turn, wages and capital rentals would also be equalized in the trading countries. Basic hypotheses underlined the validity of the theorem; an essential hypothesis was that with the same production technology in both countries, perfect competition in commodities and factor markets was assumed to prevail. In a perfectly competitive market, factors receive the value of their marginal productivity; the latter is influenced by output prices. Thus, when output prices differ between countries, so will the value of marginal productivities; consequently, wage rates and capital rentals will differ among countries. In a free trade, the one-price law applies. More specifically, commodity prices are equalized; the value of marginal products, the wage rates, and rental rates become all equal among trading countries. To analyze the effects of different factor dotation, the H–O model assumed identical production technology in trading countries. If this assumption is dropped, as in Ricardo's model, then output prices equalization would not necessarily equalize factor prices. Notwithstanding, in a free trade based on differences in factor endowments, the FPE theorem may predict a narrowing in any gap between factor prices.

4.4 The Rybczynski theorem

The Rybczynski theorem illustrates the relationship between changes in a country's factor dotation and changes in final outputs in a H–O framework. The theorem maintained that an increase in a country's supply of a factor will enable an increase in the commodity which uses that factor intensively, and a decrease in the output of the other good. For instance, if a capital-rich country enjoys a further increase in capital, it will step up the production of the capital-intensive good; at the same time, it will reduce the production of the labor-intensive good. The theorem could be useful in discussing topics such as population growth and hence labor force growth, investment, and immigration within the H–O model.

In sum, the H–O model elaborated the following principles:

- Two countries A and B will trade, if relative price of commodities X and Y are different; X and Y being produced in both A and B. The motivation for trade is the difference in commodity prices in the two countries. As in Mill (1821), the motivation underlying inter-regional trade is always that goods can be bought cheaper from outside than they can be produced at home.
- Under perfect competition, prices are equal to average costs. Thus, relative price differences arise from factor-price differences in the two countries. Factor prices are determined by factors' supply and demand. Assuming given outputs and factor demands, it follows that a capital-rich country has a cheaper capital price and a labor-rich country has a relatively lower labor price.
- Based on the H–O model, each country is better off producing commodities which are intensive in its affluent factor. If X is a labor-intensive product in labor-rich country A, it will be cheaper than in B, because labor is relatively cheaper in A. Likewise in respect to Y, the capital-intensive product in capital-rich country B, is relatively cheaper as cost of capital is relatively lower than in A.
- As a result, A will tend to specialize in X and sell its surplus. Likewise, B will specialize in Y and export its surplus. Trade arises because of factor-dotation difference and factor immobility. In a model where factors of production cannot move among countries but where commodities are allowed to move freely, free trade may be seen as a substitution for factor mobility.

5. The effects of an import tariff

Trade protection, a basic principle of mercantilism, has been and continues to be an obstacle to free trade. An awkward example of trade protection was the British Corn-Laws (1815–1848) aimed at protecting local farmers; this law turned out to be disastrous to workers and manufacturers, and elicited powerful local opposition until it was repealed in 1848. A mandate of the World Trade Organization is to lift trade barriers among countries. Governments impose duties to protect local producers (e.g., farmers or manufacturers) and employment or to collect taxes for the budget. The argument of infant industries had often been invoked. McKinnon (1973) and Shaw (1973) attacked the protection policy and called for liberalization of trade. Countries that followed the protection policy paid a high price in terms of an inability to industrialize and compete in foreign markets. Countries who followed an open export-oriented strategy were able to industrialize and gain both in terms of employment and economic growth.

To illustrate the welfare effects of a unit tariff imposed on an imported product such as corn we consider a market in a small importing country that faces an international price of P_1 in free trade. The hypothesis of small country means that demand and supply of this country have no impact on world prices. The free trade equilibrium is depicted in Figure 11.2 where P_1 is the free trade equilibrium price. At that price, domestic demand is Q_2, domestic supply Q_1 and imports are the difference Q_2-Q_1. When a specific tariff is implemented by a small country it will raise the domestic price by the full value of the tariff. Suppose the price in the importing country rises to P_2 because of the tariff. In this case the tariff rate would be $t = P_2$-P_1.

Table 11.3 provides a summary of the direction and magnitude of the welfare effects to consumers, producers, and the governments in the importing country.

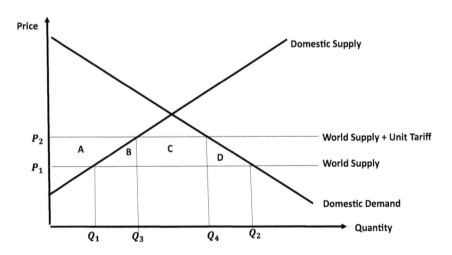

Figure 11.2 Welfare effects of an import tariff: small country

Table 11.3 Welfare effects of an import tariff

Consumer surplus = $-(A+B+C+D)$	Producer surplus = $+A$	Government Revenue = $+C$	National Welfare = $-(B-D)$

The aggregate national welfare effects is also shown. Consumers of the product in the importing country are worse off as a result of the tariff. The increase in the domestic price of both imported goods and the domestic substitutes reduces consumer surplus in the market. Producers in the importing country are better off as a result of the tariff. The increase in the price of their product increases producer surplus in the industry. The price increase also induces an increase in output of existing firms, an increase in employment, and an increase in profit and/or payments to fixed costs. The government receives tariff revenue as a result of the tariff. Who will benefit from the revenue depends on how the government spends it. These funds help support diverse government spending programs, therefore, someone within the country will be the likely recipient of these benefits. The aggregate welfare effect for the country is found by summing the gains and losses to consumers, producers and the government. The net effect consists of two components: a negative production efficiency loss (B), and a negative consumption efficiency loss (D). The two losses together are typically referred to as "deadweight losses." Because there are only negative elements in the national welfare change, the net national welfare effect of a tariff must be negative. This means that a tariff implemented by a "small" importing country must reduce national welfare.

The Corn-Laws kept food costs high, heavily penalized workers, manufacturers were harmed since they had to pay higher wages, and famine occurred in Ireland. Moreover, as trading countries could not sell cereals in the UK, they could not in turn buy UK's industrial products, which restricted the UK manufacturing exports. In sum, whenever a "small" country implements a tariff, national welfare falls. The higher the tariff is set, the larger will be the loss in national welfare. The tariff causes a redistribution of income. Producers and the recipients of government spending gained, while consumers lose. Because the country is assumed "small," the tariff has no effect upon the price in the rest of the world, therefore there are no welfare changes for producers or consumers there. Even though imports are reduced, the related reduction in exports by the rest of the world is assumed to be too small to have a noticeable impact.

6. The effects of an export subsidy

Mercantilism used the state power to protect a group of producers by securing to them a floor price for their products. In many commodity markets, international prices fluctuate and may rise as well as fall by significant margins. Domestic producers may face rigid costs, such as minimum wage laws, and many other inefficiencies, and may not be able to compete except with substantial support from the government. We consider the case of a small country for which the international price is a datum which is not affected by changes in demand and supply of the small country. Figure 11.3 shows the distortions of an export subsidy. The free trade equilibrium price is P_1. At that price, domestic demand is Q_2, domestic supply Q_1 and exports are the difference Q_1-Q_2. When a specific subsidy is implemented by a small country it will raise the domestic price by the full value of the subsidy. Suppose the price in the exporting country rises to P_2 because of the subsidy. In this case the subsidy rate would be t = P_{2-} P_1.

Table 11.4 provides a summary of the welfare effects to consumers, producers, and the government in the exporting country. Consumers of the product in the exporting country are worse off as a result of the subsidy. The increase in the domestic price of exported goods reduces consumer surplus in the market. Producers in the exporting country are better off as a result of the subsidy. The increase in the price of their product increases producer surplus in the industry. The price increase also induces an increase in output of existing firms, an increase in employment, and an increase in profit and/or payments to fixed costs. The government incurs a loss of the revenue as a result of the subsidy. Who will pay for this loss of the revenue depends on how the government finances its expenditure. This loss of revenue would undermine diverse government spending programs; therefore, someone within the country will be the

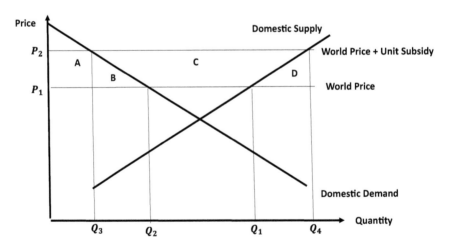

Figure 11.3 Welfare effects of an export subsidy: small country

Table 11.4 Welfare effects of an export subsidy

Consumer surplus =	Producer surplus =	Government Revenue =	National Welfare =
− (A+B)	+A+B+C	− B−C−D	− (B+D)

likely loser. The aggregate welfare effect for the country is found by summing the gains and losses to consumers, producers and the government. The net effect consists of two components: a negative production efficiency loss (D), and a negative consumption efficiency loss (B). The two losses together are typically referred to as "deadweight losses." Because there are only negative elements in the national welfare change, the net national welfare effect of a subsidy must be negative. This means that a subsidy implemented by a "small" importing country must reduce national welfare.

7. The foreign exchange markets

Mercantilism became too entrenched in foreign exchange markets and dealt a serious blow to trade and capital flows as well as to economic development. By abolishing the gold standard in 1931, industrial countries used the exchange rate as a commercial policy tool as well as an instrument of adjustment of the external deficit without a wage-price deflation; the latter was required by the Hume price-specie flow mechanism. With rigid wages and prices, exchange rate was seen as an essential instrument of internal and external deficits adjustment. This action was hailed by Keynes (1936) and followers as a triumph against the barbaric gold. In fact, an exchange rate depreciation is equivalent to an import tax and an export subsidy. The Bretton Woods fixed exchange rate system (1945–1971) brought some measure of stability of exchange rates. However, repetitive devaluations by many countries showed that countries found it more appealing to use the exchange rate as an instrument for alleviating budget and external deficits without resorting to deflation. The dismantlement of the Bretton Woods in 1971 was followed by endless instabilities of exchange rates. In a bid to stabilize exchange rates, a number of European countries established the Eurozone in 1999 to establish a common money among them.

Many countries deliberately depreciate currency to gain competitiveness in face of rigid wages and intractable internal and external deficits. Figure 11.4 shows that ultra-cheap money policy in the United States during 2002–2008 contributed to a dramatic depreciation of the US dollar vis-à-vis some key partner currencies, e.g., the Eurozone and Japan. To counter this policy, key partners either adopted an ultra-cheap money policy and excessive fiscal expansion, or prevented currency appreciation via restriction on speculative capital flows.

The foreign exchange market is an area where mercantilism seriously undermined export and economic growth of many developing countries. By forcing control and appropriation of foreign exchange, a large number of developing countries became trapped in endless external deficits and debt accumulation. Many of these countries had an inconvertible currency, forced import licensing and foreign exchange surrender, and a large number of restrictions on current account as well as capital movements. Direct foreign investment was negligible,

Figure 11.4 Euro and Japanese Yen monthly exchange rates, 2000–2015

Source: IMF, IFS

and large capital flight was under way. In such countries with foreign exchange monopolized by the government, private sector development was suffocated, and the sources of foreign exchange dried up, except from traditional exports such as primary products. The theories of Hume, Smith, and Ricardo that advocated free trade were ignored by mercantilists. These theories looked at trade as an exchange of commodities as implied by Say's law and stressed the futility of controlling foreign exchange, such as forbidding gold and silver exports and restricting imports. A country has to promote exports: it can never be short of foreign exchange in a free market context (Ricardo 1817). Many writers criticized foreign exchange control, including Mises (1953), McKinnon (1973), and Shaw (1973). To deal with the self-inflicted foreign exchange shortage, deluded governments had to rely on extensive borrowing to finance their basic imports. With repeated debt crises and an inability to repay borrowed debt, many countries fell into decline.

Based on failed control policies in many countries, a totally free foreign exchange market is fundamental for a country's economic growth. Restrictions on this market penalize heavily the economy. They undermine both trade and capital flows with the rest of world, and undermine the exports sector. Foreign exchange is exactly like any other market; if left free, it is self-correcting. A shortage of foreign exchange is only temporary. The economy will adjust through price and income mechanisms which make exports highly competitive and reduce imports. The shortage tide will be reversed. However, government intervention had diminished the automatism of the foreign exchange market; the government had to resort to borrowing as the only way to alleviate foreign exchange shortage.

Domestic credit expansion leads to an outflow of foreign exchange. During the nineteenth century, many banks were not able to provide the gold needed for settling foreign payments: they failed. Modern central banks interfere with foreign exchange movements. When there is an outflow of foreign exchange, there is necessarily a drop of money supply and a subsequent fall in prices; the central bank foils the deflation of prices and incomes and sterilizes the outflow by an expansion of credit. In contrast, when there are important inflows of foreign exchange, there is a consequent increase of money supply. To prevent inflation and an expansion of incomes and imports, the central bank sterilizes these inflows through a tightening of credit. These operations of the central bank were unnecessary.

Foreign exchange market has a demand and supply forces both operate in the current and capital accounts of the balance of payments (Figure 11.5). The current account operations supply foreign exchange from exports, services, factor incomes, and transfers. They absorb foreign exchange through imports, services, factor incomes, and transfers. The main determinants of the current accounts are prices (Hume) and incomes (Cantillon). In the capital account, the supply of foreign exchange arises from foreign direct investment, foreign demand for domestic stocks and bonds, and repayment of debt. The demand for foreign exchange arises from investment, domestic demand for foreign bonds and stocks, and repayment of foreign debt. The main determinants of capital account operations are returns on assets and expectations regarding the future movements of the exchange rate. The interplay of demand and supply forces lead to an instantaneous equilibrium of the foreign exchange market. If the government fixes the exchange rate at S_1, there will be excess demand for exchange equal to $Q_1 Q_2$ to be filled with foreign borrowing. Expansion of credit shifts the demand curve for foreign exchange rightward and depreciates the exchange rate to S_2. Likewise, structural inhibitions to exports reduce foreign exchange supply and move the supply curve leftward and depreciate the exchange rate to S_3. If the

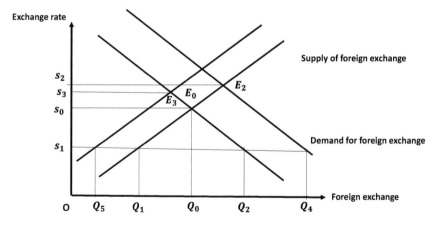

Figure 11.5 The foreign exchange market

government maintains the exchange rate at S_1, foreign borrowing expands in either case.

8. Sharia free trade and exchange model

Sharia model admits no restriction, by the government or an interest group, to the free circulation of goods, labor, and capital across countries. Duties, subsidies, and quotas all violate Sharia law. Trade is vital, always mutually beneficial between domestic or foreign traders, and should be totally free. The government has no natural right to obstruct free trade. Trade tariffs or subsidies have no existence in a Sharia model where borders between countries imply no natural restrictions on the free movement of goods. Trade has enhanced considerably the welfare of people. This needs no elaboration, and has been fully demonstrated by the classics Smith, Ricardo, and Mill, as well as Heckscher and Ohlin. Countries are endowed differently with climate conditions, natural resources, and technical and industrial advance, and would enjoy enormous gains from trade. Japan, with limited agriculture potential, would prosper by exporting industrial products and importing energy, agriculture, and raw materials. Contrary to mercantilism, a country would benefit by eliminating import restrictions and should import as much as it could, provided it could export as much as it could without barriers.

Sharia model forbids interest-based debt in financing trade. The debt model has been rejected in the 1950s in favor of "trade and not aid." Countries that relied on borrowing to finance their imports were not able to industrialize and remained thoroughly dependent on primary exports, exhibiting an endless structural, external deficit. Debt crowded out exports. Reliance on debt was partly due to trade restrictions in partner countries. Moreover, countries became debt-stressed and had to default on their foreign debt. Sharia allows foreign direct investment, which involves no interest-debt and is more efficient than debt, since capital is investment in productive projects, whereas debt often finances consumption products. In Sharia, a country which puts restrictions on imports will not be able to export, since debt financing of exports and imports is not available. Similarly, a country that is prevented to export to the rest of the world should not import with debt financing and should rely on its own production and develop its industries. Moreover, a country should necessarily develop its exports and cannot live forever on debt, as the case seems to be for most of the developing countries now.

In the area of foreign exchange, the government should not control the foreign exchange market. Any control of foreign exchange is a violation of Sharia property rights and freedom of trade. In a Sharia model, monetary policy as a trade tool is not allowed. Prices and wages are fully flexible which allows Hume price-specie flow mechanism to be fully operational in the adjustment of the external trade sector. Changes in the money supply operate through changes in the balance of payments, discoveries of precious metals, and their conversion from and back to non-monetary use. As Locke (1691) has emphatically maintained, the value of currency has to remain unaltered, with no devaluation or re-evaluation via changing the denomination in money of accounts or altering the metal content and its fineness.

Sharia model allows no policy role for exchange rate. A contemporaneous exchange rate policy that uses exchange rate as a policy instrument to prevent wage-price adjustment and force exchange rate devaluations violates Sharia, since this policy redistributes wealth and income from one group to benefit another group. Devaluation may encourage exports; however, the higher profit of exporters is not paid up by foreign buyers, but by a redistribution of income from those citizens who are penalized by the inflationary impact of devaluation in favor of the exporters who are beneficiaries of the devaluation.

9. Conclusions

Sharia model is a free trade and exchange model. Domestic as well as international trade are fully beneficial to trading partners. A basic principle formulated by Adam Smith stipulates that without trade there can be no specialization and division of labor. In a Sharia model, interest-based debt is not available; hence, it cannot crowd out export. A country has to develop exports as much as it can to enjoy an equivalent amount of imports. Tariffs and subsidies violate Sharia law of free trade and can only impede growth and employment. Structural impediments to wage and price flexibility, an element of Hume's price-specie flow mechanism, violate Sharia. Often countries become deprived of this mechanism and see inflationism and currency depreciation as the only way to external adjustment.

Mercantilism and trade obstruction prevent further international integration and gains from efficiency. Debt financing of external deficits prevent further growth of trade and keep many countries unable to develop their export sectors despite their amazing labor resources. For them, debt financing is an import of unemployment. Moreover, debt financing essentially covers fiscal deficits and higher consumption; it contributes to a consumption of capital that could have helped many countries invest and grow. Debt financing made external deficits eternal and structural, with some countries exhibiting persistent deficits over many decades. Most developed countries impose a protection of sectors where they have no comparative advantage. This policy is harmful to each trading party. Consumers in each country enjoy less of each product. If some developing countries could export freely their farm products, they would be able to import a lot of industrial products, such as medical machinery, which they lack considerably under the present system of trade restrictions.

Notes

1 Kindleberger (1973), Gandolfo (2004), Williamson (1983), Caves and Jones (1981), and Krugman and Obstfeld (2003) are useful references for the theory of trade and exchange rates.
2 We note that Cantillon (1730) incorporated the role of money incomes in the trade balance adjustment mechanism.

References

Cantillon, R., 1730, *Essay on the Nature of Trade in General*, Auburn, AL: Ludwig von Mises Institute.

Caves, R., and Jones, R., 1981, *World Trade and Payments: An Introduction*, Boston: Little, Brown and Company.

Gandolfo, G., 2004, *International Economics*, New York: Springer-Verlag.

Hume, D., 1752, *Political Discourses*, Edinburgh: Printed by R. Fleming, for A. Kincaid and A. Donaldson.

Keynes, J. M., 1936, *The General Theory of Employment, Interest and Money*, London: Palgrave Macmillan.

Kindleberger, C., 1973, *International Economics*, 5th edition. Homewood, IL: Richard D. Irwin, Inc.

Krugman, P., and Obstfeld, M., 2003, *International Economics, Theory and Practice*, 6th edition, New York: Harper Collins College Publishers.

Locke, J., 1691, *Some Considerations on the Consequences of the Lowering of Interest and the Raising of the Value of Money*, The Works of John Locke, 1824, London: C. Balwin, Printer.

McKinnon, R., 1973, *Money and Capital in Economic Development*, Washington, DC: Brookings Institution.

Mill, J., 1821, *Elements of Political Economy*, 3rd edition revised and corrected, London: Henry G.

Ohlin, B., 1933, *International and interregional Trade*, Cambridge, MA: Harvard University Press.

Ricardo, D., 1817, *On the Principles of Political Economy and Taxation*, London: John Murray.

Rothbard, M., 2006, *Economic Thought Before Adam Smith: An Austrian Perspective on the History of Economic Thought, Volume I*, Auburn, AL: Ludwig von Mises Institute.

Say, J. B., 1803, *A Treatise on Political Economy*, Philadelphia: Claxton, Kemsen, & Haffelfingee.

Shaw, E., 1973, *Financial Deepening in Economic Development*, Oxford: Oxford University Press.

Smith, A., 1776, *An Inquiry Into the Nature and Causes of the Wealth of Nations*, London: Methuen and Co., Ltd., ed. Edwin Cannan, 1904, Fifth Edition.

Spooner, L., 1886, *A Letter to Grover Cleveland*, Boston: Benj. R. Tucker, Publisher.

Von Mises, L., 1953, *The Theory of Money and Credit*, New Haven: Yale University Press.

Williamson, J., 1983, *The Open Economy and the World Economy*, New York: Basic Books, Inc., Publishers.

12 Growth policy and private sector development

1. Introduction

A number of developing countries are endowed with vast territories, rivers, natural resources, and large population, yet no sustainable growth has taken place, with unemployment remaining at worrisome rates ranging between 15–30 percent of the labor force. Since their independence in the 1950s, these countries continue to depend heavily on foreign debt. In contrast, some miniscule countries, with negligible natural resources, were able to maintain high growth and achieve annual per capita far exceeding that of industrial countries. Poverty has deteriorated so much in a large number of countries that the international financial institutions decided to initiate in mid 1990s the poverty reduction strategy; yet still no significant progress as countries are trapped deeper in poverty and unemployment. Many countries were unable to create a laissez-faire environment favorable to the domestic and foreign private sector investment. Basic conditions for private sector participation are missing; instead impediments are pervasive. These include widespread insecurity and lawlessness, unruly governments that impose high taxation on private sector incomes, and powerful labor unions that have ruined basic government services such as education and health and formal private enterprises. There may be also a lack of basic infrastructure such as power, water, sanitation, health, schools, etc. The financial infrastructure may be too shallow, which constrains saving and investment.

Adam Smith (1776), Ricardo (1821), Say (1803), and James Mill (1821) have inquired into the wealth of nations and showed that the laissez-faire model was favorable to growth. The causes of economic decline and poverty are not within the private sector; the latter is a natural body, which is responsive to the environment that surrounds it. If the environment is propitious for freedom, then the private sector is endowed with natural forces that will make it grow and create wealth; if the environment is corrupted and unsafe, then the private sector will see its energy for growth frozen and will become in a state of decay as explicated by Ibn Khaldoun. Nock (1935) contended that the more the government expands, the less the private sector can grow. This truth applies to both developed and poor countries. When the government observes no fiscal balance, keeps increasing debt, empowers labor unions, and imposes too many trade restrictions and high taxation, the domestic and foreign private sector finds no opportunity for investment.

Sharia model aims at promoting the most favorable environment for private sector laissez-faire by setting laws against absolutism, interference with free markets, excessive taxation, and crimes. It establishes a judicial system that reinforces contracts and strictly eliminates crimes. Sharia model prohibits interest-based debt: This interdiction changes completely the environment of the private sector: it fully liberalizes the financial sector, the latter becomes an efficient intermediary for mobilizing capital, and, since a country cannot borrow, it will have forcibly to export to be able to import. Moreover, wage and price flexibility prevails, which enables the economy to operate at full potential, inflation disappears, and external competitiveness increases.

This chapter covers:

- Optimal growth theory: the Golden rule of capital accumulation
- Promoting an environment conducive to private sector development
- A public private model for infrastructure development
- Public-private partnership (PPP) in infrastructure development
- Models of infrastructure financing
- Models of financing for small and medium enterprises (SMEs)
- Microfinance: a strategy for reducing poverty and creating employment
- The judicial and social environment for doing business

2. Optimal growth theory: the Golden rule of capital accumulation

The sources of economic growth are the labor force, capital, and science, i.e., technical progress. A main source of economic growth is capital; capital accumulation is a main foundation of growth theory. The capital of a nation includes housing, infrastructure of all types, plants, machinery, inventories of raw materials, etc. Capital is not a natural resource; it is built by labor; it increases tremendously the productive power of the worker. If Robinson and Friday build a canoe and a nest, they catch a far larger quantity of fish than if they continue to use a primitive rod (Bohm-Bawerk 1888). Likewise, using heavy machinery and fertilizers in agriculture multiplies considerably the agricultural output and liberates considerable manpower for industry. In the same vein, using generators produces electric power for industrial and residential use. Railroads, jumbo jets, trailers, big ships, etc. all are capital that tremendously increase the flow of traffic and shorten time between destinations.

Capital accumulation is the path to economic growth (Lewis 1954; Swan 1956; Solow 1956). Developed nations have higher capital per worker and therefore enjoy higher standards of living than developing nations. The more a country accumulates capital, the more it grows. The more the legislative and institutional environment are favorable, the more a country is able to accumulate capital and grow. Developed banking and capital markets are crucial for capital accumulation. Capital constitutes an engine of economic growth. There can be no scientific and technological progress without investing in capital. Human capital cannot be developed without material capital, such as schools, universities, and research facilities. Capital embodies scientific advances, such as satellites, machines, airplanes, and computers. The more a nation invests in capital the more it will be able to enjoy higher per capita income.

Capital arises from saving. The national income identity can be formulated as equality of resources (sources of income) and uses:

$$Y + M = C + I + X \qquad (1)$$

Where: *Y, C, I, M,* and *X* denote gross domestic product, aggregate consumption, gross capital formation – i.e., gross fixed capital plus changes in inventories – imports, and exports, respectively. Saving *S* is defined simply as national income *Y* less consumption. It can be expressed as:

$$S = Y - C \qquad (2)$$

The national income identity can be restated as:

$$Y - C - I = X - M \qquad (3)$$
$$S - I = X - M \qquad (4)$$

If the saving-investment gap *S-I* is negative, the country is importing capital. If it is positive, the country is exporting capital essentially through being a creditor.

Often saving is expressed as, $S = {}_sY$, where *S* is a structural parameter called the propensity to save. This parameter is not constant and may be influenced by many factors; such as tax legislation, interest rates, financial intermediation, saving instruments and institutions, inflation, income distribution, etc. Low taxes encourage savings, inflation is a sign of low savings, higher share of profits in national income induces higher savings, and the development of banks and capital markets encourages tremendously savings.

A simple growth model is Harrod model (1939) which is a linear relation between an increase in output ΔY and investment *I*:

$$\Delta Y = I / \lambda \qquad (5)$$

λ is the marginal capital-output ratio, called incremental capital-output ratio (ICOR). Investment may be financed by domestic and foreign resources. Dividing both sides by *Y*, we obtain:

$$g = \frac{\Delta Y}{Y} = \frac{I}{\lambda Y} = \frac{\beta}{\lambda} \qquad (6)$$

Where g stands for the rate of real gross domestic product (GDP) growth; β the rate of real investment in GDP, i.e., $\beta = I/Y$ and λ the real capital-output ratio. A simple inference of Harrod model is for the economy to sustain a given rate of real economic growth it has to invest a required percentage of its real GDP. For instance, if the economy is to grow at 5 percent per year and if its capital productivity as measured by the capital-output ratio λ is 4, then its real investment rate has to be: $\beta = g \times \lambda = 5\% \times 4 = 20\%$.

Evidently, capital is always deployed with labor and some substitution between capital and labor may exist (Solow 1956). The capital is combined with the labor force to produce the real gross product; namely, the real aggregate production function is expressed as:

$$Y = F(K,L) \quad (7)$$

Where Y denotes gross real output, K real capital, and L labor. Let real output per worker be $y = Y/L$, and capital per worker be $k = K/L$, the aggregate production function can be expressed as:

$$y = f(k) \quad (8)$$

Real output per worker y is an increasing function of K. The more capital per worker is used, the higher the real output per worker will be. This relation is illustrated in Figure 12.1. For instance, the produce of a farm could be augmented enormously through the application of machinery, fertilizers, and irrigation. Moreover, in a competitive economy, marginal products are equal to real wage rate (W) and the rental cost of capital (r) as follows:[1]

$$w = \frac{\partial F(K,L)}{\partial L} \quad \text{and} \quad r = \frac{\partial F(K,L)}{\partial K} = f'(k) \quad (9)$$

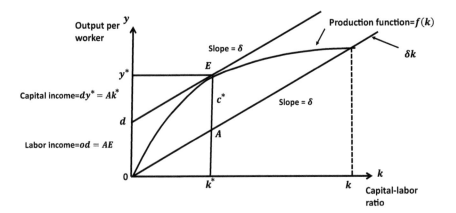

Figure 12.1 Neoclassical golden rule of growth

The output serves to compensate factors of production as follows:

$$Y = rK + wL \tag{10}$$

Dividing by L, we obtain:

$$y = rk + w = f'(k)k + w \tag{11}$$

In a competitive economy, per capita income is composed of wage and capital return. In Figure 12.1, Od is labor income and dy^* is capital income. per capita income serves two purposes: per capita consumption (C) and investment (i). We have:

$$y = c + i \tag{12}$$

Investment serves three purposes: reconstitute depreciated capital, endow new laborers with the same capital as existing workers, and augment the capital/labor ratio. Investment may be expressed as:

$$i = \dot{k} + \mu k + nk = \dot{k} + (\mu + n)k \tag{13}$$

Where $\dot{k}$ = increase in k; μ = rate of depreciation of capital; and n = rate of labor force growth. Let $\delta \equiv \mu + n$, the investment formula becomes:

$$i = \dot{k} + \delta k \tag{14}$$

Per capita income may be reformulated as:

$$y = c + \dot{k} + \delta k \tag{15}$$

In Figure 12.1, we have the production function $y = f(k)$ and the linear function: δk. The difference between the two variables is per capita consumption and net addition to k, i.e., $\dot{k}$:

$$y - \delta k = c + \dot{k} \tag{16}$$

In Figure 12.1, per capita consumption has a maximum at c^*; the associated k^* is called the Golden rule level of capital per worker, with $\dot{k} = 0$ (Phelps 1965). The Golden rule of accumulation establishes the existence of k^* at which consumption per capita is maximized; moreover, $\dot{k} = 0$, i.e., k and L are growing at the same rate n, and so is real GDP, by the virtue of constant returns to scale. The Golden rule of consumption is:

$$c^* = f(k^*) - \delta k^* \tag{17}$$

We recall the income-expenditure identity:

$$y = rk + w = c + i \tag{18}$$

This identity has essential consequences for growth and capital markets. We note that real GDP is a main source of income. We also note that the income of capital does not distinguish between debt and equity; it remunerates real capital regardless of its source of financing. Hence, both creditors and shareholders compete for the same income: rk. We observe that if the competitive assumptions are invalidated, then the income distribution is modified, and the economy may not increase saving and growth. If labor is compensated above its marginal product, then unemployment emerges. Moreover, consumption rises, and investment declines, causing a permanent decline in economic growth. Likewise, if capital is compensated above its marginal product, there will be less demand for investment.

3. Promoting an environment conducive to private sector development

Growth models have addressed the quantitative aspects of economic development. However, capital accumulation cannot proceed when the legal, institutional, and social environment is impeding private sector initiative. Statism can discourage the private sector and keep the economy in a state of decay. When the government becomes dominated by private and political power groups it becomes a major force of economic destruction. Hence, a military junta could keep the country in agony for decades as long as the junta is in power. Likewise a communist, socialist, and centrally planned system can keep the economy in state of impoverishment and bare survival. McKinnon (1973) and Shaw (1973) recognized that an economy cannot develop in a context of corrupted policies. Their message was a full liberalization of capital markets and foreign trade. A government cannot become subservient to a power group without damaging the private sector. It is very important that the government promotes competition in all sectors as well as free price mechanism in the economy. It should reinforce free entry into any industry. The abolition of minimum wage laws and interest rate setting is an important reform for a vibrant private sector and full-potential growth. Minimum wage laws are illusionary because what matters is the real wage, which can be decided only through the market with influence neither from unions nor employers. Likewise, interest rate is a key price in the economy which, if controlled by the government, will cause major distortions. The financial crises of 1929 or 2008 showed that the fixation of an interest rate by the government can never be profitable and could only be too costly. The huge fiscal deficits caused by financial crises would weight on growth and cause economic decline.

Some countries have on their tax books high progressive income taxes both on individuals and corporations. The mere existence of such tax legislation has practically discouraged private enterprise and kept the private sector confined to small shops such as small commerce, mechanical repairs, etc. High corporate tax has either discouraged enterprise, or forced firms to relocate to countries with less penalizing taxation. Hence, hostile legislation makes both the cost of labor and capital too elevated and offer no room for investment or for competing in the foreign markets.

The licensing procedures of firms could be too lengthy, and immigration laws for hiring foreign labor could be rigid. Social environment could be disadvantageous to the private sector; in some countries larceny is so widespread that farmers decide to renounce farming and livestock since a large part of their produce is stolen.

Sharia model provides a favorable framework to the private sector. Competition has to prevail, with free entry and exit, and no interference with wage and price, trade, and creation of enterprises. In a Sharia model, there is no absolute taxation nor absolute spending. Absolute taxation yields unlimited power for the government to grab income and wealth and enrich a political class which often appropriates tax resources and accumulates stolen wealth within or outside the countries such as often seen in many developing countries. Spending programs have to be within natural attributions of the government and not for extravagancy. Taxation has to be Sharia-compliant. The abolition of interest-debt leads to full liberalization of the financial sector, increases savings and investment, and eliminates trade restrictions. Foreign deficit cannot be financed by interest-based borrowing: it can be financed only through exports or non-interest capital flows such as grants or foreign direct investment. Moreover, the government will have to cut down its waste since it can no longer borrow and increase unproductive spending.

In a Sharia model, the saving rate, s, a key variable in an economic model tends to be high. The elimination of interest rate elevates the rate of return on capital for savers who are presently earning very low or no interest income on their savings deposits, and correspondingly saving; it helps financial deepening and higher mobilization of saving from domestic and foreign sources, and the stability of stock markets attract investment into shares and enlarges financial intermediation.

4. A public private model for infrastructure development

An advanced and well-maintained infrastructure would contribute to the expansion of the private sector and to sustain economic growth. Development of economic and social infrastructure is a natural attribute of the government. Because they involve large indivisibilities, large financial resources, complex legal aspects, and free-of charge services, infrastructure projects were predominantly implemented by the government. In retrospect, exclusivity of the state in infrastructure in many countries was not a socially optimal model. In fact, due to low or negative government savings and unsustainable public debt, infrastructure spending had suffered significant cuts in many developing countries, which hindered economic growth in these countries.

A Sharia model proposes a coordinated strategy between the government and the private sector in infrastructure development. The state should not have exclusivity in the construction and maintenance of infrastructure. An active participation of the private sector in infrastructure could be highly profitable for the economy. Privatization of infrastructure enables to mobilize plenty of financial resources, which cannot be easily obtained through taxation; consequently, it will step up significantly the supply of infrastructure in the economy.[2] It is a form of burden sharing and may preempt the necessity for additional taxes destined to infrastructure. Social equity is enhanced inasmuch as the cost of infrastructure is born by users and not the taxpayers which include the poor.

Infrastructure may be built by the government as well as private business. When supplied by the state, the public enjoys infrastructure services free of charge or at a price far below cost. Hence, roads and highways are free of charge; their cost is covered by taxes or by specific road funds. Likewise, state hospitals, schools, and universities impose no charge; their budgets are financed from taxes. Nonetheless, there is a large field in infrastructure for profitable private ownership and operation. In fact, private corporations had invested in railroads, hospitals, communications, airports, ports, turnpikes, universities, schools, electricity, water, and sanitation. Private investment in infrastructure would have great social benefits: it prevents interest-based borrowing by the state, it enhances considerably economic efficiency and social equity, and it lets the government develop infrastructure which serves better the social welfare, including the needs of the poor, and where a charge is not desirable or not practical. It will increase the access of the poor to education, health, water, electricity, and transport.

Two cases are contrasted in Table 12.1. Case I shows only the state invests in infrastructure, and Case II shows both the government and the private sector invest in infrastructure.

Case II is far better than case I; it may not be achieved through taxes; even if it could be, it still remains better since the collection of taxes is costly, and there is no guarantee that new taxes will be earmarked to infrastructure only. Typically, Case II describes a developing country where infrastructure is poorly

Table 12.1 Public and private infrastructure investment

Case I: Government infrastructure		Case II: Government and Private infrastructure	
Taxes	$300	Taxes	$300
Borrowing	$700	Borrowing	$700
		Private savings	$1000
Infrastructure	$1000	Infrastructure	$2000
		Public infrastructure	$1000
		Private infrastructure	$1000
GDP growth rate = 2%		GDP growth rate = 6%	
Unemployment rate = 8%		Unemployment rate = 3%	

developed and where the private sector, if enabled through new legislation, could invest far greater capital in infrastructure than the government could do.

5. Public-private partnership (PPP) in infrastructure development

Besides being developed separately by the public or the private sector, infrastructure projects may be undertaken in the PPP format with a mixed participation of both sectors. In all cases, the government is the decision maker regarding the extent of private sector participation, the identification of main risks associated with the infrastructure project, and the allocation of these risks between the government and the private sector. Under pure privatization, the government may simply devolve the project to the private sector and reserve only a regulatory role for itself. The assets are owned by the private sector and the risks are also assumed by the private sector. Under pure public procurement, the infrastructure is a fully owned, operated, and maintained by the government, all risks remain with the government, and the private sector role is limited only to the construction of the project in compliance to an awarded construction contract. Under a PPP, assets may be jointly owned and risks allocated or jointly shared between the public and private partners.

A public-private partnership is a legally binding contract between government and business for the provision of assets and the delivery of services that allocates responsibilities and business risks among the various partners and generates value for money for taxpayers. In a PPP arrangement, government remains actively involved throughout the project's life cycle. The private sector is responsible for the more commercial functions such as project design, construction, finance, and operations. PPPs take a variety of forms, with varying degrees of public and private sector involvement – and varying levels of public and private sector risk. The benefits of a PPP are that the public and private sectors will have certain advantages relative to each other, and these advantages can be exploited so as to deliver a superior project or service in the most economically efficient manner. The risks are identified from the outset and a key aspect of PPPs is that risks are placed with the party best able to manage them. Because a number of risks associated with the designing, building, and operating of the asset may be transferred to the private partner, the risks facing the government are lowered.

Realizing the potential benefits of PPPs for taxpayers – including lower costs, better service quality, and faster project delivery – depends on allocating project risks to the party best able to manage them. In fact, risk transfer from the public to the private sector is a critical element of all PPPs. The goal is to combine the best capabilities of the public and private sectors for mutual benefit. For example, if a private company assumes responsibility for financing and building a highway, it also assumes responsibility for related risks: interest rates could rise, construction could be delayed, labor costs could increase, energy and building materials cost could rise, etc. If the company also takes responsibility for highway operation and maintenance, it assumes even more risks. For example, traffic volumes might not be as high as anticipated, and unforeseen circumstances such as mudslides, snowstorms, or an earthquake could add significantly to maintenance costs.

6. Models of infrastructure financing

Sharia strictly precludes any interest-based debt. Such interdiction is indeed a benediction for a country because it prevents debt and shields the government budget from any debt service payments. In retrospect, if debt-stressed countries observed this prohibition in the past, they would have been spared the debt burden that has afflicted their economic growth. They would have avoided fiscal mismanagement and would have grown much faster than their actual slow performance.

Sharia allows equity and risk-sharing financing of infrastructure. Essentially, the government jointly with other equity owners supply long-term capital and hold common stocks; they become joint owners of an infrastructure project. Stocks may be liquidated on a secondary market. As in any joint-stock company, the government and private investors bear the same risk and share dividends. In addition to equity financing, Sharia allows issuance of asset-backed securities for financing infrastructure, namely *sukuks*, through a securitization of real assets. Sukuks have a return based on the securitized assets. They are redeemable at a maturity date and may also be traded on a secondary market. Sukuk financing of infrastructure is widely used by many governments (Iqbal and Khan 2004).

To promote Sharia compatible finance for infrastructure, a country should stress the development of stock markets as a channel for long-term resources and liquidity (Askari et al. 2012). Stock ownership is a main feature of capitalism and the stock market is an essential institution for raising long-term capital from domestic and foreign sources and minimizing the risk associated with investment. A propitious approach in infrastructure finance is to rely on an advanced stock market; the latter would enable access to long-term capital at the same time that it provides essential liquidity for investors. This approach has a number of advantages:

- It demonstrates that stock markets can be used as a tool of risk and financial management.
- It reduces the reliance of government budget on borrowing, thus imparting greater stability to the budget and mitigating the risk of "sudden stops."
- It promotes tax equity and reduces the burden of taxation.
- It has positive distributional effect in that the financial resources that would normally go to service public debt which can now be spread wider among the people as returns to the shares of government projects.
- It enhances the potential for financing of larger portfolio of public goods projects without the fear of creating an undue burden on the budget.

- It promotes ownership of public goods by citizens, which should have a salutary effect on maintenance of public goods as it creates an ownership concern among the people and to some extent mitigate "the tragedy of commons."
- It promotes better governance by involving citizens as shareholder-owners of public projects.
- It provides an excellent risk-sharing instrument for financing of long-term public-sector investment.
- It is an effective instrument for firms and individuals to use to mitigate liquidity risks.
- By providing greater depth and breadth to the stock market and minimizing the cost of market participation, governments convert the stock market into an instrument of international risk sharing as other countries and their people can invest in the stock market.

Reliance on stock exchanges for infrastructure was prevalent in the 18th–19th centuries. An example of an important infrastructure financed through shareholders' subscriptions was the Suez Canal. The project was a concession entrusted to a French Company by the Egyptian government for 99 years. The government of Egypt was paid royalties by the Company. Examples of infrastructure concessions financed through risk sharing are numerous. An infrastructure project may require the constitution of a special purpose vehicle (SPV) that will be in charge with financing; the SPV may invite financing from institutional investors, it may also float *sukuks* or shares on the stock exchange.

Governments and corporations have formulated market-determined models for long-term financing of infrastructure. Among the conduits for mobilizing capital there are the following: the equity capital markets, the debt markets, the infrastructure funds, and infrastructure banks. Some of the funding solutions are described below:

6.1 Equity capital markets

6.1.1 YieldCos, a form of asset spin-off

A model of equity financing of energy infrastructure is the Yield Companies (YieldCos). The latter are publicly listed equity vehicles established by power companies to raise capital. Being a new class of assets, YieldCos are promoted through the spin-off of energy companies' assets. Because of a relatively stable cash flow profile of the parents' companies, resulting from credible long-term power sales' agreements and a stable cost structures, YieldCos promise a relatively stable and growing yield in form of dividend income that is attractive for investors. Their aim is to raise equity capital for infrastructure assets at a higher valuation. The YieldCos mobilize money capital through initial public offerings (IPOs).

6.1.2 Infrastructure Project Corporation (IPC)

The Infrastructure Project Corporation (IPC) is a listing vehicle for raising equity financing for infrastructure companies. These companies are involved in projects with long gestation which are preferably financed with long-term equity capital. IPC offers small investors the opportunity to invest in dividend-yielding infrastructure companies. Because they are awarded government concessions, these companies generally receive a stable inflow of revenue. Equity listings of infrastructure project companies on the stock market would secure an adequate funding source for the infrastructure sector. Investors in infrastructure project companies comprise institutional investors such as financial institutions and pension funds as well as both retail and high net worth investors.

6.2 Debt capital market: bonds and sukuks

In addition to the equity markets, the bond markets were a main conduit in mobilizing capital for governments, municipalities, and corporations. They deepened financial intermediation, afforded liquidity, and enhanced efficiency in mobilizing money capital. Bonds may be guaranteed by an asset owned by the issuer, by tax revenues, or by sunk funds. Bonds are rated by rating agencies, have a fixed coupon payable every quarter or semester and a fixed maturity. They offer great investment opportunities to savers, funds, and financial institutions. Bonds are tradeable on secondary markets. High grade bonds are highly liquid. Many countries had to develop the bond markets with a view to finance long-term projects.

In order to attract investors to infrastructure investors, some enhanced bond programs were initiated by issuers. In this vein, the European Union has launched the Project Bond Initiative (PBI) to finance infrastructure projects. By providing credit enhancement, the PBI aims to mobilize private capital for infrastructure and minimize funding costs for infrastructure companies. The credit enhancement may consist of a partial guarantee of senior debt or a funded subordinated debt. Project bonds may appeal to institutional investors who expect normal returns from infrastructure projects with moderate risks.

Another model of infrastructure financing is the green bonds program to mobilize capital for projects with specific environmental benefits. These bonds are issued by financial institutions to attract investors who want to invest in infrastructure that preserves the environment.

Sukuks are the counterpart to bonds. They are Sharia-compliant assets as they avoid interest payment. Governments, local governments, municipalities, and corporations have resorted to *sukuks* for infrastructure financing. Sukuks are issued on the basis of a securitization of real or financial assets. Sukuk can be structured to satisfy long-term infrastructure financing needs in a Sharia-compliant manner, and provide an attractive alternative to bonds. Like bonds, Sukuk programs can be enhanced with guarantee features to reduce risks and attract investors to infrastructure financing.

Many governments emit *sukuks* to finance their infrastructure programs. Projects financed via *sukuks* include government hospitals, highways, airports, etc. Development banks also emit *sukuks* to raise long-term capital for infra-structure. An important application of *sukuks* is in the securitization of mort-gage loans to increase financing for housing, including low-income housing. Mortgage corporations have been founded in many countries to make housing loans more accessible and affordable to home buyers. These corporations issue *sukuks* to finance the purchase of mortgage loans from banks and mortgage companies. By providing liquidity at a reasonable cost to primary lenders of housing loans, these corporations mobilize further financing of housing and therefore reduce the borrowing cost for homeowners.

6.3 Pooled investment vehicles

6.3.1 Asean Infrastructure Fund: AIF [3]

The ASEAN Infrastructure Fund (AIF) is a model of regional cooperation in infrastructure. Its aim is to satisfy the large infrastructure financing needs of the Association of Southeast Asian Nations (ASEAN) region. The fund initially receives equity contributions from ASEAN members and the Asian Devel-opment Bank (ADB). To raise more resources, the AIF resorts to the capital market where it floats perpetual bonds and debt instruments. Through market-based financing, it mobilizes sovereign savings, global institutional investors and multilateral development banks' resources, and taps foreign exchange reserves. Structuring the fund's debt instruments so as to satisfy reserve eligibil-ity requirements may help retain members' sovereign savings for infrastructure investments within the region, and reduce dependence on external investment flows.

6.3.2 Emerging Africa Infrastructure Fund: EAIF

The Emerging Africa Infrastructure Fund (EAIF) aims to solve the dearth of long-term financing for private sector-based infrastructure development in Sub-Saharan Africa (SSA). Its objective is to finance infrastructure projects that promote economic growth and reduce poverty. The EAIF considers that the financing gap for infrastructure in underdeveloped African regions such as SSA should not be funded purely from public resources and through Official Devel-opment Assistance. The EAIF aims at mobilizing private funds on remunerative commercial terms. Accordingly, the EAIF offers long-term infrastructure loans of up to 15 years, however, on commercial terms and not concessional terms.

6.3.3 Fund of Pension Funds: IFM

IFM Investors (IFM) is an investment entity belonging to 30 largest industry-based superannuation funds (Super Funds) in Australia. It aims mainly to pro-vide long-term capital to infrastructure. It offers a range of wholesale unit trusts, pooled superannuation trusts (PSTs), and limited partnerships and segregated mandates for institutional investors globally. The pooling of resources of many pension funds has enabled IFM to constitute a large amount of investment capital and expertise which together have granted those funds investment opportunities in line with their profiles. IFM is a member in the boards of the infrastructure companies in which it holds equity capital. Prudential regulations have been enacted to enhance IFM's success. Regulations aims at channeling pension funds' money into infrastructure companies partially through PSTs. The regulations' emphasis on risk management and governance ensures high standards in infrastructure projects.

6.4 The Asian Infrastructure Investment Bank: AIIB

AIIB is a recently established multilateral financial institution which aims to pool resources with a view to address immense infrastructure needs in Asia countries. By increasing the supply of infrastructure, the AIIB will help promote growth and enhance access to basic services. The AIIB will provide financing to any government, or any agency, or any entity or enterprise operating in the territory of a member concerned with infrastructure projects. It will provide financing in different ways, including investing in the equity capital of an entity, approving loans, and loans for infrastructure. In addition, the AIIB may underwrite, or participate in the underwriting of, securities issued by any entity for financing infrastructure.

7. Models of financing for small and medium enterprises (SMEs)

In any country, SMEs constitute the bulk of output and employment; they exist in all sectors, including agriculture, fishery, industry, commerce, and services. In spite of their importance, SMEs may have difficult access to long-term financing. They constitute a higher risk for investors. There is a wide gap between supply and demand of long-term financing for the SMEs. Many countries have put in place capital market institutions specialized in mobilizing financing for the SMEs. The SMEs' long-term financing model has four main components of the capital markets: (i) the equity capital market, (ii) the debt capital market, (iii) the securitization of issued loans, and (iv) the pooled investment vehicles. In each market, there are financial institutions that mobilize finance for the SMEs, with varying effectiveness in attracting long-term capital. In each market, there are also different risks that may face each type of financial intermediaries and the investors.

7.1 Equity capital markets

7.1.1 Small business investment companies (SBIC)

SBICs are private equity and venture funds with a purpose to mobilize long-term capital for SMEs, and therefore support the growth of this sector. They are licensed and regulated by the US Small Business Administration (SBA).

Instituted by the SBA, the SBIC program intends to promote private financial institutions specialized in satisfying the capital needs of small businesses. SBICs raise equity capital: they may borrow money at a lower cost by issuing SBA-guaranteed securities to enhance investments in small businesses in conformity with SBA regulations. By regulation, SBICs may invest only in small businesses. Generally, SBICs are conceived as limited partnerships. The SBIC fund manager is appointed as the general partner. The limited partners contribute the majority of the private capital; they are typically institutional investors, including banks, and high net worth investors. The majority of SBICs are relatively small; they are privately owned and managed institutions. Nonetheless, many other SBCIs are owned by commercial banks or insurance companies. Some SBICs specialize in equity financing while others in debt financing. A main shortcoming of SBICs is the illiquidity of their investments. Investing in a SBCI is equivalent to purchasing non-ratable and nonmarketable securities. There is no formal secondary market for an SBIC investor to sell his investments to satisfy an immediate need for cash.

7.1.2 Multi-tiered stock markets: a new stock exchange for SMEs

Equity and venture capital institutions specialized in SMEs financing were hindered by the illiquidity of their investments, which constrained capital mobilization for this sector. Aware of this shortcoming, Canada and China have established a multi-tiered equity capital markets. More specifically, capital markets authorities in each country have established a new parallel stock exchange for listing and trading SMEs stocks. In 2011, China founded a new stock exchange, named the National Equities Exchange Quotations (NEEQ), to solve the capital needs of SMEs. In Canada, there are multi-tiered equity markets. Toronto Stock Exchange (TSX) is the most important trading platform for large and medium-sized issuers. In contrast, the TSX Venture Exchange (Venture) operates a junior stock exchange institution for SME issuers to raise equity capital. The junior component of the multi-tiered exchanges also serves as a steppingstone for SMEs issuers to graduate and be listed on the senior exchange.

The capital market authorities in Canada have founded the capital pool company program (CPC Program), a new initiative for facilitating SMEs access to equity financing. CPC is a corporate finance conduit developed by the TSX Venture Exchange (Venture). It enables SMEs to obtain financing from investors with financial market experience. The CPC Program authorizes an initial public offering (IPO) to be undertaken and a Venture listing obtained by a newly created company under this program. A large number of CPCs have used the CPC Program. Many companies currently trading on Venture and TSX exchanges started as a CPC.

7.2 Debt capital markets

Financial institutions, such as the European Central Bank, the European Investment Fund (EIF), the European Investment Bank, and Alibaba Group, have established loan facilities to SMEs. A principal feature of the SMEs debt financing is the securitization of the SMEs loans: securitization moves risk from banks to investors in the capital markets. In order to facilitate the securitization process, institutions such as the EIF offer guarantees to the loan-based securities. The SME loan securitization program was launched successfully in 1985 by the Small Business Administration in the United States; it preceded the European SME securitization. The advantage of securitization consists of augmenting lending by financial institutions to SMEs and reducing SMEs borrowing cost. The thrust of securitization was that banks originate loans, whereas the actual funding was mainly raised through asset-based securities issuance.

7.3 Securitization

The securitization of receivables, such as payments from franchise revenues, lease contacts, and sales transactions, has enabled the securities issuer to augment financing to SMEs, diversify its financing sources, and reduce its financing costs. Increased involvement of reputable institutions such as European Investment Bank in the Asset-Based Securities market has helped entice new investors. With such support, securitization increases the overall financing to SMEs.

7.4 Pooled investment vehicles

Business development companies (BDCs) are listed as SMEs' investment conduits. They are closed-ended investment funds that are established primarily with the aim to invest in SMEs. In addition, they provide managerial assistance to these companies. Most BDCs are publicly listed; their shares are traded on stock exchanges. BDCs appoint investment managers who invest primarily in SMEs. They mobilize long-term capital from investors, including retail investors. Hence, they provide a channel to invest in private SMEs and offer flexible and diversified investment opportunities for investors.

8. Microfinance: a strategy for reducing poverty and creating employment

Microfinance aims at diffusing capital to the informal sector. Research on this sector in many developing countries during the 1960s and 1970s showed that it was a sector of self-employment in which most of the laborers found a refuge for survival. High demographic growth, large labor surplus, and a very small formal sector all concurred to make the informal sector a dominant part of most developing economies; most of the workers turned to informal activities for a bare living. The facts about the informal sector were too severe poverty, negligible capital used in self-employment, and very low incomes. A main recommendation was to inject capital into the informal sector. Formal finance was not available to this sector. Microfinance was conceived as a type of finance aimed to inject capital in the informal sector and help operators in this sector build their businesses and improve their incomes.

Microfinance is highly versatile and aims to reach poor laborers of both genders in urban and rural activities. It can be provided through various channels and in different forms. In fact, microfinance may be provided by official aid agencies, international financial institutions, government special funds and institutions, private banks such as the Grameen Bank in Bangladesh,[4] nongovernment organizations (NGOs), local licensed financial institutions, credit cooperatives, etc. Capital provided to eligible operators may be in form of physical capital, loans, grants, or risk-sharing capital. Typically, loans are provided with no collateral and on highly concessional terms. Agencies monitor closely their individual projects to ensure success of each project; they provide advice and technical training, and follow up on the servicing of their loans. Microfinance projects penetrated deep into remote rural areas and were not concentrated in one specific town or region. They were diversified and included small farming, livestock, fishery, mechanical and electrical repairs, carpentry, construction, garments confection, handicrafts, etc. They contributed to higher output and employment, and often were profitable, which explains the keen interest in microfinance.

Promoting further microfinance is an effective mean to enhance financial inclusion and crowdfunding. It is a means to deepen financial intermediation and endow qualified entrepreneurs with seed capital to build their assets. It enables the creation of wealth and employment, and reduces substantially poverty.

9. The judicial and social environment for doing business

Sharia considers the eradication of crimes and social disorder as an utmost priority of the government as crimes inflict huge toll on the society in form of loss of lives and spread of fear. High security and an environment free of crimes are necessary conditions for economic prosperity. An environment infested with crimes and insecurity would be barbaric and would not attract local and foreign investors. Economic activity would be reduced to bare survival. Business requires strong and effective judicial system for preventing lawlessness and reinforcing property rights and contracts. Many countries lack considerably security as well as an effective judicial system. For many decades, these countries were not able to promote a sustainable private investment and a vibrant private sector. Most of the economic activity has been confined to the informal sector with low incomes and no sizable investment. The overall environment was not habitable for business, industrialization, and infrastructure development. Many people leave their crime-ridden countries and seek life in more secure and orderly countries.

Besides uncontrollable aggravation of crimes, deep penetration of powerful unions in all sectors of the economy, including small enterprises, farms, and vital economic sectors such as the government administration, health, transport, etc. has paralyzed the economy. Unions have ruined work ethics, spread workers' indiscipline, and, with prolonged and frequent strikes, inflicted great damage to the economy. In a union-infested environment, no sizeable investment in infrastructure or in industry, commerce, etc. takes place. Considerable capital is expatriated to countries where unions have no existence.

Sharia aims at eradicating poverty. Where too much poverty and human agony prevail, business cannot expand. Hence, Sharia imposes *Zakat* as a means to secure the livelihood and welfare of the vulnerable population, which includes among the poor the handicapped, the orphans, widows, the aged, etc. To enhance economic prosperity, it is mandatory for the state to levy *Zakat* as well as devote part of its revenue for the purpose of improving the welfare of the destitute people. This social priority has been neglected by many governments at a cost of aggravating poverty and hindering the growth process.

Developing a legal, regulatory, and institutional framework is a basic stage toward full-fledged private infrastructure and PPPs. The government has to devise laws regarding private sector's investment in infrastructure.[5] These laws define the sectors and areas for private sector participation, the obligations and rights of each party, the types of contracts, the methods of participations, the revenue sources, the tax laws, etc. The government has to establish the institutions that implement its PPP's policy and endow them with capacity to design projects, develop cost-benefit analysis, and analyze bids. In some countries where private sector's involvement in infrastructure was initiated many decades ago, institutions and laws are at an advanced stage. In countries where private sector's involvement is non-existent, there is a need to develop the legal and institutional framework, and build capacity for identifying projects, collaborate with the private sector, and supervise infrastructure projects.

Similarly, an advanced and innovative institutional, legislative, and regulatory framework has to be established for the development of financial institutions and capital markets. The central bank and the capital market authorities have to establish a safe financial system; they have to lead in innovating new models for financial intermediation and new products, and update constantly the regulatory framework to accommodate financial innovations. A large number of countries suffer a strong inertia in their legislative and regulatory systems and are not able to develop their banking and capital markets at the cost of restricting their growth. The development of highly advanced and diversified banking and capital markets requires an advanced legislation to regulate banks, funds, stock markets, products, securitization, issuance, investors' protection, etc. Both the central bank, the capital market authorities, and other agencies in charge of regulation have to build their legal and regulatory capacity and contribute steadfastly to an expanding and stable financial system.

Governments should organize the most favorable environment for doing business and enhance economic competitiveness as a prerequisite for investment. The World Bank evaluates regularly the business environment in each country, taking into account governance, legislation, regulations, taxation, and financial services. It analyzes the ease with which to start a business, obtain construction permits, receive access to credit, obtain access to infrastructure, effectively reinforce contracts, etc. Countries are ranked according to the hospitality of their environment to business. In the same vein, the World Economic Forum monitors the competitiveness in 138 countries and ranks these countries according to their competitiveness. Countries that implement reforms to achieve best environment for business and highest competitiveness would win confidence of business, attract considerable capital, and advance prosperity. In contrast, countries with a degraded business environment and competitiveness would deprive their citizens of growth and grow far below potential.

10. Conclusions

The comfort enjoyed by consumers nowadays far exceeds that enjoyed by consumers say half a century ago; essentially thanks to technical progress and greater efficiency of the private sector in producing consumer goods at reduced costs. Consumers enjoy far better medical services, communications, transports, housing, etc. This rise in income is attributed to capital accumulation, which makes capital per head rise. There is no limit to capital accumulation, and the more it proceeds, the higher incomes are. Models of growth have established the relationship between growth, capital accumulation, and the competitive pricing of labor and capital. Unfortunately, capital accumulation may be hindered by government policies which disable free competition and stifle the private sector development. Many developed as well as developing countries have increasingly built a legislative and institutional framework too hostile to the private sector and forced rigidities in the economy that prevent any market adjustment of the economy toward growing at full potential, with unemployment becoming intractable at higher than 10 percent. Many countries are trapped in a vicious circle of self-defeating policies which are impoverishing their economies and creating too many uncertainties.

A large number of poor countries, although very rich in natural resources, had to initiate poverty reduction strategies since the mid-1990s to address rapidly deteriorating social and economic standards. In many countries, progress in alleviating poverty and reducing unemployment was timid, and dependence on foreign aid had increased. The conditions for establishing a sustained growth had yet to be established.

A Sharia model offers a propitious environment for capital accumulation and economic growth; it prevents any impediment to the private sector expansion. It establishes perfect security, economic freedom, perfectly competitive markets, limited taxation, social safety nets, and fully liberalized labor and capital markets. In such environment, the private sector will easily advance, and capital accumulation will proceed uninterrupted. Since debt is precluded, foreign trade will have to expand through exports and imports: a country can no longer rely on foreign debt to sustain its development, it has to enhance its own creative powers and progress toward industrialization, and it has to make best use of its labor resources as well as its natural resources.

Infrastructure constitutes a predominant part of a nation's capital stock too essential for economic growth. Truthfully, an economy cannot develop if it lacks an adequate and growing infrastructure. The construction of infrastructure is a fundamental attribution of the government. In view of deteriorating fiscal deficits and difficulties of financing these deficits, a large number of governments were compelled to significantly reduce spending on infrastructure maintenance and development. Moreover, these governments were in arrears in servicing their infrastructure loans from development banks, which in turn led these institutions to curtail their loans. In retrospect, a model where only the government constructed infrastructure was not optimal. There should be a mix where both the government and the private sector construct infrastructure. In this mixed frame, a cut in government capital spending would be buffered by higher private infrastructure investment. The mix would depend on the political, legal, and institutional framework. When the business environment is hostile to the private sector, there will be limited scope to attract domestic and foreign investors into highly capitalistic projects such as infrastructure. However, if the business environment is highly propitious to private investment, large private capital will be invested in infrastructure.

Infrastructure and SMEs financing may not be favorites for banks. Hence, these two particular and important sectors may be at some disadvantage in financing compared to large corporations. Bank financing for these two sectors has even become more restrictive after 2008. Governments and corporations have formulated market-determined models for long-term financing of infrastructure as well as SMEs. These models rely on diversified conduits for mobilizing capital and attracting institutional investors and sovereign funds. They envisage tapping financial resources from the equity capital markets, the debt market which includes bonds and *sukuks*, securitization of real and financial assets, pooled investment funds, and specialized development banks. To enlarge SMEs' access to long-term financing, some countries have established a new parallel stock exchange for trading SMEs' shares.

Microfinance was actively promoted by governments, official donors, multilateral development institutions, NGOs, etc. as a vehicle to inject capital into the informal sector. By enabling qualified operators to obtain capital and establish productive projects, their income would improve and poverty would be alleviated through productive employment.

Promoting a judicial and social environment favorable for business is an essential element of a growth policy. Countries shackled with un-natural regulations, labor unions, and infested with alarming crimes, have experienced deteriorating social and economic conditions, and are totally unattractive for local and foreign investors. In contrast, economies where regulations are favorable, no labor unions exist, and crime is totally reduced have offered a highly propitious environment for prosperity.

Notes

1 The marginal product of capital is defined as increment of output per additional unit of capital. Capital has a rental cost, and a user cost which is equal to rental cost plus the depreciation cost. The rental cost measures the cost of funds. The user cost recognizes the depreciation of capital as part of the cost of capital. These measures have to be distinguished from total return to capital; the latter measures profits plus capital gains or losses.
2 High net worth investors, such as development banks, insurance companies, sovereign wealth funds, investment funds, pension funds, etc., would be shareholders in infrastructure projects.
3 ASEAN is an organization established to promote political and economic cooperation as well as regional stability among its 10 member countries comprising Brunei, Cambodia, Indonesia, Laos, Malaysia, Myanmar, the Philippines, Singapore, Thailand, and Vietnam.
4 This bank, located in Bangladesh, was founded in 1983 by Muhammad Yunus. Both the founder and the bank won the Nobel Peace Prize in 2006 for their remarkable achievements in microfinance. In 2017, the bank has 24,703 employees in 2,565 branches; it has extended its activity to health care.
5 The World Bank, Asian Development, Bank, and Inter-American Development Bank, 2014, Public-Private Partnerships, Reference Guide, Version 2.0.

References

Askari, H., Iqbal, Z., Krichene, N., and Mirakhor, A., 2012, *Risk Sharing in Finance, the Islamic Finance Alternative*, London: Wiley and Sons.

Bohm-Bawerk, E., 1888, *The Positive Theory of Capital*, London: Palgrave Macmillan.

Harrod, R. F., 1939, "An Essay in Dynamic Theory," *Economic Journal*, 49(1): 14–33.

Ibn Khaldun, 1377/1985, *Al Muqaddimah*, Beirut: Dār al-Qalam.

Iqbal, M., and Khan, T., 2004. "Financing Public Expenditure: An Islamic Perspective," Occasional Paper No. 7. Jeddah, Saudi Arabia: Islamic Development Bank, Islamic Research and Training Institute.

Lewis, A., 1954, *On Development With Unlimited Supplies of Labor*, The Manchester School.

McKinnon, R., 1973, *Money and Capital in Economic Development*, Washington, DC: Brookings Institution.

Mill, J., 1821, *Elements of Political Economy*, 3rd edition revised and corrected, London: Henry G. Bohn, 1844.

Nock, A. J., 1935, *Our Enemy, the State*, Caldwell, ID: The Caxton Printers Ltd.

Phelps, E., 1965, "Second Essay on the Golden Rule of Accumulation," *The American Economic Review*, No(4): 793–814.

Ricardo, D., 1821, *On the Principles of Political Economy and Taxation*, 3rd edition, London: John Murray.

Say, J. B., 1803, *A Treatise on Political Economy*, Philadelphia: Claxton, Kemsen, & Haffelfingee.

Shaw, E., 1973, *Financial Deepening in Economic Development*, Oxford: Oxford University Press.

Smith, A., 1776, *An Inquiry Into the Nature and Causes of the Wealth of Nations*, London: Methuen and Co., Ltd., ed. Edwin Cannan, 1904, Fifth Edition.

Solow, R., 1956, "A Contribution to the Theory of Economic Growth," *Quarterly Journal of Economics*, 70(1): 65–94.

Swan, T. W., 1956, "Economic Growth and Capital Accumulation," *Economic Record*, 32(2): 334–361.

Conclusions

The basic message of this book is to propose a Sharia-based model for reforms which is immune to the defects and instabilities of the statist model and which promotes a secure and free environment for the private sector. It presents Sharia principles in basic areas, covering the nature of government, the free market model, public finance, the nature of money, the nature of inflationary financing, financial repression, Islamic banking and capital markets, labor markets, trade theory, and growth and development policies.

A Sharia model fully embraces the naturalism of the classical model, except for the interest-debt contracts which are forbidden in Sharia. The interdiction of interest contracts has far-reaching implications on the financial sector, public finance, money, and trade. A Sharia model is a free-enterprise model that promotes fully the private sector and the competitiveness of the capital, labor, and commodities markets.

In the area of government, a Sharia model restricts the government to its natural role without which the welfare of the community will be seriously impeded. The natural attributions of the state are justice, security, defense, social work, education, health, infrastructure, and regulation. The government has to remain within the confines of its Sharia duties and not expand to areas that do not fall under its natural role. In the area of justice, the state is not allowed to circumvent Sharia laws. Justice has to be easily accessible to citizens and very efficient. Education and health are extremely important; considerable resources have to be devoted to these priority sectors, and this can be done by curtailing unproductive spending. State education has to be free for the entire population. Similarly, health care has to be free for vulnerable groups. Health coverage has to be fully developed via free health care by the state and via insurance systems. In the area of social work, the state has to promote *Zakat* collection and distribution to attend fully to the well-being of the vulnerable groups. The development of *Zakat* foundations offers significant prospects for reducing poverty and promoting the poor's welfare.

In the area of public finance, the state has to be compliant with Sharia laws. Spending has to be subjected to revenues, and not otherwise. Spending has to be Sharia-compliant, favoring essentially productive spending in education, health, and infrastructure. Government revenues have to be fully Sharia-compliant.

The government has to promote full participation of the private sector in the construction of infrastructure. This will enable the state to reduce its needs for taxation, increase considerably infrastructure, and achieve social equity.

In the monetary area, the prohibition of interest leads to a separation of money from debt. In a Sharia model, the banking system is similar to the one proposed by the Chicago Plan, Simons, and many others. It has two components: a 100 percent reserve banking for safekeeping and for payments, and a risk-sharing banking for investment. The development of a stock market is a necessity to mobilize savings and provide liquidity to investors. The central bank has to be in charge with the stability of the banking system; it should not create money out of thin air.

Capital and labor markets are competitive in a Sharia model; rates of return on capital are rates of profits of individual firms. Similarly, labor markets are competitive; wage rates in different labor markets are determined competitively and are related to the labor productivity. Foreign trade in a Sharia model aligns with Adam Smith's and David Ricardo's free trade model; capital movements are free. The foreign exchange market is also free and subject to no control.

Index

Page numbers in italic indicate a figure.

For Product Safety Concerns and Information please contact our EU
representative GPSR@taylorandfrancis.com
Taylor & Francis Verlag GmbH, Kaufingerstraße 24, 80331 München, Germany

www.ingramcontent.com/pod-product-compliance
Ingram Content Group UK Ltd.
Pitfield, Milton Keynes, MK11 3LW, UK
UKHW020955180425
457613UK00019B/696